IN SEARCH OF AMERICA:

A NEW HISTORY OF
THE UNITED STATES,
1860–2025

Peter Wallenstein

IN SEARCH OF AMERICA:

A NEW HISTORY OF THE UNITED STATES, 1860–2025

ISBN 13: 978-1-955338-41-7

Cover Illustration by Ai Le

Clint T. Eaton, Editor/Proofreader,

Book design and layout by Lori C. Graham

Printed in the United States of America

POCAHONTAS PRESS

Floyd, VA
pocahontaspress.com

Dedication

To big sister Barbara Johns

Always, Sookhan

My US Survey class, spring 2026,
for whom, as Course Request and Book Orders arrived in October,
I first dreamed it up

Members of my fall 2025 History of Virginia class,
who inquired after "newbook,"
inspired some parts,
and cheered it and me on

And the many people who have, over the years, shared their stories with me, so I can forward some bits on—including Joan Johns Cobbs, Darlene Clark Hine, Philip J. Hirschkop, Ford T. Johnson Jr. and his father and big sister, Gerda Lerner, Mildred D. Loving, Joan Trumpauer Mulholland, Raymond B. Randolph Jr., and Anne Firor Scott

Preface

I have taught US Survey courses over many years, at very different institutions. I have never found a textbook, for the first half or the second, that met my needs or wants. So, finally, looking ahead to taking on the second half of the Survey for spring 2026, I decided to write my own.

I did not want my book to be encyclopedic, stuffed full of all possible topics and a relentless rendition of facts. Instead, I wanted it to take a brisk tour and not seek to "cover" everything, nor be big or expensive.

One thing my book *would* do is tell stories to introduce readers–whether college students, high school students or teachers, or general readers—to a series of vignettes, vivid depictions of various pieces of the past. The chapters are short (I call them "modules"), on average two pages. Though moving right along, this book does tarry on occasion to more fully explore one big topic or another: the Civil War era, the World War II era, the Civil Rights Struggle.

As to approach, I tell many stories through biography—as in, some particular person did that thing. I situate some US developments in a global context. I sometimes try to convey something of how history works, how it can be done, what sources can help us revisit the past, as well as how much the study of history can illuminate.

And this book is, as you'll see, deliberately, unabashedly, multicultural as well as clear-eyed. This is, after all, *US history*, whether the theme is military history or women's history or how US presidents from one era to another have handled their obligations and opportunities.

I often challenge—even directly—prevailing understandings, whether among academic scholars or in the popular culture. If you find a module provocative, so much the better. I hope that you as the reader will engage what you find here, reconsider what you think you know or believe. Not that, in the end, anyone must become fundamentally reoriented to the wider world, but my objective is that you come away with an enhanced understanding of the past and how it might relate to the present. What *did* happen, back in that time and place, and how might it matter?

Some of the people I highlight here are scarcely household names, whether I consider them towering figures from their time or, instead, rather typical of their time, place, and situation. Others you may immediately recognize, but I might present them in ways you find unfamiliar. And whatever you might think of one facet or another of their lives—perhaps you admire them for this but cringe at that—they tend to be some combination of representative (similar to lots of other people) and consequential (they made a difference).

As you read one module or another, you might ask: What are the main ideas here? What is the point? And what facts presented here, or examples, help to clarify, or illustrate, one idea or another? The facts are not so very important on their own. How they relate to the ideas, now that's where they become significant. So let the facts help with the ideas, and then hold on to the ideas and consider what they can tell you.

Sometimes I point readers, either in the text or, more often, in the bibliography at the back of the book, toward "further reading." Regardless, online sources can usually permit an interested reader to gain ready access to a fuller discussion of any topic, once introduced here.

As for primary sources—usually documents, often records generated at the time by people who witnessed an event—a great many are available online. I have supplied a very few, at places where they build effectively on the text.

This is a first edition, meant to provide an effective introduction to a range of people, places, and events in the century and a half (and more) beginning with the Civil War era. Subsequent editions can permit reconsidering my choice of modules, as well as how to present them. Lots of topics I considered could not make their way in here.

And of course as the present changes, ways to connect past to present will likely change also. My book comes to an end when 2025 does. Twenty-five years ago, many stories here would be very different or not yet available to tell at all. A few years from now, who knows what new stories will cry out to be told.

I have divided the 70-plus modules into three sections, each emphasizing individuals and events or developments in one or another of three half-centuries: from the 1860s to the 1920s, from the 1930s through the 1960s, and since the 1970s.

At the back of the book, given that many of the modules are topical or thematic, I supply a brief timeline to help readers situate people and events, also an outline of presidents and presidential elections from 1860 through 2024.

Welcome! Let's peer into the past and see what we find.

Table of Contents

Part Two, 1930s–1960s

Part Three, 1970s–2020s

Part One
1860s–1920s

1-1
Dred Scott, Western Slavery, and Black Citizenship

In 1846, two natives of Virginia at that time held in slavery in Missouri, Dred Scott and his wife, Harriet, petitioned a local court to gain their freedom. Slavery had taken them both west, at first separately, a third of the way across the continent.

Dred Scott (c. 1798–1858) had married once before, in Alabama, but then saw his wife sold away from him. He had next labored in Missouri, Illinois, and then Wisconsin Territory, where he met and married Harriet Robinson (c. 1818–1876). One or both had later lived in Louisiana and Texas before arriving in Missouri.

They felt particular concern for their two surviving children, young daughters Lizzie and Eliza (they had lost two sons, born between the daughters). Knowing their daughters' prospects in slavery to be grim, the couple went to court in St. Louis to sue for their freedom, or rather he for his and she for hers and that of their children. If Harriet had been free—if now declared to have been free—when her daughters were born, they would have been free from birth.

Since the couple had each lived in free territory for some years, they had a plausible case. Under the Missouri Compromise of 1820, the vast area of the Louisiana Purchase north of Missouri, including Wisconsin Territory in one corner of it (today's Minnesota), was closed to slavery. As for Illinois, where he had lived for two years, the Northwest Ordinance (under the Articles of Confederation) had long ago declared it free.

Under Illinois law, Dred Scott's time in Illinois should itself have qualified to free him, though that would not help his wife and children. For them, the Missouri Compromise held the potential key to their emancipation.

Americans held in bondage had been suing for their freedom—very often with success—since the era of the American Revolution, in such varied places as Massachusetts, Maryland, Virginia, Louisiana, and Missouri. Whether the Scotts, any or all of them, would gain their freedom would hinge on how the courts understood the facts and how they interpreted the law. By mid-century, ever fewer freedom suits were proving successful.

The Scotts' two cases were combined into one. For years, their case bounced around in the state courts of Missouri, where they won once but saw their victory reversed, and then went to federal court. Both the facts of their case and the history of their efforts to gain recognition of their freedom were highly complex, but a short version goes like this: they won at trial in 1850, but their owner appealed the outcome there to the Missouri Supreme Court, which in 1852 (with the judges divided 2-1) overturned the trial decision and left them all enslaved. They were able to appeal that outcome to the US Supreme Court, but there it languished for still more years.

In 1857, Chief Justice Roger B. Taney, who hailed from Maryland, wrote the principal opinion of a deeply divided US Supreme Court. Should Dred Scott be permitted to sue for his freedom? And should his freedom be granted? No, and no. At great length, Taney worked out his argument. He determined that Scott, as a Black person, could simply never be a US citizen and therefore had no right to bring the case into federal court in the first place.

Scott's having nonetheless been permitted to bring his case, however, occasioned a declaration by a majority on the nation's highest Court that Congress never had authority under the US Constitution to enact the Missouri Compromise. So even if the Scotts could rightly have brought a case to the Supreme Court, their having lived in Wisconsin Territory, though for decades had been assumed to ban slavery, could not help them.

Wherever they might have lived, and wherever their children might have been born, had no bearing on their freedom. They would remain enslaved. Moreover, even if free, they could never be citizens. And Congress could do nothing to prevent the spread of the slave system into new territories in the West.

The Republican Party had organized in the North in response to the Kansas-Nebraska Act of 1854, in which Congress had undone the Missouri Compromise line in the West by dividing the area into two territories, Kansas and Nebraska, and leaving it up to the voters in each to determine whether it would be open to slavery.

Outraged, the Republicans now attacked the Dred Scott decision of 1857 as yet another example of law and public policy gone awry; of southern power and slavery run amok; of the North and freedom being trampled by the Slave Power; and as showing the urgent need to put the nation's politics under new management.

The Scotts had raised a question, forced a contest, that led to radically contrasting answers. The Court had ruled in such a way as to undermine the Republicans' core objective: Congress preventing the spread of slavery west. The chief justice's language in Dred Scott laid bare not only the utter irreconcilability of proslavery and antislavery approaches to American society and politics, but also the central issues that, depending on how they were resolved in the years to come, would go far to determine the future of the American nation.

Abraham Lincoln weighed in from Illinois. The Dred Scott ruling, he observed, "declares two propositions—first, that a negro cannot sue in the U.S. Courts; and secondly, that Congress cannot prohibit slavery in the Territories." He recognized that the Court had spoken, and he disputed everything it had said, from the history it claimed to draw upon to the policy outcomes it had directed.

In less than four years, he would be president of the United States.

1-2
Robert Barnwell Rhett and South Carolina's Declaration of Independence

Robert Barnwell Rhett, from coastal South Carolina, was one of the leading "fire-eaters," proponents of immediate secession by southern states, even before the 1850s. More recently, in 1859 he called for his home state to leave the Union immediately should any Republican Party candidate win the 1860 presidential election, which Abraham Lincoln did.

The South Carolina legislature promptly called for a convention to meet the next month. Delegates there unanimously approved the state's immediately leaving the Union. Their state went out alone, but delegates looked for more states to join them in seceding and forming a new nation. Rhett served as a delegate to the South Carolina convention, and then, some weeks later, in Montgomery, Alabama, he helped establish the Confederate States of America.

Why secession? Examining how states explained themselves can help answer that question.

The very first to secede, South Carolina, had a higher proportion of slaveholding families than anywhere else (about the same number as the White families holding nobody in bondage). Its enslaved population comprised a substantial majority, 57 percent of all inhabitants, higher even than Mississippi's 55 percent.

Beyond passing an Ordinance of Secession, delegates agreed to a "Declaration of the Immediate Causes which Induce and Justify the Secession of South Carolina from the Federal Union." They modeled the 1776 Declaration of Independence in stating that South Carolina had a responsibility "to herself, to the remaining United States of America, and to the nations of the world, that she should declare the immediate causes which have led to this act."

Back in 1852, the men at the convention recalled, political South Carolinians had been ready to secede, but "in deference to the opinions and wishes of the other slaveholding States" had held back. The time either to defer to anyone else or to delay taking action by itself, had ceased to be "a virtue."

According to the convention, when South Carolina entered a new Union under the US Constitution, "each State was recognized as an equal, and had separate control over its own institutions," in particular "the right of property in slaves." But now the voters in "the non-slaveholding States" had elected a president "hostile to slavery." In particular, the Republican Party platform of 1860 had insisted, as the Declaration put it, "that the South shall be excluded from the common territory" in the West. Soon, delegates fretted, "the equal rights of the States will be lost."

South Carolina was insisting on state rights, that is, that those rights be accorded full and reliable respect. And what were those rights?—the right to maintain the slave system, the right to see the system expand across the West, and the right to secede for the purpose of protecting individual slaveholders' interests and the entire system of slavery.

Referencing the *Dred Scott* decision from three years before, moreover, together with the fact that Black men had voting rights in Massachusetts and a few other states, the Declaration charged that the election's outcome had been "aided . . . by elevating to citizenship, persons who, by the supreme law of the land, are incapable of becoming citizens; and their votes have been used to inaugurate a new policy, hostile to the South, and destructive of its beliefs and safety." Black men, permitted to act as though they were citizens, had voted, and had voted Republican.

So, the protective shield against interference with slavery included a denial that Black residents of the United States could ever be citizens, let alone have political rights. Central as were the maintenance and expansion of slavery, assumptions about the only appropriate racial regime, for South Carolina and any nation it might be part of, transcended slavery itself. The slave system, perceived as in immediate jeopardy, was the preeminent issue but not all that mattered on the racial front. Even aside from slavery, Black freedom must never equal White freedom.

By the beginning of February 1861, six more slave states seceded, and all seven participated in forming the Confederacy. The Confederate Constitution made sure to guarantee slavery in any new territories it might acquire.

Would Lincoln let South Carolina and its companions go quietly? If he did, no war seemed at all imminent. Secession would have gained recognition as a legitimate political act. The independent state of South Carolina would have secured its "separate control over its own institutions," in particular "the right of property in slaves."

The seven original states to secede and form the Confederacy—all in the Deep South: South Carolina, Georgia, Florida, Alabama, Mississippi, Louisiana, and Texas—had acted without waiting for the new president to take office. Other states in the South waited to see what he would do as president. After Confederate forces subdued US troops holding Fort Sumter in Charleston Harbor, Lincoln called for 75,000 volunteer soldiers to put down secession.

In response, Virginia and three additional slave states—North Carolina, Tennessee, and Arkansas—also seceded and joined the Confederacy. So the Deep South went out first, and the Upper South followed. Even then, the states of the Border South—Delaware, Maryland, Kentucky, and Missouri—remained in the Union.

1-3
Robert E. Lee, the State of Virginia, and Secession

The combination of Lincoln's election and South Carolina's secession forced Virginians to consider their options. On 4 February 1861, delegates from six seceded states met at Montgomery, Alabama, to form a new nation, the Confederate States of America (CSA), and more, from Texas, soon arrived. Also on 4 February 1861, Virginia voters selected delegates to a constitutional convention in Richmond. There, members would monitor developments, determine how best to navigate through treacherous times, and establish Virginia's official stance as events unfolded.

Along the way, a Committee on Federal Relations proposed a series of resolutions, and all were adopted. The first echoed South Carolina in speaking of "the rights of the States" to be treated with "exact equality," and the second flatly declared: "African slavery is a vital part of the social system of the States wherein it exists." Resolution 3 spoke of federal officials as "hostile to the institutions of some of the States."

Resolution 4 declared, "The territories of the United States constitute a trust," a "common benefit" at least some of which must be open to the expansion of slavery: "If the equal admission of slave labor and free labor into any Territory, excites unfriendly conflict between the systems, a fair partition of the Territories ought to be made between them."

Regarding this central point of contention in the 1860 presidential campaign, most convention delegates had yet to decide on secession, and they still hoped not to be forced to decide. As for the westward expansion of slavery, more temperate than South Carolina, they wanted something that might look like the Missouri Compromise, some means of sorting out the West so that some parts would be open to slavery.

Resolution 5 addressed the matter of federal forts in seceded states. A contest over Fort Sumter in South Carolina threatened a flashpoint that might ignite war, but if the US government simply relinquished that facility then no violence would be occasioned. So, the administration must recognize forts in seceded states as no longer federal properties; rather, "jurisdiction reverts of right to the States," yet another state right. Delegates must also have had in mind Fort Monroe, right there in Virginia. All such forts were designed to protect "against foreign force," not "to intimidate a State."

Resolution 7 spoke directly of a "more effectual" fugitive slave law (not a particular concern in South Carolina, which lay far from any free state or territory), together with northern states repealing "their unfriendly and unconstitutional legislation" against enforcement. Most delegates looked for assurance of "the rights of the States" to secure runaway slaves, yet another state right.

Resolution 6 portrayed Virginia as eager to stay in the Union, if only the Union would not interfere with slavery: "Deeply deploring the present distracted condition of the country, and lamenting the wrongs that have impelled some of the States to dissolve their connections with the Federal Government, but sensible of the blessings of the Union," delegates "earnestly" hoped that "an adjustment may be reached by which the Union may be re-established." Amendments to the US Constitution must better safeguard the rights of Virginia and the other slave states.

Resolution 8 specified the right of a state to withdraw from the Union to safeguard those various state rights, all of them centered on slavery: the right to have slavery in the first place, the right to expand slavery into the West, the right to retrieve fugitive slaves, and the right to secede if these rights faced constant jeopardy in the Union.

On 4 April, delegates voted two-to-one (90–45) to stay with the Union—not to secede, nor join the Confederate States of America. But many of the votes against secession came from delegates who would be Unionists only until they were not. Their stance was conditional.

Then came the Confederate attack on Fort Sumter, and its fall on 13 April, quickly followed by President Lincoln's call on 15 April for 75,000 volunteers to put down the "rebellion," 2,340 of them to come from Virginia. Convention delegates responded on 17 April by voting nearly two-to-one (88–55) to secede.

One group of delegates continued to hold out, resisting secession; another group had determined to support secession well before Fort Sumter. The outcome in the two votes hinged on what the middle group did, and that middle group had reversed direction.

The Secession Ordinance repealed Virginia's ratification of the US Constitution back in 1788: "The Union between the State of Virginia and the other States under the Constitution is hereby dissolved" and is "no longer binding on any of the Citizens of this State."

The time to wait and see had vanished. On 18 April, Lincoln (through an intermediary) urged Robert E. Lee, a career Army officer who had been promoted just a month earlier from captain to colonel, to take command of an army to put down the "rebellion."

As for Lee's personal connections to slavery, for much of his adult life he had a small holding, but he appears to have had none of his own at the time of secession. Yet he managed (often from a great distance while away with the Army) huge numbers, especially as executor of his father-in-law's estate (the last of whom were slated for manumission in 1862).

Anyway, Lee quickly determined that he had to go with Virginia, whatever Virginia did, and Virginia had seceded. On 20 April, he resigned his commission in the US Army and abandoned his oath to uphold the Constitution of the United States. Escorted to Richmond two days later, he found himself offered the position of commander of the newly independent state's military forces, at the rank of major general. That day, 22 April, he accepted.

Like hosts of other Virginians, Lee represented the middle group, the sizable number who shifted from Union to secession in the days following the attack on Fort Sumter and Lincoln's call for volunteers.

Virginia soon joined the Confederate States of America. Soldiers from Virginia in the war that followed reflected the range of orientations that delegates to the convention had displayed. Many men eagerly joined the crusade for political independence. Others, hanging back at first, joined only when Union troops threatened their farms and communities. Considerable numbers went into the Confederate military because, under a draft law enacted in 1862, they had been conscripted. Yet, like the delegates who consistently voted against secession, many White Virginians wore Union blue. They all fought because a war was under way.

Forced to choose, Virginia shifted from "no," or at least wait and see, to supporting secession. War came, with Virginia, or at any rate two-thirds of it, located in the Confederacy. White men in Virginia were expected to point their weapons north, not south—to join the rebellion, not join in extinguishing it.

The establishment of a new state, West Virginia—though the process took a couple of years to play out—demonstrated that a great many voting Virginians, concentrated in the northwestern third of the state, persisted in their desire to remain in the Union. Many also acted out a chronic wish, one that had been fitfully emerging for three decades, to be separated from their eastern counterparts. The eastern and western portions of Virginia had long tussled over matters of power and policy, and back in 1832, in a great debate in the House of Delegates over the future of slavery, each side had threatened to break away if it lost.

What would often be characterized as a "war between the states" proved also, then, to be a war *within* the states, a fact that itself proved critical to the outcome. In all, Union soldiers from what became West Virginia numbered at least one-third as many as all the Confederate soldiers from the first state to secede, South Carolina, the state that forced the issue that Virginians found they had to address.

Each of those Union men from Virginia not only subtracted one soldier from the Confederate military, but also countered one more Confederate soldier in gray, so in effect subtracted two. From eastern Virginia, too, a good many men served under the Union flag, among them generals Winfield Scott and George Henry Thomas, each of whom played a prominent role in shaping the course of the war and its outcome.

With West Virginia's formal departure in 1863, Virginia's Black-White ratio suddenly resembled that of Deep South states Georgia and Alabama, with roughly 40 percent of all people enslaved. By then, whether those numbers would hold—whether the system of enslavement would survive the conflict—had become a core question in the war.

1-4
Shepard Mallory, from Slavery to Freedom (by Elliot Sheehan)

"Three negroes, field hands belonging to Col. Charles K. Mallory now in command of the secession forces in this district, delivered themselves up to my picket guard," reported Maj. Gen. Benjamin F. Butler of the US Army on the morning of 24 May 1861.

Barely a month had passed since the attack on Fort Sumter, Lincoln's call for volunteers, and Virginia's secession. Col. Mallory, CSA, who as a member of the Virginia Convention had twice voted the previous month in favor of Virginia's secession, sought the return of his property: Shepard Mallory, James Townsend, and Frank Baker, three of the 13 enslaved people who had been living on his nearby place. Butler declined—though he was prepared to comply if Col. Mallory undid his allegiance to the Confederacy and signed an oath of allegiance to the US Constitution.

Way back in 1619, a Dutch ship carrying some "twenty and odd" captive Africans had landed on the same shores, the first arrival of unfree Africans in British America. On the very ground where the seeds of slavery were planted in the colonies, the three fugitive men reached for the possibility of freedom and ignited a transformation that would eventually turn a war for Union into a war for emancipation.

Within a few days, several more men showed up. They reported that they had been put to work constructing artillery units across the James River at Sewell's Point, a spot in Norfolk that would enable Confederate forces to endanger Union ships in or near the James or even Fort Monroe across the river. With the approval of Winfield Scott, commanding general of the US Army, Butler declared that the Union could henceforth hold Shepard Mallory and other fugitive slaves as "contraband," a legal designation that allowed an army to seize enemy property, and a term soon widely adopted.

Soon, hundreds more refugees from slavery—men, women, and children—settled in what was designated the Grand Contraband Camp in Hampton. Butler promptly put the "contraband" men to work, deeming the newfound manpower "very serviceable" in satisfying the Union military's "great need of labor." Therefore, the fugitives' encounter with Union troops did not immediately result in unconditional liberation but rather left them subject to Union needs in an uncertain status. They would be contributing combat support labor for the US Army, and the military would see that the men and their families were fed and housed.

Federal law soon reinforced Butler's decision. That August, Congress passed the First Confiscation Act, authorizing the Union to seize enslaved people being used to support the Confederate war effort. A Second Confiscation Act, the next year, went further. What began as an improvised military declaration at Fort Monroe thus became federal policy, though it would be another year until the Emancipation Proclamation declared free anyone held in slavery in any parts of the Confederacy still in rebellion. Only in late 1865 did the Thirteenth Amendment bar slavery everywhere.

In the meantime, Shepard Mallory disappeared for a time from the written record, yet accounts of the Grand Contraband Camp allow for an imaginative reconstruction of his life during the war. He no doubt continued to work, but now for the Union military, not the Confederacy or his former master. His wife, Fanny, joined him in the camp. They no longer needed to fear being forcibly separated, for example by sale.

As one benefit of life in the Grand Contraband Camp, people formerly barred by Virginia law from any opportunity for schooling could get a basic education, thanks to Mary Smith Kelsey Peake, a free Black woman, an experienced teacher although previously only in secret. Confederate troops, shortly before abandoning Hampton at the beginning of the war, had torched Peake's home, so she, too, settled in the camp. She started a school there for people of all ages and held classes under an oak tree.

In January 1863, Hampton residents would gather under that same tree to hear what is thought to be the first reading of the Emancipation Proclamation in the South. And in the presidential campaign of 1864, the Republican Party platform affirmed what Butler had recognized: slavery was the "strength of this rebellion." The platform called for the "utter and complete" abolition of slavery by amending the US Constitution, and in January 1865 Congress approved the Thirteenth Amendment, which then went out to the states for ratification.

Mallory resurfaces in the written record in the 1870 Census, which shows him and Fanny as the parents of three children. The eldest, Shepard Mallory Jr., was born in the Grand Contraband Camp in July 1862, followed by younger brothers William and Frank. Mallory Sr. was working as an oysterman on the Chesapeake Bay, with Fanny keeping house.

Shepard Sr. likely arrived at Fort Monroe illiterate, but censuses later indicated that he and Fanny could read and write, perhaps because they attended Mary Peake's camp school. An 1879 article in the *Norfolk Virginian* implied Fanny's facility with reading, writing, and arithmetic when it reported her as the treasurer of the local Dorcas Society, a church related charitable organization that provided clothing for the poor.

Meanwhile, one of the first colleges in the South for Black men and Black women, Hampton Normal and Agricultural Institute, emerged in 1868 in Hampton. On the Hampton Institute campus stood the very tree—later named the Emancipation Oak— where Shepard Sr. and Fanny may have learned to read and write and perhaps also where they heard the news of Lincoln's 1863 proclamation.

Shepard Jr. enrolled at Hampton Institute in the late 1870s, exemplifying the new opportunities that the Civil War era brought Black southerners. His classmates there included Booker T. Washington, formerly enslaved in Virginia's Franklin County.

According to the 1880 Census, the Mallory family was still living on the grounds that once housed the fugitive slave camp, with their home located on the aptly named West Lincoln Street. Their youngest son, Frank, had died, but they now had a daughter, Louisa (or Louise or Lucy).

After Fanny died, Shepard Sr. married a much younger Lelia Wilson in 1903, and another Mallory daughter, Ruth, was born in 1921. Shepard Sr., when he died three years later, had continued to live in his longtime 260 West Lincoln Street home, which Lelia maintained until her own death in 1950. Meanwhile, Ruth married World War II veteran Jack Z. Styles in June 1945, and the couple moved in with her mother.

In 1951, after Jack graduated from Hampton Institute, he and Ruth had a son, Jack Styles Jr. As late as 1959—nearly a century after Shepard Mallory stole himself in 1861— family members were still living at the Lincoln Street address. Ruth worked in the cafeteria at Hampton Institute, and Jack as a tailor at Fort Monroe. When Ruth died in 2007, according to a *Washington Post* obituary, she was survived by her son, a granddaughter, and a great-granddaughter.

The saga of Shepard Mallory Sr. unfolded where Virginia's race-based bondage began in 1619, and where it began to end in 1861, as he gained his freedom, and his wife's, and the chance for them both to see their children grow up free.

1-5

Robert Smalls, Harriet Tubman, and Black Combat Troops in Union Blue

Early in the Civil War, the triracial former Virginian John Mercer Langston urged the governor of Ohio, David Tod, to authorize him to recruit Black troops there for the war effort. Tod rebuffed him: "Do you not know, Mr. Langston, that this is a white man's government; that white men are able to defend and protect it. . . . When we want you colored men we will notify you." On 1 January 1863, President Lincoln's Emancipation Proclamation directed the enrollment of Black men as soldiers in the Union military, thus making clear that the conflict was no longer (not that it ever had been) simply a White man's war to fight. Tod now reached out to Langston.

Combat units quickly formed, the best known among them the Massachusetts 54th Infantry. It is often said that the Emancipation Proclamation did not immediately free a solitary slave, since it focused on the many parts of the South still in rebellion. There, the US had as yet no authority. As Union forces continued to recapture new places in the Confederacy, however, an ever larger number of Black men, together with their families, made their way to Union lines, and a great many of those men became US soldiers. In all, some 200,000 African Americans—both already free and until recently enslaved, from the Northeast and the Midwest as well as state after state in the South—served in the armed forces of the US during the war.

Robert Smalls, enslaved from birth, dramatized the kinds of roles that Black participants in the Union war effort could fill. He grew up in the South Carolina Lowcountry, in the Charleston area, and by the time the Civil War came along he had gained extensive experience piloting vessels around Charleston Harbor. He continued to do so during the war, in support of Confederate operations. In the early hours of 13 May 1862, however, the 23-year-old Smalls put his formidable experience to a very different purpose. He had to plan carefully. Then, sailing with the rest of his Black crew and their families, he successfully piloted the CSS *Planter* past all the Confederate defenses, including Fort Sumter, and on out to the US Navy, which was blockading the area.

Smalls thereby freed himself and his wife and children, at the same time delivering an armed ship that was perfectly designed to make its way up coastal rivers. Knowing where mines had been laid and how much manpower each Confederate facility had, Smalls himself contributed mightily to Union operations in the months that followed. His exploits also made it easier for President Lincoln to move toward incorporating Black men in the Union forces in a combat capacity, starting there in coastal South Carolina. Smalls himself was at the scene of one military engagement after another through the war. In December 1864, he and the USS *Planter* moved down the coast to support Gen. William Tecumseh Sherman at Savannah, and in April the next year he participated in a ceremonial re-raising of the US flag at Fort Sumter.

Meanwhile, many thousands of Black men had long been contributing to the Union war effort on the battlefront, in critically important combat *support* roles. Carrying and firing weapons, however, participating as *combat soldiers*, gave Black men a more direct way of altering the outcome of one battle or another—and helping bring the war itself to a triumphal end.

Actually, those Black soldiers, sailors, and scouts might not only be men. One dramatic scene in the war's last two years had Harriet Tubman helping lead some 300 soldiers of the South Carolina Volunteers, men who had previously stolen themselves and joined the US Colored Troops (USCT), on a venture up the Combahee River on 2 June 1863.

Two steamships (a third ran aground) successfully made their way some 25 miles up the river, stopping at a series of big rice plantations and destroying as they went, meanwhile collecting hundreds upon hundreds of people taking advantage of this once-in-a-lifetime opportunity to escape their enslavement.

What they called "Lincoln's gunboats" provided a ticket out. Among them, 88-year-old Minus Hamilton explained: "I was gwine to de boat"; "neber too ole for leave de land of bondage." Another man, Friday Barrington, was returning to the plantation where he had long been enslaved, and there he found his parents and sister.

Harriet Tubman is widely known for her heroic efforts in leading fellow Marylanders out of slavery to freedom in Pennsylvania during the 1850s on the Underground Railroad. Yet, on that one day in June 1863, she helped liberate more people, over 700, than all those many she had led to freedom before the war. Moreover, more than 160 men newly freed during the Combahee River Raid joined the US Colored Troops, thus bolstering the Union's military successes going forward.

Interviewed in Virginia in the 1930s, by then in his 90s, Union Army veteran Cornelius Garner peered back into his recollections of the wartime 1860s in the Upper South. Born into slavery, when he turned 18 in February 1864 he promptly made his way to Union-held Norfolk and enlisted in the USCT. He first told tales of some of the fighting that ensued over the next year. Then he recounted a key moment in April 1865, when the Capital of the Confederacy fell at last: "Our regiment was de fust into Richmond."

Regarding Black soldiers more generally, he declared: "Dey won de war for de white man. Yessuh." More precisely, Cornelius Garner and his Black comrades helped win the war for the Union side.

1-6
MIA: Black Combat Soldiers in Confederate Gray

Enslaved men had no choice but to contribute mightily to the Confederacy, throughout the war, on both the home front and the battlefront. On the home front, they grew the corn that fed the army and the cotton that clothed the men away at war. Many accompanied their masters' sons to war as personal servants. Far more were drafted, along with free Black men, as combat support personnel—as cooks, teamsters, all-purpose laborers.

But that was *combat support, not combat*, building fortifications, not firing weapons at the enemy—working with shovels, not shooting with guns.

In the aftermath of the Confederate victory at First Manassas in June 1861, early voices did emerge in support of enlisting Black troops in Confederate gray. Gen. Richard S. Ewell raised the thought; but Jefferson Davis, the new president of the new Confederacy, called it "stark madness." Far to the west in Arkansas, when citizen W. S. Turner offered to raise a Black regiment to support the bid for Confederate independence,

CSA Bureau of War chief Albert Taylor Bledsoe—echoing Ohio governor Tod's response to John Mercer Langston's offer to raise troops for the US Army—said he was "not prepared to accept." As of mid-1861, only White soldiers would wear either blue or gray.

So the idea of Black combat Confederates appeared early, and again from time to time over the next three years and more. But it went nowhere, even after US President Lincoln's Emancipation Proclamation on 1 January 1863 soon led to the enlistment of many tens of thousands of Black soldiers in the Union's armed forces. At that point, the US military moved beyond Black *combat support personnel* to the deployment of *combat troops*. The Confederacy did not.

In January 1864, after a disastrous Confederate defeat at Chattanooga, Gen. Patrick Cleburne argued that the Confederacy had to tap enslaved men as a major new source of combat personnel, which might at the same time, perhaps, bring France and England over from supporting the Union. Despite the serious and growing shortage of White manpower, jeopardizing the entire Confederate project, Cleburne's idea went nowhere.

But then came Union Gen. William T. Sherman's occupation in late 1864 of Atlanta and then Savannah. Even so, in early January 1865, Confederate stalwart Howell Cobb of Georgia denounced any proposal to arm enslaved men as "the most pernicious idea that has been suggested since the war began." "If slaves will make good soldiers," he went on (a premise he found preposterous), "our whole theory of slavery is wrong."

In those early weeks of 1865, however, a rising chorus—including Virginia Governor Billy Smith and CSA Gen. Robert E. Lee himself—supported adoption of a revolutionary new policy, to incorporate Black men into the Confederate military as combat soldiers. The Confederate Congress earnestly debated a bill to do that. On 20 February, the House of Representatives narrowly approved it, but then it went to the Senate, where it languished. February turned into March.

Here, the Virginia General Assembly stepped in to break the logjam. By 4 March, both Virginia houses had accepted the core features of the bill in front of the Confederate Congress. Now they directed Virginia's two Confederate senators to vote for this radical shift in policy (both senators had resisted it). At the same time, Virginia suspended its law against Black men carrying weapons, provided that they were "organized as soldiers" and "in active military service" "during the present war with the United States."

This tipped the balance in the Confederate Senate, where, on 8 March, a measure that would otherwise have failed instead narrowly passed, by a vote of 9–8. The next day, the Confederate House, having already accepted the outlines of the bill, approved the Senate version, and on 13 March 1865, President Jefferson Davis signed it.

Soon, reports came in of a small number of Black prospective soldiers drilling in the Confederate capital. There had been talk of 100,000, maybe 200,000, even 300,000 total Black soldiers entering the war on behalf of the Confederacy. The Virginia bill had authorized enrollment of up to 25 percent of all Black men in Virginia of military age. The actual number in Virginia reached only a few dozen, and those men never finished training, let alone saw action.

In recent years, Confederate re-enactors and other facets of popular culture have sometimes featured Black combat soldiers in gray. Historian Kevin Levin has a book exploring the origins of this notion, this emerging myth, which he explains as a post-1960s reaction to the mainstreaming of historians' demonstration that slavery constituted the core of the Confederate project. Levin recounts how in the 1860s, and in the generations that followed, somehow the presence of such a military force never gained recognition as even plausible, let alone ever understood as real.

Levin was asking when, why, and by whom the modern version had taken shape. He focused less on the actual developments between 1861 and 1865, the great resistance to enrolling Black combat troops in Confederate gray. That it took so long to approve such a policy, and even then by so bare a margin, should put an end to any notion that legions of Black soldiers ever fought against the Union.

The Confederate statute that finally authorized Black troops carefully limited the reach of this radical gesture. It made any promise of freedom dependent on the approval of both state authorities and individual owners. Moreover, what might that "freedom," if any, mean? The typical experience of a "free person of color" in prewar and wartime Virginia offered clear clues to the conception of Black freedom being assumed, how very limited any such freedom would have been.

Black Confederate combat soldiers had not gone missing in action from Robert E. Lee's army. They had never been there.

1-7
Abraham Lincoln, the Republican Party, and the War for Union

As political, military, and cultural conflict unfolded through the 1850s and '60s, the Republican Party responded to radical shifts in the situation.

The party originated in 1854 as fury erupted in the Northeast and Midwest over the Kansas-Nebraska Act. All hopes that somehow the controversies over slavery had been resolved disappeared when suddenly the sacred Missouri Compromise of three decades earlier came unglued. A vast region, divided into Kansas Territory and Nebraska Territory, would be open to slavery or closed to it, entirely depending on how voters decided in each territory. Already in 1856, after adopting the name Republican, the party ran a campaign for the presidency on a platform denouncing that new policy, though it lost to Democratic candidate James Buchanan.

The following year, when the Supreme Court ruled in the *Dred Scott* decision that Congress had in fact no constitutional authority to regulate slavery in the territories, it only reinforced a widespread perception that the national government had come under the control of radical proslavery advocates. A growing number of northerners feared what they came to call the "Slave Power." They saw the system of slavery as threatening to invade all parts of the nation where it did not already exist.

Adding to the fury, northerners began to see quite clearly how in practice the Slave South demonstrated no principled commitment to state rights. To the contrary, under the new Fugitive Slave Act of 1850, citizens of any non-slave state could at any point be conscripted to join a posse to capture alleged slave runaways, and southern spokesmen expressed outrage when northern state legislatures passed laws to protect their citizens from being drafted in such fashion. On top of that, in the interests of safeguarding slavery, the Slave Power was prepared to suppress White northerners' free speech and free press.

All of this was background to the 1860 presidential campaign. In its platform, the Republican Party attacked the notion that the western territories had somehow become open to the expansion of slavery. At the same time, the platform made clear that the federal government had no constitutional authority to tamper with slavery in the states where it already existed.

As to the legitimacy of secession, the party made clear that this was not an option and would be resisted if attempted by any state. When Abraham Lincoln won the presidency, and 11 states did secede, most southern Democrats left Congress, leaving substantial Republican majorities in both houses. When the war began, Congress moved expeditiously on all fronts that seemed open to action. First, it banned the expansion of slavery into the territories, thus enacting the party's core policy. Second, it opened the door to a general emancipation in the nation's capital, albeit with restrictions.

With the war grinding on, President Lincoln considered his options. In September 1862, he issued the Preliminary Emancipation Proclamation, declaring that, in any areas still held by rebel forces on New Year's Day 1863, slaves were to be deemed free.

No Confederate state accepted these terms for peace. Commander-in-chief Lincoln therefore issued the Emancipation Proclamation on 1 January, declaring all slaves in rebel-held territory free. Beyond that, he authorized the enrollment of Black soldiers into Union combat units. Thus were US war aims transformed as wartime conditions unfolded.

The next year, 1864, Lincoln ran for reelection. This time the Republican Party's platform expressly embraced the Emancipation Proclamation, including the enrollment of Black men as combat personnel in the US Army and Navy. More than that, it called for a constitutional amendment to end the system of slavery throughout the nation, and it did so in terms that spoke not only to military necessity but also to the imperatives of morality and of democracy.

Secession had led to a war for Union, and the war had gone on until it became a war for both preserving the Union and abolishing slavery. Lincoln won reelection on this platform.

The following April, the world suddenly shifted again. As organized military action came to an end, and as the Thirteenth Amendment made its way toward ratification between January and December that year, new questions arose. If no longer enslaved, who were these four million people in the South going to be? They were not citizens if the doctrine from the *Dred Scott* ruling held sway, that no person of African lineage could ever be a citizen. Were they entering the liminal status of "free persons of color" in the pre-war South, that is, not owned by any individual, but circumscribed in all manner of ways as to their legal rights and prospects?

How similar to *White freedom* would *Black freedom* turn out to be?

1-8
Civil Rights, Three-Fifths, and the Fourteenth Amendment

In early December 1865, for the first time since the previous spring, Congress came back into session. Since it had last met, Confederate armies had surrendered to Union forces, an assassin had killed Abraham Lincoln and put Andrew Johnson in the White House, and legislatures in the recent Confederate states had begun creating new legal regimes to maintain as much control over Black southerners as could be managed in the absence of slavery.

With ratification of the Thirteenth Amendment, slavery was declared abolished. A universal emancipation had lifted all people formerly held in slavery into some new status. But what would that new status look like? Congress initiated action toward a civil rights bill, plus an omnibus collection of clauses to put into a proposed constitutional amendment, all designed to address issues that went beyond the Thirteenth Amendment, surpassing a simple declaration that enslavement had ended.

State legislatures in the recent Confederacy, one after another in late 1865 and early 1866, were enacting severe limits on what Black freedom would look like. Mississippi's new legal regime, for one, curtailed the prospect that any freedman could buy rural land. That meant that freed people, notwithstanding their purported emancipation, would continue to be landless, dependent on White landowners for employment, working not on their own land but someone else's, not temporarily but permanently, a situation that appeared, to most northerners as well as to people recently declared free, entirely too much like slavery.

The Republicans' civil rights bill, if it became law, would establish a set of federal rights to override state restrictions. The Civil Rights Act of 1866 would rebut the 1857 *Dred Scott* ruling by declaring anyone born in the United States, i.e., to include Black southerners, to be US citizens. For one thing, that would mean that African Americans would have the right, unlike Dred Scott, to go into federal court to protect their rights. A bill of that sort might be vulnerable to judicial override as beyond the authority of Congress to enact, or it might be repealed in the advent of a hostile Congress. Therefore, these provisions had to go into the Constitution, all before the current Congress could safely readmit congressmen and senators from the 11 seceded states.

Other issues, too, had to be satisfactorily resolved. Lest there be doubt, as there continued to be, no compensation would ever be paid for the loss of property in slaves. In addition, congressional Republicans were determined to ban repayment of debts that Confederate state governments had incurred to prosecute the war, and they had also to guarantee that the federal debt incurred in that war would be safe from repudiation. Perhaps far and away more immediately significant than all the other provisions, they saw it as imperative to fix the Three-Fifths Clause.

By that point, Republican in Congress had come to recognize that an end to slavery gave the Constitution's Three-Fifths Clause a radically new meaning. Under the US Constitution, enslaved people had always counted as three-fifths of a person for purposes of establishing the population figure that determined how many members of Congress any state's voters could elect. All other people counted full value.

People formerly held in slavery, but now free, would automatically count full value in terms of representation in Congress, and therefore in the Electoral College. And yet the electorate in each of those states remained categorically White.

In the absence of a very big change, White southerners would come back into the Union with far more power in national governance than before, far more capacity to cause serious mischief, as Republicans understood the matter, than the enormous power they had enjoyed in the 1840s and 1850s, before secession and war and Union victory. In death as in life, in short, southern slavery roiled national politics.

Congress in early 1866 did two main things. It passed a civil rights bill, and when the new president, Andrew Johnson, vetoed it, overrode that veto, so the Civil Rights Act of 1866 went into effect. And it set in motion a proposal for a Fourteenth Amendment.

As proposed by Congress, Section One, the one that in modern times has gained the most attention, aimed to place key elements of the 1866 Civil Rights Act beyond the reach of invalidation by a federal court or repeal by a future Congress. Almost all African Americans, by virtue of having been born in the US, were now citizens. And, reaching even beyond the rights of citizens, no state shall "deprive any person of life, liberty, or property, without due process of law; nor deny to any person within its jurisdiction the equal protection of the laws." *Any person.*

Section Two, central to Republicans' determination not to lose the fruits of the victory won in a ghastly war, addressed the Three-Fifths Clause and, at the same time, prodded the seceded states to consider Black enfranchisement, though not demanding it. White legislators in southern states must choose between two alternatives: grant Black men the right to vote, and all Black residents would fully count for purposes of representation; or retain an all-White electorate, but forfeit representation for Black residents. In short, five-fifths or zero-fifths; Black men vote; or they do not.

The states must choose one of those options. Black men would vote their own representation, or nobody would.

When the proposed amendment went out to the states for ratification, among the 11 recent Confederate states only one, Tennessee, accepted its terms. Tennessee alone ratified it. Republicans in Congress did not conceive ratification as somehow optional—its terms provided the only acceptable basis for bringing the seceded states safely back into the Union. Yet without some of the 10 resistant states, the Fourteenth Amendment could not secure ratification. What to do?

And so began "Congressional Reconstruction," as enacted in March 1867. In each of those 10 states, the US military would supervise new elections, in which Black men as well as White men would participate, to select delegates to a new state constitutional convention. The new constitutions to be crafted, and put into operation, must include voting rights for Black men. And that was only the first condition that must be satisfied.

Legislatures elected under those new constitutions must ratify the Fourteenth Amendment, and only then might those states be fully "restored," meaning that their voters could once again participate in federal elections, and men chosen from those states could once again take their seats in the US Senate and House of Representatives.

In sum, in 1860, voters and their electors chose the Republican candidate for president. Eleven states acted upon three principal "state rights": (1) the right to own people as slaves; (2) the right of a state's citizens to take their slaves to settle in western territories; and (3) the right to secede, committed as they were to safeguarding the first two rights. In 1865 the war put an end to all three of those "state rights." Instead, Black Americans, whether previously free or, until recently, enslaved, picked up new rights.

During the 1860s, the US moved from widespread Black enslavement to universal Black freedom from slavery, then to Black citizenship under federal law in 1866, albeit without any guarantee of voting rights, to Black citizenship with all the kinds of political rights that most White men had long enjoyed. The Fifteenth Amendment, ratified in 1870, recognized Black voting rights throughout the US; but Black suffrage had already come to the 10 "reconstructed" states back in 1867.

To summarize, ten years after the Anti-Nebraska Party formed in 1854 committed to keeping the slave system from further expansion, the (renamed) Republican Party had adopted a full abolition approach to the future of Black Americans everywhere. It certainly did no such thing in 1860 or 1861. But the war came.

And then the war dragged on, and the Republican Party came around to a full commitment to universal emancipation in 1864 or 1865. After 1863, 1864, or 1865, not only would slavery be forbidden in new areas of the West, but it would also come to an end where it had long existed in the South.

By 1867, 10 years after the ruling in *Dred Scott*, Congress had gone much farther. It had proposed a constitutionalized recognition of Black citizenship; and in fact, Black men, under Congressional Reconstruction, began exercising their political rights as citizens in at least 10 additional states by going to the polls, in some cases gaining election, and then participating in the making of public policy.

By 1870, every former Confederate state had achieved "restoration." The Fourteenth Amendment had become part of the US Constitution in 1868. In addition, the Fifteenth Amendment joined it in 1870, declaring that no state, North or South, could deny the right to vote on grounds of race. By then, of course, hundreds of thousands of Black men had already voted, both in 1867 to elect members of their state's new constitutional convention and, in 1868, in the presidential election that put another Republican candidate, former Union general Ulysses S. Grant, in the White House.

During a decade of radical discontinuity, Congress had generated the legal basis—both statutory and constitutional—for a dramatically different nation. What might the future bring?

1-9
Document: Republicans on Slavery and Race, 1860 to 1864 to 1868

The Republican Party's platforms reveal the Republicans' rapid movement through the 1860s on matters of race, slavery where it was, slavery where it might be spreading, Black men as combat soldiers fighting against the Confederacy, Black citizenship and civil rights, and Black men voting.

In 1860, the party's platform took an adamant antislavery stance regarding the territories, that is, against the spread of the institution into new lands in the West. At the same time, however, it voiced an anti-abolition, proslavery approach when it promised no assault on slavery in the states where the institution had long been rooted:

> 4. That the maintenance inviolate of the rights of the states, and especially the right of each state to order and control its own domestic institutions according to its own judgment exclusively, is essential to that balance of powers on which the perfection and endurance of our political fabric depends . . .

> 7. That the new dogma that the Constitution, of its own force, carries slavery into any or all of the territories of the United States, is a dangerous political heresy . . . ; is revolutionary in its tendency, and subversive of the peace and harmony of the country.

8. That the normal condition of all the territory of the United States is that of freedom: That, as our Republican fathers, when they had abolished slavery in all our national territory, ordained that "no persons should be deprived of life, liberty or property without due process of law," it becomes our duty, by legislation, whenever such legislation is necessary, to maintain this provision of the Constitution against all attempts to violate it; and we deny the authority of Congress, of a territorial legislature, or of any individuals, to give legal existence to slavery in any territory of the United States.

By 1864, by contrast, the war had both permitted and mandated a radical change in national policy regarding slavery in the states where it had existed in 1860. That year, the party platform deployed a combination of powerful rhetoric, strategic thinking, political necessity, and moral mandate to rid the nation of slavery once and for all everywhere. It expressly approved the Emancipation Proclamation, both what it said about slavery in Rebel-controlled places and what it said about incorporating Black men as combat soldiers wearing Union blue:

3. Resolved, That as slavery was the cause, and now constitutes the strength of this Rebellion, and as it must be, always and everywhere, hostile to the principles of Republican Government, justice and the National safety demand its utter and complete extirpation from the soil of the Republic; and that, while we uphold and maintain the acts and proclamations by which the Government, in its own defense, has aimed a deathblow at this gigantic evil, we are in favor, furthermore, of such an amendment to the Constitution, to be made by the people in conformity with its provisions, as shall terminate and forever prohibit the existence of Slavery within the limits of the jurisdiction of the United States.

5. Resolved, That we approve and applaud the practical wisdom, the unselfish patriotism and the unswerving fidelity to the Constitution and the principles of American liberty, with which ABRAHAM LINCOLN has discharged, under circumstances of unparalleled difficulty, the great duties and responsibilities of the Presidential office; that we approve and indorse, as demanded by the emergency and essential to the preservation of the nation and as within the provisions of the Constitution, the measures and acts which he has adopted to defend the nation against its open and secret foes; that we approve, especially, the Proclamation of Emancipation, and the employment as Union soldiers of men heretofore held in slavery . . .

The Republican Party Platform of 1868 voiced a commitment to Black citizenship and the right of Black men to vote, in the reconstructed states, that is—while at that time leaving the matter of Black suffrage in the loyal states to those states. The Party was not yet ready to move to what became the Fifteenth Amendment. But it voiced an absolute commitment to the Fourteenth Amendment, recently adopted:

First—We congratulate the country on the assured success of the reconstruction policy of Congress, as evinced by the adoption, in the majority of the States lately in rebellion, of constitutions securing equal civil and political rights to all, and regard it as the duty of the Government to sustain those constitutions, and to prevent the people of such States from being remitted to a state of anarchy or military rule.

Second—The guaranty by Congress of equal suffrage to all loyal men at the South was demanded by every consideration of public safety, of gratitude, and of justice, and must be maintained; while the question of suffrage in all the loyal States properly belongs to the people of those States.

Fourteenth—We recognize the great principles laid down in the immortal Declaration of Independence as the true foundation of Democratic Government; and we hail with gladness every effort toward making these principles a living reality on every inch of American soil.

1-10
W.E.B. Du Bois, Public Schools, and the Benefits of Reconstruction

The African American scholar and activist W.E.B. Du Bois (1868–1963) published a journal article, a jaunty specimen titled "The Benefits of Reconstruction," in 1910 in the *American Historical Review.* In an era when most academics shared a nationwide commitment to White supremacy, the title itself constituted an act of temerity, suggesting that the Reconstruction era, the highly contested period that followed the Civil War, really did bring "benefits."

Du Bois's historical reassessment represented one among a great many battles he fought on the civil rights front in a lifetime that stretched from his birth during the presidency of Andrew Johnson to his death on the cusp of Lyndon Johnson's time in the White House. A few years after the article's appearance, African American scholars would find that Carter G. Woodson's new *Journal of Negro History* offered a far more welcoming venue for research reports on Black history whether by Black writers or Whites.

Then again, "The Benefits of Reconstruction" went well beyond Black history. As the era's top "benefits," Du Bois pointed to an actual democratic experiment in southern governance in every "reconstructed" state, plus a state system of public schools. The new educational opportunities became available not only to Black children but also to what, in most southern states, was a White majority.

Outside the South, public elementary schools arose early everywhere. The Northwest Ordinance of 1785 stipulated that land in that vast area be set aside in every township to provide a financial basis, and a physical location, for a school. Horace Mann famously championed a system of public schooling for Massachusetts decades before the Civil War. But as late as 1860, no state in what soon became the Confederate South supported such a system. State law often criminalized Black schooling, and opportunities even for White children generally proved sparse.

Then came the war and its aftermath, including the deliberations in Congress over what should happen in the restored states of the former Confederacy, as well as what the Black-and-White Republican coalitions demanded in the late-1860s constitutional conventions and the legislative sessions that followed.

Florida's new constitution, for example, declared: "It is the paramount duty of the State to make ample provision for the education of all the children residing within its borders." Virginia appearing uncertain in its commitment to establishing and maintaining a school system, Congress conditioned the state's political restoration on a pledge that it never "deprive any citizen or class of citizens of the United States of [their] school rights and privileges."

Each of the 10 states undergoing "reconstruction" should, and did, inaugurate a system of public elementary schools, open to all children, Black and White. Every one of those states embarked on such a system by 1870 or soon after.

Would White children and Black children go to school together? Most states started out with, and all states soon had, two systems of schools. South Carolina and Louisiana struggled over establishing schools in which Black children and White children could be classmates. But those two states soon joined all the others in requiring segregation, with some schools only for Whites, others only for Blacks, thus establishing segregation by law long before the 1896 Supreme Court ruling in *Plessy v. Ferguson* approving "separate but equal."

In a time when public funds, never abundant, were especially hard to find and allocate, much public money went into this new social good. In every state, the new system/s, no matter the challenges, took root and became public benefits that most Whites and virtually all Blacks swore by.

In a graphic example of how important the schools became to Whites as well as Blacks, a great coalition arose in Virginia at the end of the 1870s that for a time toppled the state's traditional rulers. White voters, especially in western Virginian, combined with Black voters in eastern Virginia to elect an insurgent state government that reversed what had become a downward slope in school funding and pushed it to unprecedented heights.

When the "Readjusters," as they were called, were thrust back out of power, the new fiscal arrangement survived, and the school system made its unsteady way into ever greater social importance and fiscal prominence. In Virginia, again a good example, the burgeoning school system, in great need of trained teachers, led—just during the 1880s— to an investment of substantial state money into a new institution for Black students (male and female), Virginia Normal and Collegiate Institute (today's Virginia State University); a new school to train young White women to become teachers (today's Longwood University); and a teacher program for White men at the College of William and Mary.

In 1906, going beyond elementary schools, Virginia mandated at least one high school in every county and city. That meant two things. First, if a county supported just the minimum single high school, then clearly White youth would be attending that one, and Black communities and their youth would be left to their own devices. And second, the new high schools would need many more teachers, with greater preparation than elementary schools demanded, so the state created three new colleges for young White women (today's James Madison University, Radford University, and University of Mary Washington) to train as high school teachers.

By the time Du Bois wrote in 1910, public school systems even in the South were reaching their 40th anniversary. So much had changed there in those four decades as to make it hard to comprehend how undeveloped and exclusionary was the educational landscape back at the time the Civil War and its early aftermath led to a vast renovation of possibilities.

Du Bois celebrated beginnings. The 20th century brought the entire nation a vast expansion of educational opportunities, from high schools to junior colleges to four-year colleges and beyond, plus all the attendant physical and institutional infrastructure.

1-11
Thomas A. Sykes and Special Education in Black and White, 1865–1900

Modeled on innovations in France, special schools in the US for children and youth who were deaf or blind originated in New England by the 1830s and soon appeared in other states. The vast changes in the South in the 1860s raised the matter of offering such opportunities, for the first time in the region, to Black youngsters, too.

Would any of the southern states permit both races to attend these schools together, and if not, would they establish separate facilities? Most states created comparable opportunities for African Americans at some point between the 1870s and the 1890s. Rarely, however, did the two groups attend together, and even then, not for long. Examples will illustrate different facets of the South's move from absolute exclusion to segregated access.

In South Carolina in 1873, Republican state school superintendent Justus K. Jillson directed the school for deaf or blind youth to admit both Black and White children on fully equal terms, with students living, eating, and taking classes together. Here was a southern state taking an avowedly integrationist approach to social policy during Reconstruction. But the teachers, all of them White, all withdrew, and the school closed for three years. When it reopened in 1876, it had only White students, but in 1882, South Carolina provided for a separate "colored department."

Louisiana began with a similar approach, but there the experiment failed even more spectacularly. In compliance with the Reconstruction state constitution, the legislature directed in 1871 that Black children as well as Whites be admitted to the schools for blind or deaf youth. Apparently, though, no Black child ever gained admittance to either type of school before the 1920s.

In Mississippi, Black students took classes at the state's only deaf school, with the same teachers as Whites, and in the same building—but at different hours. In 1882, with students both White (54) and Black (14) enrolled, the legislature established a "colored department" for deaf children. A half-century later, in 1929, Mississippi finally opened a school for blind Black children.

After Florida finally established its first school for any deaf or blind people, both Black and White children appear to have taken classes there between 1888 and 1895, in the same building. In 1895 the legislature banned that practice and funded a new building for a separate Black department.

In Washington, DC, what would become Gallaudet University, but mostly its feeder school, Kendall Green, enrolled a few Black students along with Whites in the 1890s. Yet opposition from some White students or their parents made the arrangement untenable, and Congress provided for the transfer of Black students in the District to

Maryland's segregated Black school for deaf youth.

Most such schools, however, operated on a segregated basis from the very beginning. Considerations that drove the establishment of educational opportunity for Black youth included state leaders' understanding of their constitutional responsibilities under post–Civil War conditions, the pleas of Black parents and communities, and Black legislators' initiatives.

North Carolina, mandated by its Reconstruction constitution of 1868 to accommodate "all" blind or deaf youth, led the South with a segregated Black school for deaf and blind youth that opened in 1869. Maryland followed in 1872.

Thomas A. Sykes, a formerly enslaved man who had been in the North Carolina legislature when that state established a school for deaf and blind Black children, gained election in 1881 to the Tennessee legislature. There he promptly pushed, with success, for Black access, with provision for "proper and suitable separate accommodations," at both the school for the blind at Nashville and the school for the deaf at Knoxville.

In Georgia, Black citizens sought access at both the Asylum for the Deaf and the Academy for the Blind. Authorities at the school for the deaf, after pointing out in 1873 that state law prohibited children of both races from being schooled "in the same house together," noted nonetheless that "humanity, charity, and the Civil Rights bill" all pointed toward some kind of legislative action. "Colored" departments went into operation at both schools in 1882, on condition that the Black and White branches would be kept "as distinctly separate" as if "in different towns."

Other states—Kentucky, Texas, Arkansas, Alabama—also established schools for deaf and blind Black children in the 1880s or '90s. Scholars have traditionally considered Reconstruction to have ended by 1877, and the post–1877 regimes to have featured sharp reductions in state spending. Yet, against both understandings, much of the legislation tracked here took place after 1877. The continuing presence of Black legislators in most former Confederate states through the 1880s, as in Tennessee, spurred establishment of some facilities.

When did Black students begin to have Black teachers, and when did Black schools first have Black administrators? In Texas, when the Deaf, Dumb, and Blind Institute for Colored Youth opened at Austin in 1887, William Holland, formerly enslaved, presided over the institution and hired Black teachers, trained at other southern states' Black schools.

Segregated access constituted a vast improvement over categorical exclusion. But it was scarcely the same access, and it enabled states to fund schools for Black citizens at less than those for Whites.

1-12
John Henry and Slavery under the Thirteenth Amendment

On December 8, 1866, in Annapolis, Maryland, a crowd gathered for an auction. A recent advertisement in the *Annapolis Gazette* had announced: "Public Sale . . . a Negro man named Richard Harris, for six months, convicted at the October term, 1866 of the Anne Arundel County Circuit Court for larceny and sentenced by the court to be sold as a slave.

Terms of sale—cash."

The Thirteenth Amendment, ratified a year earlier, in December 1865, had banned slavery "except as a punishment for crime whereof the party shall have been duly convicted." Richard Harris's sentence under the terms of that exception provides a glimpse of what grew into a regionwide system of unfreedom, whether the convict lease or the chain gang, that lasted into the Great Depression and New Deal 1930s.

Enslavement before the war enormously damaged millions of people's bodies, lives, prospects, families, and communities. The new form of enslavement snared fewer people, but across time and space they numbered in the many tens of thousands, and for those caught up in it, it proved much more deadly—its inmates had no cash value to an owner that might buffer them against deadly treatment. Moreover, it disrupted and contorted countless families and communities much as prewar slavery and the old slave trade had, and it wrought terror that it could reach anyone at any time. Two examples can illuminate the larger phenomenon.

Legend has it that John Henry, a Black man in the post-emancipation South, died while racing a machine to drill a railroad tunnel through a mountain in the Appalachians. John William Henry was a real person, born in New Jersey, who turned 18 near the end of the Civil War. Arrested in Richmond, Virginia, on the charge of a petty crime in April 1866, he found himself consigned to the incipient convict leasing system. Sentenced to 10 years in the state penitentiary, then in 1868 leased to work on the Chesapeake and Ohio Railroad, not only did he not remain in the custody of Virginia authorities, he did not even remain in Virginia. He died in 1871 laboring in West Virginia.

According to the Thirteenth Amendment, people born as slaves in the prewar South were supposed to live free in the postwar world. John Henry, however, born a free man in the North before the Civil War, fell into slavery in the South soon after that war and died there a slave.

Another Black man, John Davis, while on his way home from work in Central Alabama in September 1901, encountered a White man, one of many in a sprawling network, employed to conscript Black workers who looked like promising convict labor material. Detained on no particular charge, and sentenced to no set length of time, Davis found himself whisked off to work on a huge cotton plantation alongside many other Black men secured the same way.

Thus, John Davis left farming one day as a free man, then suddenly became an unfree man, still in the agricultural business, but reflecting one of the South's great industries, the manufacture of unfree workers out of free men. His gravely ill wife, Nora, and their children, bewildered and terrified that he had not returned home that evening, were forced to fend for themselves.

1-13
George Henry White and Black Electoral Power, 1865–1900

The Thirteenth Amendment (ratified in December 1865), when declaring people formerly enslaved now free in every state, left Black men in the South with no more claim on the right to vote, or to run for election to political office, than a White woman or child had.

But that changed in 1867, when Congress, intent on getting the Fourteenth Amendment ratified, directed that Black men be included as voters in the election of delegates to a new constitutional convention in each of 10 southern states. And the new constitutions that came out of those conventions had to enfranchise Black men. Soon, Congress also proposed the Fifteenth Amendment, and enough states ratified it by 1870 that no man anywhere in the US could constitutionally be denied the right to vote on racial grounds.

Black men, therefore, no matter whether they had always been free or had just very recently gained their freedom, could, and sometimes did, win electoral office—for the next 20 or 30 years, anyway. Many Black men were elected as state legislators or even as members of Congress.

It is often said that Reconstruction came to an end in the aftermath of the 1876 presidential election. But the facts, in state after state, paint a different picture. Tennessee offers a great example. There, one Black candidate gained election to the legislature before 1877; 12 did so in the 1880s, in some cases for two or three consecutive terms.

In many of the other states of the former Confederacy—Texas, Louisiana, Arkansas, Mississippi, Georgia, South Carolina, North Carolina—African American legislators served even after 1890.

As for the US House of Representatives, from 8 of the 11 former Confederate states (all but Arkansas, Tennessee, and Texas), at least one Black candidate gained election to Congress at some point between 1870 and 1898. One or more did so, in the 1880s or 1890s, in Virginia, North Carolina, South Carolina, and Mississippi. The very last Black congressman from anywhere in the South—until after Congress passed the 1965 Voting Rights Act—was George Henry White of North Carolina (1852–1918), who served from 1897 to 1901.

Putting an absolute end to this pattern of continuing Black electoral power took extraordinary efforts on the part of White supremacists, including horrific White-on-Black violence, as in Wilmington, North Carolina, in 1898. Flagrant violations of the Fourteenth and Fifteenth Amendments brazenly denied the right to vote based on race—and with no resistance from any branch of the federal government.

Congress had required Black enfranchisement by constitutional conventions in 10 states in 1867. In the years around 1900, one state after another effectively undid that handiwork and established a new pattern that would hold for most of a lifetime.

Also during those years, however, states outside the former Confederacy displayed a sufficient degree of Black electoral power to send Black candidates to state legislatures. As in both the Deep South and the Upper South, Black candidates elsewhere typically attracted some support from White voters, though (again typically) not a lot, or not enough to carry them to victory. The first Black state legislator elected in Massachusetts came in 1866, in Illinois in 1876, in Ohio in 1879, and in Indiana in 1880. And those patterns persisted.

Nor did such victories come to an end everywhere in the South by 1900. On the contrary, in every state of the Border South—in contrast to every former Confederate state—Black candidates won legislative office: in West Virginia beginning in 1898, in Oklahoma in 1908 (a one-off until the 1960s), in Missouri (Walthall Moore Sr. served four terms in the 1920s), in Kentucky beginning in 1935, in Delaware in 1948, and in Maryland by 1954.

With Black migration out of the South, people who had lost the right to vote by 1900 picked it up again, resulting in the election of the first Black state legislator in California in 1918, the first in New Jersey in 1920, and so on. The next successful Black candidate for Congress after George Henry White of North Carolina was Oscar DePriest, a native of Alabama elected to Congress in 1928 by his constituents in Chicago, Illinois, many of them Alabama-born.

From then on, at least one Black congressman served in every term into the 1950s, and soon the numbers became more substantial. An early change came in 1934, when Arthur W. Mitchell, a Black Democrat, defeated Oscar DePriest, as Black voters began to move from the party of Lincoln to the Democratic Party, a trend that started with the New Deal and became more pronounced when President Harry Truman became a champion of civil rights in the late 1940s.

In the former Confederate South, many elderly people in the years after World War II could remember the years before 1900 when Black men in places across much of the region had been able to vote Black candidates into political office. Many Black southerners had previously seen what they hoped might come back, what many worked to bring back. Many White southerners, having witnessed that long-ago Black political power, did their best to prevent its return.

The Voting Rights Act of 1965 brought back both Black voting and Black office holding, another new beginning.

1-14
Justin Morrill and the Land-Grant College Acts of 1862 and 1890

The year 1862, amidst the Civil War, brought a new era in higher education, one that, over time, transformed both applied research and social mobility across America. Three years earlier, Vermont congressman Justin Morrill had managed to get a bill through Congress to fund new colleges, but the president had stopped it with a veto. This time, though, a new president, Abraham Lincoln, signed it into law. We know it as the Morrill Land-Grant College Act.

In the Confederate states at the time, schools had stopped operating, as the war effort redirected funds and manpower alike, and college buildings often served as military hospitals. By contrast, the Morrill Act served as one indicator of the vast superiority of resources available in the states that remained in the Union.

The 1862 law allocated what it called "public lands" in the West to each state, based on its congressional representation, 30,000 acres for each congressman plus each senator, to be converted into an endowment to support

Justin S. Morrill, Representative from Vermont, Thirty-fifth Congress the operating expenses of one or more "land-grant colleges." States had considerable discretion, but the curriculum had to feature training in at least agriculture and engineering. The Morrill Act aimed to democratize access to higher education, with a constituency that contrasted with the traditional members of elite social groups aiming for a classical education or to be trained for law, medicine, or the ministry.

Already by 1865, when the war finally ended, some states had inaugurated this new type of college, and by 1872 virtually all other states, including those that had been in the Confederacy in 1862, had done so as well. Since the funds made available under the Morrill Act did not permit the construction of any buildings, many land-grant schools represented a repurposing of schools already in existence, like (to use today's names) Virginia Tech, Maryland, Michigan State, and Kansas State. Others reflected fresh starts, among them Purdue University and the University of Maine. Around the end of the 19th century, some states revisited their original decisions and moved the funds and designation to new institutions, and thus originated such schools as Clemson University and the University of New Hampshire.

In 1890, having moved over to the Senate, Morrill secured passage of another law to support land-grant colleges, one that accomplished two main goals. First, the 1890 Morrill Act roughly doubled each state's land-grant funding. Second, it conditioned those new funds on African Americans' access to a land-grant school, although it permitted a state (along the lines of what would soon become known as the "separate but equal" policy) to support two such schools, one of them designated for Black students. These "colleges of 1890," as distinguished from "colleges of 1862"—eventually one in each of 17 segregated states—included what are today's North Carolina A&T University and South Carolina State University.

At roughly the quarter-century and half-century marks, Congress substantially enlarged the functions of land-grant schools. The Hatch Act of 1887 provided funds for each state to conduct applied research at an agricultural experiment station; a later law promoted pure research. And in 1914, Congress authorized a "cooperative extension" program, under which extension agents would bring, to citizens across their state, the benefits of the research being done on campus. Home demonstration agents worked with farm women on tasks like canning foods for the winter, and farm demonstration agents worked with the men on those farms to address problems like diseases related to crops or farm animals.

Southern states divided demonstration agents by race as well as gender. Therefore, Black home demonstration agents worked with Black families, as did Black farm demonstration agents. In Virginia, for example, the Black demonstration agents operated out of Hampton Institute at first, and then out of Virginia State College. The apex of cooperative extension across Virginia stood at the White land-grant school, Virginia Polytechnic Institute. Its annual catalogs typically listed all four groups of staff members, often distinguished between "white" and "colored."

The land-grant college system offered growing numbers of citizens access to higher education, especially in technical fields. It supplied society and the economy with people trained as civil engineers, crucial to the further developments of roads, railroads, and bridges, as well as mechanical engineers and, over time, electrical engineers and so on. It trained teachers for the elementary schools—and professors to teach in the land-grant system. And it provided a tremendous range of research as well as training that enhanced the productivity of America's farms. The extension ethos aimed to benefit rural families at a time when most people still lived on farms.

Especially in the 1960s, land-grant schools that stood alone, separate from their state's flagship university, broadened their curricula and constituencies well beyond agriculture and engineering and took new names like Colorado State University, New Mexico State, and North Carolina State.

1-15
Red Land, Black Labor, White Colleges

Every college dorm room or classroom in the US is located on land that, for thousands of years—until within the past 100 or 200 or 300 years or so—served as the home of Indigenous individuals, families, communities, and nations, whether a place of residence, a trail for hunting or trading, or a place to be especially revered.

That constitutes the "Red land" without which no college could exist whether to enroll in or teach at. In recent years many colleges and universities have adopted a "land acknowledgment," a statement recognizing that the school is located on what formerly was Native land. From a wider perspective, land-grant institutions in particular exist in a *national* context, stretching to the Pacific Coast.

In March 2020, the magazine *High Country News* published the results of a two-year investigation into the financial underpinnings of what it called "land-grab universities." A collection of stories, with vast supporting data, declared a bold thesis, one that, once declared, became obvious: "Expropriated Indigenous land is the foundation of the land-grant university system."

High Country News thereby highlighted how the federal government acquired the so-called "public lands" in the Trans-Mississippi West that it then made available to states to finance their portions of the land-grant system—each selling its acreage, investing the proceeds, and then disbursing the annual income from the resulting endowment to whatever college or colleges it identified as a land-grant school.

Virginia illustrates the report's central thesis, and Virginia Tech exemplifies the land-grant system, especially its historically White southern variant. Virginia's land-grant acreage—300,000 acres in all—was located in a dozen states west of the Mississippi River, with nearly half of it in California alone.

The California portions of Virginia's acreage came from pieces of territory ceded by Native groups in 18 treaties during the early 1850s (soon after statehood)—none of which did the US Senate ratify, so all of which went uncompensated, denying the traditional occupants both a reservation and an annuity.

The Los Angeles Memorial Coliseum sits on one of the great many tracts of land that went to Virginia under the 1862 Morrill Act. Dedicated in the 1920s to memorialize soldiers lost in the Great War, it has been the site for multiple Olympic competitions and countless football games, as well as rock concerts and political rallies.

Without exception, all land-grant schools founded in the 1860s, '70s, or '80s, Virginia Tech among them, benefited directly from Native lands in the US West. That is equally true of the University of Maine in the East and Montana State University in the

West.

As for "Black labor," huge amounts of it, provided by force from unfree Black workers, generated the wealth that made many early colleges possible. Every one of the original 13 states featured some number and proportion of enslaved people. Scholars have demonstrated how, throughout the country—even in later states that never had slavery—the trans-Atlantic slave trade, or the manufacture of goods either based on the work of enslaved labor or produced for sale to the owners of enslaved people, contributed mightily to building up local wealth.

Some of that wealth went to the establishment and maintenance of schools at every level. In Virginia, moreover, as in many other states, Black workers continued to do a great deal of the support work that kept campuses going long after slavery.

Virginia Tech as a land-grant school had a predecessor institution, the Olin and Preston Institute, an academy for White boys. Enslaved Black workers—well over 20 percent of Montgomery County's total population—generated the local wealth that financed its beginnings. Those workers produced the wealth that enabled the owners of Monacan land and African laborers to establish local schools for White children.

After the Civil War, with the names switched to Preston and Olin, it still had one big building on five acres of land. The Morrill Act did not permit a state's endowment to go toward any structure—and only so much toward the purchase of land—and therefore most state legislatures, like Virginia's, selected a location that already had real estate—some land and a good school building—in place. This, the Preston and Olin Institute—with its large structure, designed for a school—could supply.

After 1865, moreover, Black Virginians performed essential support work from the day Virginia Agricultural and Mechanical College opened in October 1872. Throughout the years, Black residents of Blacksburg and the surrounding area continued to do so, even if neither they nor their children or grandchildren, into at least the 1950s, could ever enroll for classes, let alone teach there.

Among these contributors to the life of the institution, some were custodial staff in campus buildings, among them Gordon Trigg Mills in the 1910s and '20s. Others were laundresses who looked after cadets' uniforms, or dining hall personnel who kept them fed. Preston Mays worked for a half-century in the infirmary, helping cadets to recover from disease or injury. The many Black workers on an "all-White" campus also included barbers to the cadets, among them John Sears, Fred Caldwell, and Charles A. Johnson. Andrew Oliver worked as a janitor at VAMC from its beginnings in 1872; the 1880 US Census identified him as "Janitor VA+MC," a job he had held ever since the school was still Preston and Olin.

"Record linkage," making educated guesses about tracking a person from one document to another, divulges the identity of one of the young men who helped construct the building without which Virginia would never have established a land-grant college in Montgomery County.

When the trustees of the Olin and Preston Institute arranged in 1854 for construction of a big new building for the school, they contracted with two White men to look after the brickwork and two others for the timber and carpentry. John N. Lyle, who took up the masonry work, owned at that time about 10 enslaved people, predominantly young and male.

Of particular interest is the young man listed in the Slave Population schedule for

1850 at age 14 and again in 1860 at age 24. The Slave Population schedules almost never give names, but a Freedmen's Bureau document—a "cohabitation record"—from February 1866, shortly after emancipation, lists a 30-year-old man named Felix Johnson, who identified his most recent owner as John N. Lyle and his own occupation as bricklayer, a craft that he continued to follow, as shown in subsequent censuses.

In short, Red land and Black labor combined to foster White colleges, which thereby benefited from subsidies that brought wealth across the racial line from Black or Native to White. Emphasizing the emergence and development of Virginia Tech as a land-grant university, but pulling in all other colleges, facilitates a reconsideration of the broad trajectory of US history and, more particularly, of higher education in America, especially the land-grant system. Each land-grant school has evolved and grown; the twin foundations of Red land and Black labor continue to supply the basis for every enhancement.

1-16
Toward a New American Empire, 1865-1915

At the time of the US Civil War, few people anywhere envisioned that, by around 1900, the US would claim as its own territories both Hawai'i and Alaska or, for that matter, include the Caribbean island of Puerto Rico, the central Pacific island of Guam, and even the western Pacific archipelago the Philippines.

After colonists settled the coastal parts of what would become the original 13 states, they began pushing westward. After gaining independence as citizens of a new nation, Americans began settling ever nearer the Mississippi River and then, by the 1850s, along the Pacific Coast. Building an empire during those years had Americans moving west, securing a vast territory from France in the Louisiana Purchase (1803), then securing another vast tract in the US-Mexican War in the 1840s, and obtaining big chunks of those territories a second time from the Native nations that had occupied them for many thousands of years.

Despite talk in the 1850s of seizing additional land, this time in the Caribbean (today's Dominican Republic) or Central America (especially Nicaragua), US territory remained limited, until after the Civil War, to what would become the contiguous 48 states. By 1900, however, the US had claimed distant territories in the Caribbean and even places much greater distances away, in the Pacific Ocean.

First, the US purchased Alaska from Russia in 1867. Later, in the 1890s, the US dislodged Native control, under the reign of Queen Lili'uokalani, of the islands that make up Hawai'i. And in the early years of the 20th century, the US frequently intervened in the affairs of various nations in the Caribbean, or Central or South America, and built a canal, completed in 1914, through its Panama Canal Zone, which until recently had been part of Nicaragua.

During that same half-century, Europeans were carving the African continent into territories with names like French West Africa, the Belgian Congo, and German East Africa, each of which might supply raw materials for industrial production and serve as markets for manufactured products. Nations were also jousting for economic and military control over much of East Asia and Southeast Asia. Medical breakthroughs and technological innovations helped propel an international contest for control of new lands. US expansion during those years can be considered part of that global phenomenon.

During that same time, the US contributed mightily to the disintegration of what remained of the Spanish Empire. People in some Spanish colonies—Cuba, the Philippines—were challenging Spain's continued control, and Americans had their own interest in investment, commodities, and trade. The US went to war with Spain in 1898 in what Secretary of State John Hay called a "splendid little war," one that led quickly to Spain's losing such places as Cuba and Puerto Rico in the Caribbean, and Guam and the Philippines in the Pacific.

Against an "insurrection" led by Emilio Aguinaldo, the US then conducted a major military campaign, the Philippine-American War, to secure control of those islands for itself. And in 1903, while controlling Cuba, the US extracted a perpetual lease at Guantanamo Bay, in the far southeastern corner of the island, for a naval base that it was still using in the 2020s.

1-17
Theodore Roosevelt and the Varieties of Progressivism

Historians continue to call the early years of the 20th century the "Progressive Era." It was a hydra-headed phenomenon, with progress in the eye of the beholder, on any number of issues and at every level of government. In whatever way one periodizes the era—whether from the 1890s to the 1920s, or just between Teddy Roosevelt's taking the nation's helm in 1901 and the outbreak of the "Great War" in 1914—his presidency, covering most of two terms (1901–1909), lay neatly inside the timeframe.

TR's presidency manifested an era of "progressivism" in many ways. It featured the Pure Food and Drug Act of 1906, a breakthrough piece of legislation addressing public health and consumer safety, and the Hepburn Act (also 1906) to regulate railroad corporations. In environmental terms, Congress established Mesa Verde National Park (1906) and passed the Antiquities Act (also 1906), which authorizes the president to establish national monuments; TR established eighteen.

TR was a Republican. Woodrow Wilson, a Democrat, also promoted progressive reforms. His first term featured the Federal Reserve Act (1913), which brought a vast innovation in banking that, through the next century and beyond, would play a major role in shaping the economy, and the Clayton Antitrust Act (1914). Innovations on Wilson's watch also included the Smith-Lever Act (1914), which established a Cooperative Extension Service operating out of the land-grant colleges in every state to benefit all citizens; the National Park Service (1916), to oversee national parks and national monuments; and the wartime National Highway Act of 1917, which launched the federal government into new roles in interstate auto and truck transportation.

Amendments to the US Constitution during the Wilson years authorized a federal income tax (undoing a Supreme Court ruling that such a tax was unconstitutional); inaugurated direct popular election of US senators (instead of being chosen by state legislatures); introduced stringent restrictions on the manufacture, distribution, or sale of alcoholic products (looking to curtail drunkenness, industrial accidents, and impoverished families, but an amendment that would be repealed in 1933); and recognized a right for women to vote in all state and national elections.

Wilson's presidency also showed a penchant for what historians have termed "progressivism for Whites only." His cabinet members expunged many Black workers from the federal bureaucracy and segregated the facilities used by those who remained.

In presidential electoral politics, TR, after being denied nomination by the Republicans in 1912, ran as a candidate of the Progressive Party and came in second to Wilson. In 1924, Senator Robert M. La Follette, of Wisconsin, ran on a new Progressive Party ticket—with support from the Farmer-Labor Party, the Socialist Party of America, and the American Federation of Labor—and won even more votes (though a lesser percentage of the total).

Much, however, of what is meant by the Progressive Era took place at the state and local levels. States embarked on efforts to rein in what seemed like untrammeled power of railroad companies to set freight rates and endanger livestock. Throughout the period, states embarked on crusades to bring about "good roads" and "good schools." Reforms at the local level featured municipal parks and playgrounds, as well as enhanced educational systems that brought kindergartens on-stream as well as far more robust curricula in high schools, indeed high schools at all, since those were mostly a recent innovation. In the South, though, the funding of Black schools and their White counterparts diverged into the 1930s, just as the new improved roads tended to rely on chain gang labor.

In the matter of allegedly purifying politics, one example of progressivism, in its conservative guise, came when changes to city elections converted a ward basis to an at-large basis, making it less likely that ethnic enclaves, for example, would be successful in electing candidates to seats on city councils. More drastically, the years around 1900 saw one after another of the former Confederate states combine state law and mob violence to end the Black electoral power that had originated in the late 1860s and had to some extent persisted. Those states also sculpted the electorate by targeting White folks who could not be counted on to vote the right way. White leaders could limit them by the same laws they deployed against Black men—not expressly racial, given the Fifteenth Amendment—including the poll tax. The method for choosing candidates for state and congressional office by primary election, itself a reform, took another shape when the Democratic Party barred Black participation.

Along another dimension, laws to protect children or women in the workforce might make it through the legislative process but then run into a judicial blockade, as court rulings declared such legislation an illegitimate exercise of legislative authority, as when Congress tried to restrict child labor or to establish a minimum wage for women.

Theodore Roosevelt's progressive presidency reached far beyond US shores when he brokered a conclusion to a war in East Asia between Japan and Russia. Woodrow Wilson's "Fourteen Points" proposed progressive ideas for Europe in the aftermath of the First World War.

1-18
Johnny Got His Gun and Went to France

One man died in Serbia, in the Balkans; many millions died in the aftermath.

In the early 20th century, many people hoped and even believed that the era of big wars had ended. But the August 1914 assassination of Franz Ferdinand, heir to the imperial throne of the sprawling polyglot Austro-Hungarian Empire, touched off a war that extended across Europe and far beyond. Threading through Europe, a web of alliances bound one nation to come to the aid of another, and soon Germany, the Austro-Hungarian Empire, and the Ottoman Empire were at war against Britain, France, Russia, and other nations.

New weapons, from submarines to poison gas, combined with interminable trench warfare (mostly in northern France), led to horrific bloodletting, wiping out much of a generation of young men, quite aside from millions of civilian casualties. More than that, France, Germany, Britain, and other countries had overseas colonial possessions, so the war involved Asia and Africa as well as Europe, and both the Atlantic and Pacific Oceans. W.E.B. Du Bois contended that actually "the ownership of materials and men in the darker world is the real prize" at stake.

Americans, coming as they did from a constellation of geographical places and ethnic identities, were themselves scarcely of one mind in their loyalties, but early on virtually nobody favored US entry into the war. Regardless, the American economy prospered or faltered depending on trade with Europe, and the war produced new opportunities for bankers to make loans to combatant nations and for industries and businesses to make and sell military items as well as peacetime goods.

To prevent sale of military goods to Britain and France, German submarines destroyed seagoing vessels, sometimes with great loss of civilian life. In May 1915, the sinking of the British passenger ship *Lusitania* while it was crossing the Atlantic led President Woodrow Wilson to protest so forcefully that Germany agreed to suspend its attacks. For the US, the crisis subsided, and Wilson won reelection in November 1916 as the man who "kept us out of war."

In early 1917, though, Germany calculated that it would soon vanquish both Russia and France, then starve Britain into submission, before American troops could mobilize in force. Germany resumed unrestricted submarine warfare, including against US merchant ships. Moreover, what became known as the "Zimmermann telegram" came to light, according to which Germany promised to help Mexico regain its vast territory lost to the US back in the 1840s.

In April 1917, Wilson called for the US to make the world "safe for democracy," and Congress declared war. Not for another year and more, however, did US troops land in great force in France. Eventually they numbered two million men in all, plus women in such combat support roles as nurses, ambulance drivers, and telephone operators. Meanwhile, the US Navy went after German submarines and convoyed ships carrying supplies and soldiers, so goods continued to flow to the Allies.

Contrary to German calculations back in early 1917, the American Expeditionary Forces made the difference, though it was not at all inevitable. Countless stories of heroism, as with Medal of Honor awardees Earle Davis Gregory and Lloyd W. Williams, altered one outcome or another, and cumulatively they defeated the mighty Germans.

On 11 November 1918, accepting terms that Wilson had proposed (part of his "Fourteen Points" plan for a postwar world), Germany surrendered. In the end, though, Britain and France imposed far harsher terms on Germany, including gargantuan reparations and the loss of its overseas colonies.

The war had huge consequences for the world. One was the Russian Revolution, leading to the establishment of the Union of Soviet Socialist Republics (USSR). In another, given the severity of the peace treaty, the intractable economic impossibilities and towering resentment that emerged in Germany led to the rise of Adolf Hitler and his Nazi Party in 1933. Moreover, a tier of newly independent nations emerged in central and eastern Europe, including Czechoslovakia, Austria, Hungary, and Yugoslavia.

Back in the US, meanwhile, college campuses pretty much emptied out as students left for war-related jobs or entered the military. Women's participation in wartime economic roles heightened the push for women's voting rights throughout the nation, something soon achieved.

Black Americans, while in the grip of Jim Crow, had to determine how to approach a fight for democracy overseas. W.E.B. Du Bois, briefly optimistic about the prospects for democracy at home as well as the dire threat that Germany posed for "all darker races," urged his fellow African Americans to "close ranks" in support of the Allies. They generally did so, with the hope that their sacrifice would gain recognition of their rights, something not achieved.

A figure given as 53,402 American military personnel died in combat. More than that died of disease. A great many others suffered from having been wounded or gassed, quite aside from long-term battles with what would later come to be called post-traumatic stress disorder. And every casualty reverberated far beyond the specific person involved in those numbers.

Although nothing like the far more generous GI Bill that greeted returning veterans from the Second World War, the Soldiers' Rehabilitation Act of 1918 aimed to assist disabled veterans to prepare to return to the workforce, including, for many, college classes. Program director Charles Allen Prosser, in an item he published in *The New York Times* titled "Two Hundred Ways to Salvage Wounded Men," expressed the goal as providing the means for wounded veterans to "emerge able men again, full of hope and purpose and ambition."

In the late 1930s, even as global events appeared ever more ominous in both Asia and Europe, many Americans came to think they could and should have stayed out of the previous war and must stay out of the next. A best-selling novel by Dalton Trumbo, *Johnny Got His Gun* (1939), reflected the deep skepticism, indeed horror, at the thought of US involvement in yet another big war.

In that book, the fictional Joe Bonham had shipped out late in the Great War to France, where, on 11 November 1918, he became the very last US soldier badly injured on the very last day of the war. Trapped inside of what was left of his body, his arms and legs blown off, blinded, unable to speak, in fact with touch his only remaining sense, he desperately wanted to die but could not make it happen or, for a very long time, communicate his wish to anyone who might help.

1-19
Eugene Debs and the Quest for Economic Democracy

Rarely does an inmate in a federal penitentiary get close to a million votes for president of the United States. Eugene V. Debs (1855–1926) accomplished the feat in 1920, and his journey to that point illuminates much of US economic and political history between the Civil War and World War I.

Born in Indiana, the son of immigrants from France, Debs proved to have vast energy as well as oratorical and organizational skills, plus a social conscience attuned to transformations in the American economic system in the generations after the Civil War. Laid off during the 1870s depression from his job as railroad locomotive fireman, he became aware of deep poverty around him as he followed a career that took him through the burgeoning railroad industry of the Gilded Age.

He started out believing in social harmony and a widespread potential for upward social mobility. The railroad industry offered good jobs during prosperous times, though many were very dangerous.

But the bullying behavior of railroad corporations, the economic giants of the time, which refused even to discuss with workers their wages or working conditions, increasingly disenchanted him and moved him, by the early 1890s, toward helping organize the American Railway Union (ARU). As an industrial union, the ARU sought to include all railroad workers, no matter their skills, jobs, ethnicity, or location.

Cataclysm came in 1894, during another big economic downturn, in a great strike focused on Chicago, a tremendous railway hub, where workers were looking to restore their wages, which had recently been slashed. President Grover Cleveland sent federal troops to break the Pullman Strike, and federal judges issued injunctions that made even trying to organize the strike a crime. For ignoring such injunctions, Debs spent six months in jail for contempt of court.

Debs had already run for public office, and won, first on the local level as city clerk in his hometown, Terre Haute, then as a state legislator in 1884. By 1897 he identified with the Socialist Party of America (SPA) and its promise of a more democratic economic system. In 1900, he ran as the SPA candidate for the presidency of the US, the first of five such campaigns. He picked up 88,000 votes in 1900, more than 400,000 in 1904 and again in 1908, and 902,000 in 1912, 6.0 percent of the national total.

Debs, though too sick in 1916 to run again that year, shared the nearly universal hope for world peace and, at any rate, strong resistance to the US possibly entering the Great War (World War I). He continued that opposition even after President Woodrow Wilson, who campaigned for reelection in 1916 as the man who "kept us out of war," seemed to betray his pledge when he urged Congress, in March 1917, to declare war and bring the US directly into the conflict.

Rallying from his illness, Debs gave a series of fiery antiwar speeches in 1918 that led to his arrest, under the new Espionage Act of 1917, for undermining the nation's war effort. Sentenced to 10 years in federal prison, he ran a final campaign for president in 1920 and, as Federal Prisoner 9653, received 914,000 votes.

1-20
Alice Paul and a Woman's Right to Vote

A gathering in 1848 in an Upstate New York town, Seneca Falls, issued a "Declaration of Sentiments" listing all kinds of rights that laws in the US denied female citizens, solely by virtue of their gender. Modeling the Declaration of Independence, it charged: "The history of mankind is a history of repeated injuries and usurpations on the part of man toward woman, having in direct object the establishment of an absolute tyranny over her."

The first two out of sixteen grievances, or indictments, focused on political rights: "He has never permitted her to exercise her inalienable right to the elective franchise," and "He has compelled her to submit to laws, in the formation of which she had no voice." In addition, women should have access to a college education and to the professions of law and medicine, and married women should have the right to control their own property.

Seventy-two years later, in 1920, the Nineteenth Amendment to the US Constitution said women had the right to vote in all elections, state and federal. Moreover, the right to vote carried with it the right to run for public office and participate in making public policy that governed everyone.

The Nineteenth Amendment often also prompted a wider access to higher education, whether in undergraduate programs, law schools, or medical schools. And the numbers of women in the legal and medical professions, though early on nowhere more than tiny fractions of the numbers of men, grew across the 1920s and beyond, for the next half-century, before the 1970s brought the beginnings of a surge toward parity.

But nobody at Seneca Falls in 1848 could have known when, if ever, such opportunities would come their way. Over the years, suffragists—Black, White, Asian, Native, Latina— would come from every region, North, South, and West. They would petition, lobby, publicize their mission, and engage in civil disobedience, to test the possibilities, dramatize the matter, and secure sympathetic support.

Key people early on included Seneca Falls stalwarts Lucretia Mott (1793–1880) and Elizabeth Cady Stanton (1815–1902). Both would long champion the issue but not see the big day come. The campaign for women's rights, interrupted during the Civil War, resumed afterwards and never let up.

Proponents of women's political rights found themselves sorely distressed when the Fifteenth Amendment outlawed race as the basis for denying anyone the right to vote—but excluded gender: "The right of citizens to vote shall not be denied or abridged by the United States or by any State on account of race, color, or previous condition of servitude." Black men, as well as White men, now had the constitutional right to vote in every state. Women, regardless of their racial classification, nowhere did.

In November 1872, Susan B. Anthony had the temerity of showing up in New York State to vote, went on trial for her crime, and was convicted. Sojourner Truth also tried to vote for U.S. Grant that year, in Michigan, and was rebuffed. Virginia Minor tried to register to vote that year in Missouri and, when turned back, went to court, but the US Supreme Court ruled in 1875 that the Fourteenth Amendment, despite all its guarantees, did not make her a voting citizen. Thus began a very long campaign for the "Susan B. Anthony Amendment," which would expressly guarantee voting rights for women.

Even as the Fifteenth Amendment made its way into the Constitution, the territorial legislatures of both Utah and Wyoming granted "woman suffrage." State by state, women gained the right to vote, continuing in the West: Utah (resumed after a lapse), Colorado, and Idaho in the 1890s; then (after a long break) Washington, California, Oregon, Arizona, Kansas, Nevada, and Montana between 1910 and 1914; and just a few other states, including New York, by 1917.

The state-by-state approach, where successful, made a big difference. The very first female legislators were elected to the Colorado House of Representatives in 1894: Clara Cressingham, Carrie Clyde Holly, and Frances S. Klock. The next states where a female candidate won state legislative office before 1920 were Utah in 1896; Idaho in 1898; then (after the break) Wyoming in 1910; Washington in 1912; Arizona and Oregon in 1914; Montana in 1916; and California, Kansas, Nevada, and New York all in 1918.

Most states, however, had yet to budge. Only an amendment to the US Constitution could reach many of those states, especially in the South, let alone soon.

Alice Paul (1885–1977) grew up in a Quaker family in New Jersey and often accompanied her mother to meetings of the National American Woman Suffrage Association. After graduating from Swarthmore College, she studied in England, grew passionately committed to women's voting rights, and earned a PhD at the University of Pennsylvania with a dissertation titled "The Legal Position of Women in Pennsylvania."

In England she had learned the tactics of non-violent civil disobedience and had been arrested and jailed. She had also endured her first experience of going on a hunger strike and then being force-fed, with a rubber tube forced down her throat or up through her nose. Back in the US, like the women of Seneca Falls she demanded that sex discrimination end and that women be recognized as equal citizens. She began with women's political rights but aimed for far more.

In a major early project, she planned and carried out the 1913 Woman Suffrage Procession, a huge event that took place in DC the day before Woodrow Wilson's inauguration as the new president. Breaking with more moderate suffragists, in 1913 she co-founded (with Lucy Burns) the Constitutional Union for Woman Suffrage, which became the National Woman's Party in 1916.

In the 1916 presidential campaign, Wilson did not necessarily oppose woman suffrage, so long as it was on a state-by-state basis. Committed to state rights, however, and uncommitted to the issue, he refused to endorse a constitutional amendment to nationalize the right. Charles Evans Hughes, the Republican candidate, by contrast, came out in favor of the amendment. So, Alice Paul campaigned against Wilson in the West, where women could already vote.

But he won. In January 1917, she was back in DC, this time picketing the White House, dramatizing the mission with a "Silent Sentinels" approach, where a line of women, 12 at a time, stood their ground, every day except Sundays, month after month, carrying banners and gaining visibility for their call for a constitutional amendment. Their signs bore slogans like "Mr. President, how long must we wait for liberty?" And then, after the US entered World War I in April, they kept getting arrested.

The "Night of Terror," the most dramatic event, came 14 November 1917. Alice Paul had been sentenced to seven months in jail, in DC. Dozens of other protesters, with sentences ranging from six days to six months, were sent to the Occoquan (Virginia) Workhouse (later the Lorton Reformatory), where they protested the grim conditions of their confinement—and then met much worse. On top of cold and filthy cells and disgusting food, they faced harmful forced feeding and life-threatening physical assaults. Some of the women described the treatment in a book that Doris Stevens, a silent sentinel herself, published in 1920, *Jailed for Freedom*.

Voters in New York, all men, had just passed a referendum approving women's suffrage; public outrage at the protesters' treatment mounted; the president could not abide the prospect of dozens of White middle-class women succumbing on his watch to their hunger strike. In late November, all the women were suddenly freed.

They went back to protesting. The next fall, in a special address to the Senate on 30 September 1918, Wilson gave a strong public endorsement of the Nineteenth Amendment. He based his central argument on what he termed the "world war" then raging. As "commander-in-chief," he called the amendment "a vitally necessary war measure," for "it is my duty to win the war and to ask you to remove every obstacle that stands in the way of winning it." He inquired of the senators whether, "having made partners of the women in this war," "shall we admit them only to a partnership of suffering and sacrifice and toil and not to a partnership of privilege and right?"

Critical to the eventual success in Congress were men representing states where women already had political rights, including California and New York. In spring 1919, the amendment obtained the two-thirds vote in each house necessary to send it off to the states for possible ratification. Reflecting a struggle a half-century old, it replicated the Fifteenth Amendment, except for the final phrase, "on account of sex."

On 18 August 1920, Tennessee became the last state needed to reach the three-fourths threshold, 36 states out of 48. When election day came, less than three months later, women had the constitutional right in every state to vote for the presidential candidate of their choice, as well as candidates for Congress and other offices.

Still, not all women could vote even then. Many states had a poll tax that deterred poor women as well as poor men. As for Black women, even the wives of Hampton Institute professors, when attempting to register to vote that year, saw the registration windows suddenly close as they approached. Utah, New Mexico, and other western states barred Native women from voting, even after the Indian Citizenship Act of 1924, if they lived on tribal lands. Ethnic Chinese women, by contrast, if citizens (because they were born in the US), might vote, as Tye Leung Schulze did in California in 1912.

Already by 1925, a female candidate won a seat in almost every state legislature. The very last "first," Doris Lindsey Holland, appointed to the Louisiana senate in 1936 (replacing her husband, who had died in office), won election to the lower house in 1940.

As for Alice Paul, during the 1920s she studied law to better grasp the many remaining legal disabilities imposed on women. And for the next half-century, she led the National Woman's Party and campaigned to add the Equal Rights Amendment to the Constitution. But no more hunger strikes.

1-21
Women's Access to Higher Education, 1860s–1920s

From the founding of Harvard College, in Massachusetts in 1636, and the College of William and Mary, in Virginia in 1693, higher education remained solely available to White men, and in fact very few of them, into the era of the American Revolution and beyond. As late as the Civil War, access remained highly restrictive, by both race and gender (as well as class), whether regarding White women, Black men, or Black women. Between the 1860s and the 1920s, however, access greatly increased to both private colleges and publicly supported institutions.

Quite a few new private colleges for women, mostly in the Northeast, opened between the 1860s and the 1890s. Their founders envisioned them as providing curricular opportunities that would rival those in the best men's colleges. Most notably, these included the cluster that became known as the Seven Sisters colleges: one, Bryn Mawr, in Pennsylvania; two, Vassar College and Barnard College, in New York State; and four in Massachusetts, Wellesley, Smith, Radcliffe, and Mt. Holyoke. Their approximate counterparts in the South, established in the 1880s or 1890s, included Agnes Scott in Georgia, Sophie Newcomb in Louisiana, and Randolph-Macon Woman's College in Virginia. None of these southern schools would enroll a Black student before the 1960s, but some of the Seven Sisters occasionally did, although often with race-based restrictions, among them Harriet Rice, an 1887 graduate of Wellesley; Alberta Scott, an 1898 alumna of Radcliffe; and Otelia Cromwell, who finished at Smith in 1900.

Meanwhile, the Morrill Land-Grant College Act of 1862 created many new opportunities for young women. Outside the South, new schools established under the Morrill Act granted access to young women, in some cases from the very beginning and in others delayed, albeit generally accompanied by some gender-specific social restrictions. Iowa State Agricultural College (later Iowa State University) began operations as a coeducational school in 1869. The University of Maine, Ohio Agricultural and Mechanical College (later Ohio State University), Indiana's Purdue University, and Illinois Industrial College (later the University of Illinois) each waited two to four years before enrolling women as well as men. In New York, Cornell University explicitly made enrollment open to students regardless of race or gender from the beginning.

Money from the 1862 Morrill Act also flowed shortly after the Civil War to a very few new places in southern states that Black women could attend. Virginia allocated a portion of its land-grant funds to Hampton Normal and Agricultural Institute, a coeducational Black school from the beginning; Mississippi and South Carolina took comparable actions. This was federal money, not state funds, though the states were responsible for determining which schools would benefit. As the "colleges of 1890" opened in other racially segregated states, funded by the Morrill Act of 1890, there, too, Black women gained access, often to train in such fields as teaching, agriculture, and home economics, sometimes in the liberal arts. Black women also might attend private Black colleges in the South, including Fisk University in Nashville, Tennessee.

A widespread new phenomenon, originating in the late-19th century and expanding in the early-20th, brought state-supported teachers' colleges (though not at first really colleges) to train young women to become teachers in the public schools. Virginia offers an excellent example of how, between 1880s and the 1910s, states opened new schools with limited curricula designed expressly for female students to prepare for the profession of teaching in elementary schools. What would become Longwood University opened in the 1880s, and in the decade prior to World War I, the legislature established three new such schools, to train teachers for the new constellation of high schools opening across Virginia, mostly after 1906. Aside from opening new employment opportunities for women teachers, those high schools themselves represented a more advanced education than available earlier, plus they better prepared youth to go on to college.

Another burst of new female opportunity developed in the years around 1920, during or soon after the "Great War," and often reflecting the Suffrage Amendment's ratification in 1920. Again, Virginia supplies a great example of the timing and nature of enhanced female access. During the war, in fact precisely because of it, the College of William and Mary began admitting White women, as did the Medical College of Virginia (part of today's Virginia Commonwealth University), in each case an innovation that never went away.

In 1920, the University of Virginia ended the categorical exclusion of women in its programs in law, medicine, and graduate studies, but not for undergraduates. The dean of the law school displayed his skepticism at the innovation when, reporting later to the university president, he referenced the radical experiment of enrolling three of "these new and strange beings." In 1921, Virginia Polytechnic Institute, the state's White land-grant school, with a curriculum emphasizing science and technology, opened its doors to a handful of White women. Mary Brumfield, who transferred in as a junior, graduated in 1923 and promptly became a graduate student. But at neither of the two schools would the doors open very wide for about another half-century.

All these schools, put together, supplied opportunities for a small but increasing number of young American women. Those kinds of opportunities, emerging through the half-century or so after the Civil War, greatly enhanced female access (though it remained tiny) to the profession of law, for example, and to master's and doctoral programs as well.

A much greater expansion of female opportunity in higher education waited in general until the 1970s, another half-century in the future, when all manner of changes took place in society and culture, and Title IX (in 1972) mandated a dramatic expansion of female opportunity.

1-22
Senda Berenson and Women's Sports

The 1890s brought a new era in men's intercollegiate sports, mostly football, plus the invention of men's basketball as a new sport. It also brought the beginnings of women's basketball, with rules considerably different from the men's version. Beginning in the 1890s, Senda Berenson became a central figure in young women's physical education and team sports.

Berenson was born in 1868 in eastern Europe, in the old Russian Empire, under the name Senda Valvrojenski, to a Lithuanian Jewish family. Her father moved in 1874 to Boston, Massachusetts, where dozens of families from his home area, some of them relatives, had already settled. He also changed his name to Berenson. The following year, he sent for his wife and young children to join him.

Senda was a frail child, often ill, with considerable interest in painting and piano, but very little in physical activity. New ideas percolating at the time, from Sweden to Boston, were promoting gymnastics and other physical activity for young women, and these led her in 1890 to enter the new Boston Normal School of Gymnastics, where her health might improve and she might even train as a phys ed teacher.

At first, she found the physical rigors of her new curriculum virtually unbearable, but she stuck with it and gradually saw great improvement in her health and general physical well-being. She then gained an opportunity to teach physical education, at first at a nearby elementary school, and beginning in early 1892 at Smith College and a nearby high school.

Seeking a way to make phys ed more enticing to the young women in her charge, Berenson read about a new game recently invented by James Naismith and set about adapting it for female play. She did not see competition as the main point, so intercollegiate play had no place in her scheme, but playing first-year students against sophomores promoted a sense of community.

Developing a set of rules to govern "basket ball for women," Berenson divided the playing court into three sectors, one at each end, the other in between; players would each be restricted to a single zone. Female people could scarcely be expected to run the full length of the court, and anyway she wanted to discourage "roughness." In subsequent years, she incorporated other sports—fencing, field hockey, volleyball—into her program at Smith.

Berenson's rules for basketball, though modified at different times and places, generally characterized high school and college female basketball past the mid-20th century. Typically, the court would be divided into halves, with three players bringing the ball up to half court, then the other three responsible for taking it to the basket. Scores tended to be low.

From New Hampshire to Tennessee to California, these rules governed female basketball almost everywhere, through the 1950s, with the exception that girls and young women at Black high schools and colleges were more likely to play according to the men's rules.

1-23
Marshall "Major" Taylor and the Color Line in Sports

Jackie Robinson exemplified the athletes who broke the color line in American sports in the years after World War II. Yet lost in his characterization as a "first" is the roster of Black athletes who had participated with White teammates and rivals considerably earlier in high-profile competitive sports, including baseball.

Each demonstrated that a time existed when it was permissible for a first-class Black athlete to compete against Whites and on the same team as Whites. Each also faced extreme resistance, as Black athletes found themselves soon pushed out of "White" sports organizations. One such athlete, Jack Johnson (1878–1946), emerged in the early years of the 20th century as the dominant heavyweight boxer, before he was forced out of the sport and even sent to prison.

Back in the 1880s, in the early years of Major League Baseball, then the top team sport in the US, Moses Fleetwood Walker (1856–1924) was a star catcher. Walker played in organized baseball through much of the decade, though he often ran into challenges as a Black man in a "White" arena, like when opposing teams refused to play against him. A key moment in major league play occurred when he took the field on 1 May 1884 for the Toledo Blue Stockings of the American Association. Later in the season, his brother Weldy briefly joined him. And then it was over, until Jackie Robinson.

Marshall "Major" Taylor (1878–1932) exemplified a Black athlete's worlds, lost and found, between the 1870s and the 1930s. The son of a Civil War USCT soldier, he dominated competitive bicycle racing, or shared top billing, for years. Forced out of the sport as a Black man in a White supremacist America, however, he took his prowess across the Atlantic Ocean to Europe, even around the world to Australia, and there his career continued. Commentary on his few years competing in the US offers glimpses of the social psychology at work in a sports world of White supremacy and Black exclusion.

As a teenager in the early 1890s, during the great bicycle boom of that era, "Major" Taylor worked in a bike shop in Indianapolis and took up the sport of bicycle racing. Early on, his many victories mostly took place against Black competition. A former champion racer, a White man named Birdie Munger, took him under his wing, offered him training, supplied him with first-rate equipment, and encouraged him to find and test himself against White competition.

Finding his opportunities to race White athletes in the Midwest very limited, Taylor and his mentor moved in 1895 to Worcester, Massachusetts, where he turned professional in 1896 at the age of 18. He experienced the best of sportsmanship and merit-based acceptance one time when, invited to join four White riders from Boston in a race against a team from Philadelphia, he helped his team readily win.

But the bigger races took place in every region, and it was often worth his life to take his prowess elsewhere, especially to the South. "Taylor rides in all his big races in deadly fear of his racing companions," reported a New York paper, the *Sun*, in 1897, continuing: "Taylor now ranks among the fastest men in the country, but the racing men, envious of his success and prejudiced against his color, aim to injure his chances whenever he competes."

In 1898, the *Syracuse Telegram* said of Black athletes like Taylor: "His color should not weigh against him. If he can ride a bicycle or a horse as well as a white man, he should not be denied the privilege of displaying his abilities."

More representative of the wider culture, though, came in comments from the *New York Morning Telegraph*: "It is, of course, a degradation for a white man to contest any points with a negro." But, the paper went on, it is even "worse than that, and becomes an absolute grief and social disaster when a negro persistently wins in the competition." This in the same breath as exulting over a boycott of Taylor as an "emphatic assertion of the superiority of the Caucasian over the Ethiopian." The term "superiority" in this context meant artificial elevation, deliberate subordination, categorical exclusion.

Taylor set many world records in time trials, which did not feature human competitors on the track. He became world champion in the one-mile sprint in Montreal, Canada, in 1899. He also won the League of American Wheelmen's national championship in 1900, then left for a more welcoming environment to live and compete in. In Europe in 1901, he found himself treated everywhere as a star, with his competition fully accepting him and appreciating his accomplishments. He found adulation in France, Belgium, the Netherlands, France, Germany, Denmark, Austria, Italy.

Taylor continued to race in Europe, then in Australia. Retiring after the 1904 season and returning to the US, there he encountered, he later wrote, a "new epidemic of

Colorphobia." After three years of retirement, he returned to Europe in 1908, where he went out a victor in his last big race the next year. He briefly raced competitively again in 1910, in Salt Lake City, then, at the age of 32, left the sport.

He had been a world champion in North America, then both a champion and a celebrity in Europe and Australia. In the US, even the first of those put him in chronic danger in an already dangerous sport. He could have both in Europe.

As for Jack Johnson, he had hoped to model the great Major Taylor and become a world champion in cycling. Instead, he took up a less hazardous sport and in Australia, in 1908, became world champion in boxing. Back in the US, Johnson's victories over White boxers, combined with his flamboyant lifestyle and his marrying a White woman, led to his being hounded by the law and also a proposal in Congress for an amendment to the US Constitution outlawing Black-White marriage in every state.

In a very different sport, the early years of the National Football League featured 10 Black players in the 1920s, and three more in the early 1930s. But after 1933 they could no longer join (or remain on) any NFL team, no matter how good they were. These 13 players included Paul Robeson, Fritz Pollard, Duke Slater, Joe Lillard, and Ray Kemp.

After 12 years with no African Americans in the NFL, the 1946 season featured four Black players, and the numbers soon went up from there.

1-24
Andrew Carnegie, from Rags to Riches

Andrew Carnegie (1835–1919) embodied the mass immigration into the US between the 1840s and the 1920s, the transformation of the American economy during those years, and the rise of mega-philanthropy.

After arriving in New York City from his native Scotland at the age of 12 in 1848, he soon went to work in a textile mill, next at a telegraph company, and then for a railroad corporation. In 1861, at the age of 25, he worked for the US War Department in the first year of the Civil War, overseeing military transportation and telegraph communications, notably at First Bull Run. In the 1870s he embarked on a career in the steel industry.

Carnegie's parents, like millions of other Europeans during his lifetime, decided to leave their homeland for the greater opportunities that the New World seemed to offer. Like most immigrants of their time, his family followed relatives and neighbors who gave them some idea of what to expect in the US and helped with shelter and work when they arrived.

Typical as the Carnegie family may have been, Andrew proved unique in the stunning success he achieved. He embodied the myth of "rags to riches," that with enough effort, gumption, and good fortune, one could start at the bottom and work up to the top. Unlike most immigrant children, he moved much farther than from "rags to respectability," the theme in Horatio Alger's book *Ragged Dick* (1868).

Carnegie's career mirrored, as it promoted, the development of the 19th-century US economy. He began work as a bobbin boy in a cotton mill, so the mechanization of textile production, which had cost his father his job in Scotland, supplied young Andrew's first employment in America, in the first industry of the industrial revolution. At the same time, he participated in the tremendous economic opportunities in the North related to enslaved workers' production of agricultural commodities, most notably cotton, in the US South.

In the 1850s, he next worked at jobs in the "communications revolution" and "transportation revolution," first in the telegraph business, then in the nation's "first big business," the railroad (the Pennsylvania Railroad). Finally, he rose to great heights, along with the American economy, as he led the new steel industry into the 20th century.

Carnegie was a leader in the late-19th century process of "vertical integration," an effort to bring under one big company's control all the major components of a business, including the raw materials to be processed, the various stages of the production process itself, and the marketing. By the 1890s, his steel company operated its own coal mines, iron fields, shipping and railroad lines, and steel mills. Such a huge business had as its central concern the cutting of costs through efficient management, the latest technology, and large-scale operations: "big trains, loaded full, and run fast," as Carnegie put it.

As the railroad system neared completion, Carnegie turned to the cities as the next major source of demand for his product. He successfully sought contracts to supply the steel for the Brooklyn Bridge, America's first skyscraper office building (Chicago's Home Insurance Building), the Washington Monument, and the elevated railroads of Chicago and New York City. These big projects reflected the dramatic growth of American cities, together with a new architecture for the new age. And they depended on the emergence of a material that permitted such construction, as well as the deployment of electricity to light skyscrapers and power the elevators that moved people many stories up and down.

The strike at Carnegie's steel plant at Homestead, Pennsylvania, in 1892 resulted in bloodshed and a public outcry. At the same time, he succeeded in destroying the Amalgamated Association of Iron and Steel Workers, so that Carnegie Steel could operate without unions, itself emblematic of the late-19th century.

In an 1889 essay, titled simply "Wealth" and included later in his book *The Gospel of Wealth* (1900), he laid out his conviction that people possessing a great fortune should be constantly putting it to work to improve society. As to hoarding it, or passing it on to one's children, he insisted: "The man who dies thus rich dies disgraced." Carnegie spent the first half of his adult life making a fortune, the second half giving it away, converting philanthropy into a big business with an investment of some $350 million.

His legacy provided thousands of library buildings and church organs, and millions of dollars supported higher education or the cause of peace. He remembered Pittsburgh, the city of his greatest economic triumph, with gifts to establish the Carnegie Institute of Pittsburgh and the schools that are now part of Carnegie Mellon University, and he contributed lavishly to education and other causes back in Scotland. With the bulk of his fortune, he founded the Carnegie Corporation of New York, the largest of its kind before the Ford Foundation.

Carnegie had a profound impact on higher education in America. He contributed funds to several southern Black or Appalachian schools, including Hampton Institute, Tuskegee Institute, and Berea College, and he also operated at wholesale through the Carnegie Foundation for the Advancement of Teaching. In 1905 he inaugurated the first pension fund for college and university teachers, which in 1918 became TIAA (Teachers Insurance and Annuity Association). After the "Flexner Report" of 1910, the Carnegie Foundation also had a huge impact on medical education.

Carnegie developed a deep aversion to war. In the great days of the international peace movement that preceded World War I, he worked to promote arbitration as a non-military way to resolve international disputes. He created the Carnegie Endowment for International Peace and financed construction of three "temples of peace": the Hague Peace Palace in the Netherlands, a Central American Court of Justice in Costa Rica, and the Pan American Union Building in Washington, DC. The catastrophe of World War I devastated Carnegie's optimism, crushing his belief that war had become avoidable, even outmoded. No longer could he assume that "all is well since all grows better."

1-25
Appalachian Mountains, from Obstacle to Bonanza

As 18th- and 19th-century settlers from the East looked to go beyond the Appalachian Mountains, they saw an enormous challenge to their safe and commodious passage. Getting a wagon up a mountain, then safely down the other side, made for difficult and dangerous travel. The mountains were therefore a huge obstacle to their safe passage. That's why gaps, offering easier passage, in particular Cumberland Gap, proved so popular.

But the mountains also supplied new homes for people who desired the kind of environment to be found there and saw no need to continue. Valleys or hollows could offer land for grazing and growing, forests beckoned hunters as well as livestock, and rivers and streams offered opportunities for fishing and a means of moving people or things. As plantations and enslavement increasingly characterized much of the South, the Southern Appalachians constituted a second South, with slavery and commercial agriculture both much less in evidence.

Until deep into the 19th century, whatever commodities might come into view, from coal to timber, could prove extremely valuable, but only for local use, whether for cooking or heating, home or church construction, farm tools, furniture, or fencing. No transportation system offered a feasible means to get such items to distant markets.

That began to change even before the Civil War. Examples of prewar infrastructure innovations included the Erie Canal in New York from the 1820s and the Western and Atlantic Railroad in Georgia from the 1850s. But each meant primarily to reach the hinterland, not tap the area along the route: the canal aimed to connect the Hudson River with the Great Lakes, and the railroad connected Atlanta on the Chattahoochee River with Chattanooga on the Tennessee River.

Unlike those transportation improvements, the late-19th century changes emphasized tapping the country in between. They focused on transit facilities and market demand related to the riches of the mountains, and revolutions in both transit and the market drove up the supply coming out of Appalachia.

Tremendous growth in the iron and steel industries generated prodigious efforts to find the raw materials that a rapidly industrializing nation could put to productive use, whether for railway construction, bridges, skyscrapers, automobiles, or other new uses, including all the machinery used in a range of emerging industries.

Local railway construction in the 1880s and beyond made it possible to reach into the mountains and haul away vast quantities of both coal and timber. New machinery for cutting trees and hauling them—or trimming them onsite—provided another big dimension of the extractive process. King Coal towered over most other economic activities in Southern Appalachia between the 1870s and the 1940s, but timber was huge too.

Clearcutting timber, a one-and-done approach, served as a metaphor for how extraction benefited outside interests but not so much the residents of Appalachia. After World War II, the coal industry moved aggressively toward less labor-intensive means of extracting countless tons of black gold, including strip mining and mountain top removal, which proved catastrophic for both the environment and the people living there.

Coal towns and timber towns brought new amenities and new people. Company towns might feature a lightbulb hanging from the ceiling, an innovation typically appearing in cities long before rural areas. New arrivals to work the mines included Black migrants from the Deep South, as well as Italian and eastern European single men or entire families. For a time, Appalachia became, as it had been earlier with non-Native settlement, an area that attracted newcomers.

New railroads constituted the local key. By the 1880s, the Norfolk and Western began seriously building branch lines to tap local resources. Beginning in the 1890s, the Chesapeake and Ohio Railroad, intended primarily to reach beyond the mountains (and the line John Henry was cutting a tunnel for in West Virginia in 1871 when he died), also did so.

Large stands of hardwood trees had grown thin across the North by the 1880s, so Southern Appalachia looked ever more enticing. Early on, individual trees were cut selectively, and the work permitted local families to work seasonally and supplement their income from other sources. Increasingly, though, rail lines reached further, timber camps emerged, sawmills were located onsite, large tracts clearcut.

Some areas supported mostly coal, others mostly timber operations. Reaching after 1903 into chunks of eastern Kentucky as well as eastern Tennessee, however, the Stearns Coal and Lumber Company, headquartered in Michigan, developed both kinds of operations according to local conditions. Its operations featured a lengthy private railroad, a giant lumber mill, mining towns and timber towns, all quickly, voraciously, moving natural wealth far from where the company found it.

A related phenomenon had to do with the working conditions and wages that employees of the coal and timber corporations experienced. Literal battles took place between workers and a combination of corporate power and local officialdom. The best known, among a great many, is the Battle of Matewan, in West Virginia, in 1920.

So, the combination of railroads, timber operations, and coal mining has profoundly reshaped much of Southern Appalachia. In some respects, those economic activities promoted the well-being of area residents. Overall, they came more to represent an obstacle to well-being; others, outside the region, benefited from the bonanza. In view of the form of economic modernization that came to the mountains, Appalachian people often subsidized other people, in other places.

1-26
Confederate History and Black History

Two historians during the first half of the 20th century, both natives of Virginia, demonstrated highly divergent ways of reconstructing and remembering the past. Both relied on deep research in primary sources, but they asked very different questions regarding very different aspects of US history. Working mostly between the 1910s and the 1940s, they represented a second generation of scholars trained at the nation's relatively new research universities.

Douglas Southall Freeman (1886–1953), a native of Lynchburg and the son of a Confederate veteran, excelled as both a journalist and an historian.

As a teenager, Freeman accompanied his father to Petersburg to witness a reunion of aging Confederate troops and a reenactment of the Battle of the Crater there. Already inclined to the study of history, so moved was he by the experience that he concluded: "If someone doesn't write the story of these men, it will be lost forever," and in fact "I'm going to do it." He later wrote: "They say it is a lost cause. Perhaps it was; but it still lives in the hearts of the Southern people. Its career of arms ended these forty years ago; we only live for its justification. And this is not to be done in any other way than through the careful collection and statement of calm historical fact."

Freeman's work as editor of the *Richmond News Leader* gave him a megaphone to broadcast his thoughts, something he literally did by radio programming. Very early each morning on his way to work at the newspaper, he stopped briefly to salute smartly at the statue of Robert E. Lee on Richmond's Monument Avenue. He revered the Confederacy's fight for independence and Lee's Army of Northern Virginia. Armed with a PhD in 1908 from Johns Hopkins University, he wrote many books on the Civil War, chief among them the four-volume *R. E. Lee: A Biography* (1934–1935) and the three-volume *Lee's Lieutenants: A Study in Command (1942–1944).*

He also wrote multiple volumes on George Washington. And from what he learned studying those two very different generals from America's two biggest wars before then, he distilled broad concepts regarding matters of military strategy, which he took to the Naval War College and elsewhere. Weighing in on terminology, he is credited with having successfully urged that the World War II entry of US troops into Western Europe at Normandy be called, not an "invasion," but the "liberation" of Europe.

Carter G. Woodson (1875–1950) was born in Buckingham County, midway between Lynchburg and Richmond. His mother had learned to read and write while still enslaved; his father, who had not, freed himself as a young adult during the Civil War and served in the Union Army in the Richmond area.

Woodson graduated in 1903 from Berea College, one year before the Kentucky legislature banned non-segregated education even at a private college. He then taught for four years in the Philippines, which had recently become a US territory. After earning a PhD in history from Harvard University in 1912, he set out to evangelize the gospel of Black history, or, as it was called in those days, Negro history.

In 1915, Woodson co-founded the Association for the Study of Negro Life and History and established the *Journal of Negro History* as an outlet for scholarship on all topics related to African American history. Especially in its early years, the *Journal* provided, if not the only outlet, certainly one of the few, in which scholars, both Black and White, could publish their findings in the field he championed, for example "The Negro in the Reconstruction of Virginia."

Woodson edited the *Journal of Negro History* during much the same time as Freeman edited the *Richmond News Leader*. He also initiated the *Journal of Negro Education*, focused on the curriculum in the South's segregated Black schools. He aimed to put into teachers' hands materials that they could take into their classrooms and use effectively in shaping the world view of their young charges, whether in elementary schools or increasingly also in high schools, which, for Black youth, were often called "training schools," featuring curricula often sparse in academic subjects.

Woodson's people, those he wrote of and celebrated, Freeman's armies had fought to keep enslaved. Woodson, focusing on Black Americans, emphasized the bottom of the social structure, not the great political and military leaders. His many books included *A Century of Negro Migration* (1918), *A History of the Negro Church* (1921), and *The Negro in Our History* (1922).

He developed the idea of Negro History Week (today's Black History Month), first celebrated in 1926 and marked during the second week of February to commemorate the birthdates of Abraham Lincoln and Frederick Douglass. Beginning in 1937, he also edited the *Negro History Bulletin*, designed to circulate the ongoing research on Black history to a wide audience.

Two very different historians, Carter G. Woodson and Douglas Southall Freeman were each foundational in their field of inquiry and in their influence on the wider world.

1-27
Perfecting US Society and Politics, 1924 Style

The second Ku Klux Klan peaked in influence around the year 1924. In its first incarnation, in the late 1860s, the KKK had targeted Black southerners—the men, the women, their schools, churches, political power, and labor. Suppressed for a time, the Klan never went entirely away. The new version—which emerged in Georgia in 1915, took off in 1920 in Texas and Oklahoma, and reached new levels of political influence in Indiana and elsewhere in 1922—was more of an equal opportunity hater, as well as a national phenomenon rather than restricted to the South. It cropped up in cities as well as rural areas, and it controlled politics in some entire states ranging across the nation, whether in the Northeast, the Midwest, the South, or the Pacific Northwest.

King Klan the Second aimed his wrath not only at African Americans and their allies, but also people who practiced what Klan members perceived as aberrant religious faiths, Jews and Catholics in particular, and aberrant sexual behavior. The new improved Klan harked back to a world that never entirely was—but that had at one time, say the 1880s, been far more in evidence than was true by the 1920s. The time had come to return to a preferred past—time to make America great again.

The Second Klan embodied a nationwide impulse that could be seen in various ways that took legislative form, especially in immigration restriction. It also embodied a more regional dimension, as some states in the South inaugurated the White-only

Democratic primary election to further curtail Black political influence, and some legislated a narrower definition of White racial identity—made it harder to qualify as "White"—as in Virginia, Georgia, and Alabama, and applied that new definition to such realms as marriage and schooling.

Each of these measures, state or federal, had powerful allure, as promising a much-improved society, culture, or politics. The new laws constituted significant attempts at social engineering, at seeking to make the world more congenial to the individuals and social groups that promoted them. All these measures, building on earlier versions but more thoroughgoing, set out to sculpt society and politics.

Congress set out to shape the future of American society by cutting off further immigration almost entirely from places other than Europe, and more particularly northern and western Europe, like Britain and Germany. A cartogram, or cartographic diagram, is a map-based geographical depiction that measures space in terms of magnitude. In a cartogram that captures the intent and impact of the Immigration Act of 1924, the world simply vanishes outside of Europe; and Europe itself appears very much contorted, with Britain and Germany tremendously inflated in size, and with sharply reduced areas representing the old Russian Empire, the old Austro-Hungarian Empire, and the Eastern Mediterranean nations of Italy and Greece.

All of this was happening in the context of a global phenomenon of migration of Italians, for example, not only to Philadelphia, USA, but to Buenos Aires, Argentina, and of people looking to leave China for Southeast Asia, not just North America. The 1924 law emphasized *the eastern and western borders*, not the *southern one*, though a companion bill, the Labor Appropriations Act of 1924, focused on Mexicans, who collectively comprised a large group critical to agriculture in the Southwest.

Law would profoundly shape demography, labor markets, and electoral and legislative politics. Immigration restriction constructed barriers intended to be very high and durable, designed to curtail population growth of unwanted people through immigration and thus also through subsequent natural increase. The legal regime also maintained a bar to naturalization by non-White non-citizens, a ban that blocked the right to vote everywhere and excluded most ethnic Asian residents from the purchase of agricultural lands in California.

The new immigration law did not go into immediate effect, in the sense that what Congress had mandated proved immensely difficult to provide a formula for. Who belonged to which social group, by geographical origin, as of the Census of 1890? In the end, however, the numbers derived are astonishing.

The United Kingdom received an annual immigrant quota of 66,000; Germany 26,000; the Irish Free State 18,000. Those three figures total 110,000—a greater allocation than the entire rest of the globe.

The next nations got bigger numbers than framers might have wished. After Ireland with its 18,000, Poland got 7,000, Italy 6,000. The only other countries with caps as high as even 3,000 were Sweden, the Netherlands, and France. Several other countries had caps as high as 1,000: Czechoslovakia, Russia, Norway, Switzerland, Austria, Belgium, and Denmark. The caps for Asian countries held at zero.

The formula for admitting new residents to the US remained mostly in place for four decades, until the Immigration Act of 1965, though some limited relaxation took place regarding one group or region or another during the 1940s and 1950s.

Meanwhile at the state level, legislators in some southern states took an alternative approach to reclassifying people, sorting them out, determining who could marry whom, who could sit where in so-called public transit, or who could attend which school.

Across the 19th century, Virginia had defined as "colored" or "negro" anyone with as much as one-fourth Black lineage, one Black grandparent. A 1910 law moved the boundary between White and Black two generations, with a new demarcation of one-sixteenth, or one Black great-great-grandparent. The Racial Integrity Act of 1924 moved the boundary yet again. It classified as "colored" (or "non-Caucasic") anyone not "of pure white race." To be a "white person" now required having no forebears classified as "Negro, Mongolian, American Indian, Asiatic Indian, Malay, or any mixture thereof."

Accordingly, "It shall hereafter be unlawful for any white person in this State to marry any save a white person." While it is easy to assume that the law targeted people classified as Black, and it certainly did, the law that made it a felony for two people to marry across the line separating "White" from anyone else just as fully targeted any White person involved. Nobody should entertain the conceit that he or she had permission to violate the racial code in the realm of marriage. It applied to everyone.

Other Southern states followed Virginia's lead. Georgia had long defined "persons of color" as one-eighth Black. Beginning in 1927, such people were redefined as "having any ascertainable trace" of nonwhite ancestry. A "white person" was a "Caucasian," and, to secure that designation, people had to have "no ascertainable trace" of "Negro, African, West Indian, Asiatic Indian, Mongolian, Japanese, or Chinese blood in their veins."

In 1907, Alabama jumped the racial boundary by two generations, from one-eighth to one-thirty-second. A further definition in 1927 defined a "negro" as a person "descended on the part of the father or mother from negro ancestors, without reference to or limit of time or number of generations removed." This was all a far cry from what the Alabama Supreme Court had determined back in 1850, balking at any definition that would go beyond one White parent and one Black parent, unless, that is, the legislature should make such a determination. Either way, Alabama law continued to insist that there be two races, but where to divide the two had moved a great deal.

Back in 1901, future president Woodrow Wilson, wearing his academic hat as historian, or rather writing as a public intellectual, and an apologist for a racial regime to which he held a deep commitment, published an article in *Atlantic Monthly* to mark what he celebrated as the end, "at last," of Reconstruction. "At last," he wrote, "the whites who were real citizens got control again" of southern politics and governance.

If a state reclassified mixed-race people from White to Black, they faced exclusion from political life there, considered by those who supported it a wholesome outcome. At the top of all priorities in much of American life stood a commitment to White supremacy, Black subordination, Black exclusion. In addition, people from southern Europe or eastern Europe, many of them Jews or Catholics, were suspect candidates for Whiteness, immigration, and citizenship, and Asians even more so.

In a 1955 ruling related to the 1924 Racial Integrity Act, the justices of the Virginia Supreme Court all agreed that the legal restrictions on interracial marriage must stand: "Regulation of the marriage relation is, we think, distinctly one of the rights guaranteed to the States and safeguarded by that bastion of States' rights, somewhat battered perhaps but still a sturdy fortress in our fundamental law, the tenth section of the Bill of Rights." Surely, they contended, a state could not be prevented from "enacting legislation to preserve the racial integrity of its [white] citizens." A state must be free "to regulate the marriage relation so that it shall not have a mongrel breed of citizens."

1-28
Did Homer Plessy Die a White Man?

US popular culture in the 21st century often insists that anyone of US descent over many generations is Black whose lineage from the past 400 years tracks at least in part from Sub-Saharan Africa; that Latinos are either White or Black, or all are nonwhite; or that all groups except "Whites" are "colored," or "nonwhite," and as a rule lumped together as "minorities" (even if in the majority). Let's take another look.

Homer Plessy brought the case that occasioned the US Supreme Court's language in 1896 about "separate but equal" (or, rather, "equal, but separate"), the leading constitutional marker for the long regime that followed slavery in the South. Born in New Orleans of free parents in March 1863 (midway through the Civil War), Plessy lived into the 1920s, when he died just as the system of Jim Crow segregation and disfranchisement reached its greatest strength.

In 1896, the Court paused in the majority opinion in *Plessy v. Ferguson* to remark about this light-skinned thirty-something with a smidgen of African ancestry that it might be "a question of importance whether, under the laws of Louisiana, the petitioner belongs to the white or colored race."

In the next two census enumerations, those of 1900 and 1910, census takers in New Orleans recorded "M" for mulatto next to the names of Homer Plessy and his wife, Louise. Yet for 1920, the census schedule records them both as "W" for White.

Many southern states, Louisiana among them, were moving in a direction that, under changes in state law that redefined the "races," made some "White" men and women into "colored" men and women. But (according to the census) Mr. and Mrs. Plessy had moved in the opposite direction, from "colored" to "white."

When he died in March 1925, Plessy was buried in St. Louis Cemetery No. 1, in Tomb 619, just off Conti Street. It was a segregated facility, distinguishing people by their *religious* identity: not far from his final resting place, in the Catholic section, is the smaller "Protestant Section."

Plessy was sufficiently fair featured that he had to publicly self-identify as Black for the conductor to direct him in 1892 to the "colored" car, an assignment to which he then, as planned, took exception. The "Citizens' Committee to Test the Constitutionality of the Separate Car Law" wished to bring a test case against Louisiana's railway segregation statute of 1890, which required "equal, but separate" accommodations. Plessy's racial identification under the law did far more than determine that he could sit—or had to sit—in one railroad car instead of another. At one time or another in the post–Civil War world, it might mean he could vote, or not; attend one elementary school or college, not another; or, in Louisiana after 1894, marry a woman from one racial group, not another.

There might be room for doubt, whether in the 1890s or the 1920s, what Plessy's racial identity really was. *But he had to have one.* There was no doubt that it mattered, that it often mattered greatly, as it had mattered for the generations of southerners who preceded him, and as it would continue to matter for the generations that followed.

The Court left the matter of Homer Plessy's racial classification up to Louisiana authorities, as it did not affect the outcome of his case, in which the Court told the states that they could do what they liked regarding segregation, so long as the people on each side of the boundary had "equal" access to public goods. States might segregate, or not; and if they did, they could locate the dividing line wherever seemed appropriate.

Litigation across the South often arose regarding where the boundary lay, and whether one particular person should be located on one side of it or the other. Mississippi used different definitions as to whether, on the one hand, two people were both White enough to marry each other and, on the other hand, whether their children were White enough to go to a White school. So, the Mississippi Supreme Court, in a case from 1917, took in stride a lower court finding that, while the parents were both White enough to marry, their children might be excluded from the local school for Whites. The Grandich family responded by moving to New Orleans, where the children could attend White schools.

People in Oklahoma were "White" unless they had some African ancestry. Thus, the law classified Native people as White, if all four of their grandparents were Native, or at least not Black. Jesse "Cab" Renick, a Choctaw Indian, starred in basketball at the "all-White" Oklahoma A&M College (today's Oklahoma State University) before enlisting in the Navy during World War II. In 1948, he was generally taken for White when he won an Olympic gold-medal with the US basketball team. Meanwhile, Don Barksdale gained notice as the first African American to play Olympic basketball.

In Texas, an ethnic Japanese person could legally marry a White person, since neither was Black, so both were White. In California, when two people who wished to marry in the 1940s found themselves barred by the state law against "interracial" marriage, it was because that law classified Sylvester Davis as African American, but Andrea Perez, who was Mexican American, as White. Mexican Americans' lived experiences, however, often profoundly belied the racial privilege implied in the legal classification.

The 1890 Mississippi state constitution classified ethnic Chinese residents as "colored," not White. Nonetheless two sisters, Berda and Martha Lum, attended the local White school for several years; only when they went back to start a new school year in 1924, and someone complained, were they told they could no longer attend there. The Lum family went to court, won at trial in the local court, then lost at the Mississippi Supreme Court, then lost again at the US Supreme Court. Gong Lum moved his family across the Mississippi River into Arkansas, where the children enrolled at a White school.

Not only might Chinese children in the 1920s move back and forth between White and "colored," their 20-year-old counterparts migrated between the 1920s and the 1940s from colored to semi-White: non-Black for purposes of going to college, but not White when it came to who they could legally marry. Shortly after World War II, the University of Mississippi enrolled its first ethnic Chinese student, as did Mississippi State. From then on, each school always had Chinese students. Yet when "Negro James Meredith," as news stories always called him at the time, won a court order in 1962 that Ole Miss enroll him, a deadly riot ensued. He was not taking classes as the first nonwhite student at an "all-White" institution, but rather as the first African American to enroll at that non-Black university.

In Virginia, even after the Supreme Court's 1954 ruling against school segregation in *Brown v. Board of Education*, no Black student could enter a public K-12 classroom with a White student before at least 1959. Yet at mid-century, well before *Brown*, ethnic Japanese sisters Irene and June Iwata, both of them natives of California, recent World War II internees in Arizona, and classified as "colored" under Virginia's Racial Integrity Act, found an accepting school home at Washington-Lee, an "all-White" high school in Arlington County.

Part Two
1930s–1960s

2-1
Frances Perkins and the Social Security Act

The New Deal brought to Americans perhaps the most far-reaching legislation of the 20th century when the Social Security Act went into effect in 1935, part of the "Second New Deal," reform legislation enacted that year.

The Social Security Act's leading architects included Frances Perkins (1880–1965), as well as Arthur J. Altmeyer and Edwin E. Witte. Perkins, the first female American ever to join a president's cabinet, served as Secretary of Labor during Franklin D. Roosevelt's entire 12-plus years in the White House.

She brought to her new responsibilities a lifetime of preparation. She completed her undergraduate work in 1902 at Mount Holyoke College, in Massachusetts, where she discovered the suffrage movement and learned about the sorry state of mill workers, especially women and children.

She later studied economics and sociology, first at the University of Pennsylvania's Wharton School and then at Columbia University, where she completed a master's degree in 1910. Along the way, she worked with Jane Addams at Hull House. Beginning in 1910, Perkins worked with Florence Kelley, heading the New York office of the National Consumers League (NCL), an assignment that soon had her working closely with New York state legislators, especially Al Smith and Robert F. Wagner.

That early work stemmed in large part from a life-changing class she took at Mount Holyoke her final semester in college. A course in economic history, taught by Annah May Soule, introduced her to the industrialization of Britain and the US and directed them to visit nearby mills to observe the working conditions there. Many years later, in an autobiography, she described how the conditions of work for women and children in those factories "horrified" her and just "seemed very wrong."

In a related formative experience, Mount Holyoke students organized a chapter of the National Consumers League and invited its head, Florence Kelley, to come and speak. According to Perkins, hearing Kelley "first opened my mind to the necessity for and the possibility of the work which became my vocation."

Those college epiphanies led to her working in New York City, where she watched in horror after an upper-story fire broke out in March 1911 at the Triangle Shirtwaist Factory. There, 146 people died, including many killed when they leapt from upper-story windows to escape the inferno. Perkins was soon heading a local citizens' Committee on Safety, which successfully lobbied legislators Al Smith and Robert F. Wagner to appoint a state Factory Investigating Commission. Perkins left the NCL to lead the commission, which proposed a host of labor reforms, some designed to prevent such grotesque tragedies in the future.

Women first voted in New York elections in 1918, and Perkins campaigned that year for Al Smith for New York governor. Smith in turn appointed her as a member of New York State's Industrial Commission and a new governor, Franklin D. Roosevelt, appointed her in 1929 to run the commission. Her work there, for more than a decade, continued her preparation for work on a grander scale.

When Roosevelt moved from the governor's mansion to the White House in 1933, he asked Perkins to become secretary of the Department of Labor. She conditioned her acceptance of the post on FDR's commitment to support a long list of reforms, modeled in part on what she had fought for in New York but building out various policies for the entire nation.

The economic crisis cried out for immediate relief to keep people alive, plus public works jobs to get them employed again. Longer-term reforms, to be made permanent, included unemployment insurance, workmen's compensation, maximum hours coupled with a minimum wage, and a ban on child labor, plus—a very high priority—a social security program. The only reform on the list never enacted in the 1930s was a national health system.

Secretary Perkins played key roles in the early New Deal—the "First New Deal," programs created in 1933—as Congress established the Federal Emergency Relief Administration and passed the National Industrial Recovery Act and the Emergency Conservation Work Act (which created the Civilian Conservation Corps). Not only would the CCC projects leave an enduring legacy in national parks, but money for the huge public works programs, aimed at creating millions of jobs, should be spent on schools, housing projects, post offices, and other permanent infrastructure.

Appointed in 1934 to chair the President's Committee on Economic Security, Perkins played a central role in formulating the Social Security Act, which became law in 1935. One key provision had the federal government supplying states with funds to assist destitute elderly people, a particularly pressing problem during the Great Depression. Other funds aimed to provide aid to dependent children, to blind people, and for maternal and child well-being.

The Social Security Act's long-range centerpiece, the measure that most commonly springs to mind when one hears the term "Social Security," provided for old-age retirement pensions, rather than the emergency funds made immediately available to states for distribution to the destitute elderly. This aspect of Social Security should be self-sustaining, with workers paying a small percentage of their salaries as a "premium" into the Social Security Fund, and employers matching that premium.

If workers could look forward to a guaranteed basic monthly retirement income, they would be more likely to choose to retire and thus leave open a job for someone else, so Social Security in that respect was also a jobs program to address unemployment. Regardless, the new national policy was intended to assure very large numbers of Americans of a basic standard of living in their more advanced years.

The system left out the large numbers of people in domestic service or agriculture, in part because of the administrative difficulties of reaching their often paltry incomes, and in part because of political opposition by conservative members of Congress, especially from the South. Therefore, this towering reform reached only so far.

In its intentions of lifting the incomes for vast numbers of people, the Social Security Act aligned with the National Labor Relations Act of 1935 (the Wagner Act), as well as the Fair Labor Standards Act of 1938 (part of the "Third New Deal" from that year), which established maximum hours and minimum wages for many workers who could not benefit from unionization under the Wagner Act.

The early 1940s turned Perkins's attention toward the International Labor Organization (ILO), conceived as a global umbrella, to extend far beyond US national borders the kinds of labor reforms that the New Deal had brought to Americans. The ideas percolating around the ILO, which originated just after the First World War as part of the League of Nations, can be seen as premonitions of the post–Second World War period's UN Universal Declaration of Human Rights.

The Frances Perkins legacy reverberates through more than a century down to the present. Life in the US in the 2020s features a constellation of programs that reach back to job safety reforms she worked to secure after the Triangle Shirtwaist Factory fire in the 1910s and on to such 1930s worker and "safety-net" innovations as the Social Security Act, unemployment insurance, workmen's compensation, and the eight-hour workday.

2-2
Industrial Workers, the Right to Unionize, and the Sit-Down Strike

Eugene Debs knew, back at the time of the Pullman Strike in 1894, that workers had no widely recognized right to organize unions and engage in collective bargaining with their employers over wages or working conditions. Some skilled workers did organize, according to their specific crafts, in unions with the American Federation Labor. Other workers joined the United Mine Workers (UMW), which included all mine workers of whatever craft. Four decades after the Pullman Strike, the New Deal's early years offered a glimmer that perhaps things might change much more.

Steelmaking exemplified the mass production industries in which craft skills were of secondary importance. Meat packinghouses in Chicago were little different, especially as processing became ever more mechanized, and the work was, by its nature, always dangerous to health and utterly exhausting, regardless of injuries.

One of the initial big programs of the New Deal, created in 1933 under the National Industrial Recovery Act (NIRA), sought to help both with unemployment and, by raising wages and thus purchasing power, with the broader economy. The NIRA's Section 7a stated that workers had the right to organize, and then bargain collectively through those unions, to achieve higher wages. Partly because of this, John L. Lewis, head of the UMW, along with other leaders, formed the Committee for Industrial Organization, to unionize other mass production industries.

Like some other early New Deal laws, the NIRA fell when the US Supreme Court, in the case *Schechter Poultry Corporation v. United States* (1935), declared it unconstitutional, beyond the authority of Congress to enact. Congress tried again.

US Senator Robert F. Wagner of New York, for one, embarked on an effort to enact a new law that might pass the scrutiny of the Supreme Court and enshrine workers' rights in US law. The National Labor Relations Act of 1935 (Wagner Act) did just that, and it established a National Labor Relations Board to monitor compliance. Corporations went to court to challenge the Wagner Act, too, but the Supreme Court ruled in favor of it, in *National Labor Relations Board v. Jones & Laughlin Steel Corporation* (1937).

Even then, the law itself brought no immediate change on the shop floor at any large industrial plant, whether in Pittsburgh, Akron, or Detroit, in steel, rubber, or autos. To put flesh and blood around the legal skeleton, workers would have to get fellow workers organized.

But how to do that? Historically, when workers went out on strike, employers brought in strike breakers. If I employ you and you choose to leave your job, I can readily find someone else who will step in as a substitute. Especially in times of steep unemployment, and in what were relatively unskilled jobs requiring limited training, industrial workers were easily replaced.

Moreover, racial and ethnic tensions heightened the difficulties of labor organizing. White workers often refused to labor alongside Black workers or join unions together with them, which is why Black workers often came in as strike breakers. But the social fractures went far beyond Black and White. Poles and Russians, for example, or Irish and English, brought ancient hatreds from Europe to their US workplace.

More than that, in the words of Chicago reporter Mike Royko, a Catholic "Irishman who came here hating only the Englishmen and Irish Protestants soon hated Poles, Italians, and blacks," and a Polish Catholic "arrived hating only Jews and Russians, but soon learned to hate the Irish, the Italians, and the blacks." And then there was gender. In the words of Chicago labor organizer Victoria Kramer (also known as Stella Nowicki), "Women had an awfully tough time in the union because the men brought their [gender] prejudices there."

So, workers had the federal government's new labor policy on their side, but they still had to overcome the social tensions and stick together. On all counts, what happened was simply amazing—it went some distance toward realizing the dream, dating back to the Industrial Workers of the World, of one big union. That said, the deep racism of many of the White workers, coupled with the persistent reluctance of many Black workers to trust organizations that had no history of supporting them, put limits on the degree of change. But change did come.

Workers at meatpacking houses in Chicago exemplified the Wagner Act's significance, as the Packinghouse Workers Organizing Committee reached with effectiveness across lines of race, ethnicity, and gender. Interviews from the New Deal's Federal Writers' Project captured some of the workers' experiences and perceptions. White union member Elmer Thomas recounted the story of an Irish worker rebuffing a White manager's denigration of a Black worker, saying he's "my friend. He works with me. He's a union brother." A Black union member, Jim Cole, reported: "I'll always believe they done the greatest thing in the world getting everybody who works in the yards together, and breaking up the hate and bad feelings that used to be held against the Negro."

And then there was the sit-down strike. Come to work; take your place on the shop floor; then refuse to do the assigned work. By staying at your workstation, make it hard for employers to recruit replacement workers to come in and keep the factories operating. In the struggle to gain union recognition, sit-down strikes took place in factory after factory, industry after industry, city after city, especially in 1936 and 1937.

All those scenes depict big factories in the urban North. Lucy Randolph Mason, a labor activist descended from an elite Virginia family, went to work in 1937 for the CIO, mostly in the Deep South, as a public relations representative. "Miss Lucy" discerned early on that, as she wrote in a letter at the time, "the domination of the Negro had made it easier to repeat the pattern for organized labor." A former suffragist and later the head of the National Consumers' League, she saw the CIO as a means of addressing problems of race and gender and poverty in the South. For a dozen years and more, she found ways to soften the resistance to union formation among political, industrial, and cultural leaders, among them church groups and newspaper editors. Allies she publicized regional violations of civil rights and civil liberties, included Eleanor Roosevelt. Unions, increasingly biracial, took root.

In 1955, the American Federation of Labor and the Congress of Industrial Organizations (renamed from Committee for Industrial Organization) merged as the AFL-CIO. Old rivalries had largely subsided. The older craft unions and the newer industrial unions joined forces with other sectors to represent a broad spectrum of workers, though not in agriculture.

The United Auto Workers (UAW), especially, headed out of the 1930s and into the years that followed with leadership, an ethos, and a commitment to workers' rights and social solidarity—and to some degree racial justice, too—that helped change America in the years during and after World War II.

Walter Reuther's leadership and behavior exemplified and enhanced the changes under way in the three decades between the New Deal and the Great Society. As the UAW president from 1946 to 1970, he embodied a White version of A. Philip Randolph in representing both civil rights and labor rights.

For example, Reuther brought in the AFL-CIO as a key organizer of the 1963 March on Washington for Jobs and Freedom, where, as one of the speakers, he called for economic justice and an end to racial discrimination, the dual aims of the March. Later, he marched with Martin Luther King Jr. at Selma, Alabama, and also provided financial support to the United Farm Workers in California and to the first Earth Day in 1970.

2-3
Susie Byrd and the Voice Gatherers

The Great Depression's nearly countless unemployed included a small constellation of writers, teachers, and other middle-class folk, and the New Deal brought some of them, too, welcome jobs and renewed hope. At the same time, it set in motion the collection of first-person experiences that give 21st-century readers access to the lives of individuals from a century and much longer ago.

In the late 1930s, the life histories program of the Federal Writers' Project deployed a small host of people to interview their fellow countrymen about their lives. Best known are the so-called slave narratives, interviews with African Americans most of whom had lived in slavery more than 70 years before.

These came into widespread awareness among historians after 1972, when George P. Rawick published the initial set of what by 1979 became 41 volumes, filled with copies of typescripts that had been stored away shortly after being recorded decades earlier.

Anthropologist/folklorist Charles L. Perdue Jr. and his collaborators brought out a separate volume, *Weevils in the Wheat: Interviews with Virginia Ex-Slaves* (1976). As with the Rawick volumes, most people being interviewed faced questions from White writers, and thus their responses might prove circumspect. But *Weevils* includes the results of 35 interviews that Susie Rosa Catherine Byrd, a Black woman—in her forties, far younger than the people she was speaking with—conducted, many with people she had come to know in Petersburg, Virginia. Together, the typescripts provide revealing examples of daily life often filled with lifelong anguish but also punctuated with exhilaration at the end of slavery.

Rev. James Boatman observed, according to Byrd's rendition, that the group she was visiting with and collecting memories from wanted to "help dem chillun to git all dat slave stuff jus' like twas, 'cause us ole folks will soon be dead."

Rev. Israel Massie, a teenager at the time of emancipation, told her, "Lord Chile, ef ya start me I kin tell ya a mess 'bout reb times, but I ain't tellin' white folks nuthin' 'cause I'm skeer'd to make enemies. Lord chile, dar wuz mo' grievin' and mo' crying over de family partin'—jes like de grief when ya sister or brother dies. . . Speculatin' on us humans! . . . Dem wuz terrible times! I had two brothers sold away an' ain't never seen 'em no mo' til dis day."

One night, the state project director, a White woman, stopped by the group's meeting, and Massie, with his impaired vision, kept on telling his stories, it never occurring to him that the group was no longer all-Black. The next day, he told Byrd, "Lawdy, Honey I ain't knowed I was talkin' to a white 'oman. I jes' tole dat thing jes' like hit was."

Mr. Beverly Jones told another Black interviewer about a very elderly man at church one Sunday:

Uncle Silas got up in de front row of de slaves' pew an' halted Reverend Johnson. "Is us slaves gonna be free in Heaven?" Uncle Silas asked. De preacher stopped an' looked at Uncle Silas like he wanta kill him 'cause no one ain't 'sposed to say nothin' 'ceptin' "Amen" whilst he was preachin'. Waited a minute he did, lookin' hard at Uncle Silas standin' there but didn't give no answer.

"Is God gonna free us slaves when we git to Heaven?" Uncle Silas yelled. Old white preacher pult out his handkerchief an' wiped de sweat fum his face. "Jesus says come unto Me ye who are free fum sin an' I will give you salvation." "Gonna give us freedom 'long wid salvation?" ask Uncle Silas. [Getting no better answer that time, he remained standing, silent, through the rest of the service.] . . .

Uncle Silas died fo' nother preachin' time come roun'. Guess he foun' out whether he gonna be free sooner dan he calculated to.

Louise Bowes Rose, who turned 12 the year emancipation came to her plantation near Ashland, described for her Black male interviewer a certain baptism into a new life of freedom: "Daddy was down to de creek. He jumped right into de water up to his neck. He was so happy he jus' kep' on scooping up han'fulls of water an dumpin' it on his haid an' yellin', 'I'se free, I'se free! I'se free!'"

Lost in the frequent focus by historians on the slave narratives, compelling as they are, is the fact that many other writers made their way all around the country collecting the voices of a wide cross-section of Americans, from a Penobscot Indian or granite craftsman in northern New England to longtime residents of the mountain West or desert Southwest, most of them White and living far from the South.

Ann Banks published a sample of these in *First Person America* (1980). Rather than attempt to be comprehensive and present everything, as Rawick did with the slave narratives, Banks did an expert job of selecting and introducing a tiny percentage of all possible voices. From Chicago, for example, we hear a heterogeneous group of men recounting how the Congress of Industrial Organizations had just recently pulled them together, despite all the differences of race, ethnicity, language, and task, and, against great resistance from employers, made a real difference in wages and working conditions.

We hear, too, from women reporting on experiences related to moving across the prairie, mining in Montana, or living in a dugout house and setting up ranching in Texas.

Tom E. Terrill and Jerrold Hirsch published a related collection of Federal Writers' Project materials, but they focused on the South and included voices both Black and White, in *Such As Us: Southern Voices of the Thirties* (1978). Nancy J. Martin-Perdue and Charles L. Perdue Jr. brought out *Talk about Trouble: A New Deal Portrait of Virginians in the Great Depression* (1996).

These varied collections draw attention to the vast riches of work done most of a century ago under the auspices of the New Deal. This remarkable legacy brings to life people who can take us back to the Great Depression years of the 1930s and even to the mid-1850s, a gesture toward the democratization of Americans' historical understanding.

2-4
A. Philip Randolph and the Greatest March That Never Happened

A. Philip Randolph (1889–1979) finished college in his native Florida in 1907 and, finding no jobs for Black men aside from manual labor, migrated in 1911 to New York City. There he took classes at City College, met a fellow young Black man, Chandler Owen, joined the Socialist Party of America, gave soapbox speeches supporting Black unionism, and, after trying out a variety of jobs that enabled him to buy food and pay rent, operated an employment office in Harlem for other new migrants from the South. He also met Lucille Green.

Lucille Campbell Green also arrived in the city in 1911. A child of William and Josephine Campbell, both formerly enslaved in Montgomery County, Virginia, she and her new husband had recently graduated from Howard University, in Washington, DC, and he started a new job that took them to New York, but he soon died. She began operating a Madam Walker beauty salon, met Randolph, and, it turned out, shared with him both a commitment to socialism and a passion for Shakespeare, and they married in 1914.

In 1917, Philip Randolph and Chandler Owen began publishing *The Messenger*, a labor periodical that they described as "the only magazine of scientific radicalism in the world published by Negroes." As Mr. Randolph later explained, without his wife's money the pair "couldn't have started the *Messenger*." And then the *Messenger* brought Randolph to the attention of the Pullman Car workers who, in 1925, asked him to take the lead in organizing the Brotherhood of Sleeping Car Porters (BSCP), a labor union forever after the basis of his power as both a labor leader and a Black spokesman.

Under President Franklin D. Roosevelt's New Deal, the National Industrial Recovery Act of 1933 made it the nation's public policy that workers had the right to organize labor unions and engage in collective bargaining with their employers. And then came the National Labor Relations Act (1935), which spawned the Congress of Industrial Organizations. Eventually, in 1937, the BSCP signed a contract with the Pullman Company, a victory that made a big difference to sleeping car porters in their compensation, job security, and working conditions.

Even as the Pullman victory enhanced Randolph's prominence, he looked for wider change. In 1941, jobs were opening in defense plants, as the US sought to supply war material to support Britain in its war against Germany, all the while perhaps keeping the US out of the war, though in the meantime preparing for being drawn into the war. Employers, however, maintained a "White only" employment policy.

Demanding equal access to defense jobs, plus desegregation of the armed forces and opportunities in federal white-collar employment, Randolph organized the March on Washington Movement, with a large-scale all-Black march on the nation's segregated capital city scheduled for July 1941. Through intermediaries—among them first lady Eleanor Roosevelt, New York City mayor Fiorello La Guardia, and his omnipresent aide Anna Rosenberg—President Roosevelt sought to persuade Randolph to call off the march. That failing, FDR met with Randolph, Rosenberg, and others in the White House, where Randolph refused to budge unless FDR issued an executive order. Consequently, Executive Order 8802 directed that jobs in defense industries be made available to workers regardless of their race and that a wartime Fair Employment Practices Committee (FEPC) monitor compliance.

After the war, Randolph pressed for a permanent FEPC and resumed his push for a desegregated military. As leverage, in 1948 he urged young African American men to refuse to comply with a new draft law, inaugurated in peacetime but as a Cold War initiative. Facing a difficult reelection campaign, and following his own inclinations as well, President Harry Truman, in Executive Order 9981, mandated desegregation in the US military, which soon became the nation's most integrated social environment. At the same time, Executive Order 9980, addressing Randolph's third demand from 1941, ordered the desegregation of the federal bureaucracy.

The greatest march that never happened had tremendous consequences for America. And many years later, a march did take place, even much bigger and this time multiracial. Randolph, together with Bayard Rustin, planned a mass rally for 28 August 1963, the March on Washington for Jobs and Freedom, the occasion for Martin Luther King's "I Have a Dream" speech.

In the run-up, Randolph sent a letter to President Kennedy requesting an appointment the morning of the big day and pointing out: "This action is designed to focus nationwide attention on the plight of millions of Negro Americans 100 years after Emancipation and to press for a redress of their intolerable grievances in the present session of the Congress." Those grievances included job discrimination, school segregation, systematic denial of voting rights, and police brutality (especially evident that year in the Deep South).

Kennedy met that morning with Randolph and other leaders. That day's program at the Lincoln Memorial included Marian Anderson returning to lead the throng in singing the National Anthem, opening remarks by Randolph as March director, "Tribute to Negro Women Fighters for Freedom" including Rosa Parks and the recently widowed Mrs. Medgar Evers, labor leader Walter Reuther, and the national leaders of SNCC, CORE, the NAACP, the National Urban League, the National Catholic Conference for Interracial Justice, the American Jewish Congress, and King's Southern Christian Leadership Conference.

2-5
Double-V, Rosie Riveter, Tuskegee Airmen, Code Talkers

In the late 1930s, as Japan in Asia and Germany in Europe grew ever more aggressive against their neighbors, Congress tried, by expressly adopting a stance of neutrality, to minimize the likelihood of US entry into what became World War II. But the global situation kept changing, and that stance periodically edged beyond keeping the US out of the war while trying to keep Great Britain in it.

In June 1940, President Roosevelt gave a commencement speech at the University of Virginia, where he asked "what the future holds for all peoples and all nations that have been living under democratic forms of Government—under the free institutions of a free people," and "what the extension of the philosophy of force to all the world would lead to." A "military and naval victory for the gods of force and hate," he continued, "would endanger the institutions of democracy in the western world." The US must do what it could to supply "the material resources of this nation" to "the opponents of force" (Britain in particular) and must itself prepare for "any emergency and every defense."

Eighteen months later, the US found itself in a two-front war, with some hope of prevailing given that Germany had invaded the Soviet Union and therefore must also fight on two fronts. African Americans, however, knew something about "the gods of force and hate" in domestic affairs, whatever was happening on the foreign front. A great many, as in 1940 and 1941, pressed throughout the war for progressive change on the racial front *within* the US.

At the end of January 1942, some weeks after Pearl Harbor, the *Pittsburgh Courier*, a leading Black newspaper, published a letter it had received from a 26-year-old Black man in Wichita, Kansas, urging a wider focus for the war. James Gratz Thompson assured his readers that, "like all true Americans," his "greatest desire" for "my country" was "a complete victory over the forces of evil."

But he offered a different slant to his desire than FDR seemed to have in mind when speaking of the stakes in a war in defense of democracy. "Being an American of dark complexion," he sought a good answer to his question: "Should I sacrifice my life to live half American?" He thought it a question that "every colored American" wanted a good answer to. And he had a proposal for all Americans, especially Black Americans.

Speaking of the "V for victory sign" being displayed, he said, "in all so-called democratic countries," he proposed that all "colored Americans adopt the double VV for a double victory. The first V for victory over our enemies from without, the second V for victory over our enemies from within"—victory over fascism abroad, over racism at home.

Thompson concluded that, yes, "I love America and am willing to die for the America I know will someday become a reality." For an America in prospect, that is, not so much the current edition. (He did not die for his country, but he did spend three years in uniform, much of it in the India-Burma Theatre, in a segregated quartermaster unit getting supplies to soldiers on the front lines.)

Thompson was voicing a desire, a commitment, that African Americans widely felt. The *Courier* immediately took up the call, as did the *Chicago Tribune* and other Black newspapers, and the "Double V Campaign" became a prominent wartime feature in the months that followed.

A push for Black inclusion, and the pull from wartime need, opened new possibilities in American life in the early 1940s. The "greatest march that never happened," which resulted in one (but only one) of A. Philip Randolph's three great demands of FDR, exemplified both the enhanced opportunities and the severe limitations placed upon them.

Randolph's planned march for June 1941 took place against a backdrop in which FDR had bluntly stated in October 1940 that no desegregation of the US military would take place, followed by such pushback in an election year that he promoted Benjamin O. Davis Sr. to brigadier general, a first for any African American.

Enhanced inclusion in the war effort perhaps reached gender more than race. "Rosie the Riveter," a hit song from 1942, depicted a phenomenon that brought millions of women into new jobs both in defense industries—factories and shipyards—and elsewhere throughout the economy. Many were moving up from more traditional female occupations, others newly entering the workforce. Black, White, and Latina, their experiences varied greatly. But they worked at a time that ascribed great importance to their work as an essential contribution to winning a global war.

Fanny Christina Hill, a Black woman from Texas, had moved to Los Angeles and was employed by a White family until she went to work in 1943 for North American Aviation. A combination of wartime labor needs, A. Philip Randolph's success with FDR on jobs at defense plants, and the local CIO, in her twenties she represented both "Rosie the Riveter" and other changes in the realms of race and labor. As she put it wryly, "Hitler was the one that got us out of the white folks' kitchen." She encountered racial discrimination time and again but ended up spending a career at her wartime job.

The Tuskegee Airmen embodied another dimension of great but limited change. Early on, all indications pointed toward a complete maintenance of segregation in all branches of the military, a concept that in operation did not imply anything along the lines of "separate but equal" but, rather, Black exclusion from all but some kinds of combat support roles, often menial.

In January 1941, though, an announcement came that an all-Black squadron would soon begin training at Tuskegee Institute in Alabama, located about an hour's drive away from the White base, Maxwell Field. Benjamin O. Davis Jr., West Point class of 1936 and son of the newly promoted Gen. Benjamin O. Davis Sr., had been detailed to teach military science at Tuskegee Institute, whereas his classmates, none of them Black, moved into leadership roles in the military. The younger Davis now became one of the initial cohort of Black men to train at Tuskegee as a military pilot.

Tuskegee Army Airfield quickly became an animated hive of Black mechanics, nurses, and pilots in training. On base and off, however, rank discrimination followed them all everywhere, in the face of which Davis did all he could to encourage the others, to keep up their morale. In March 1942, Davis and four other men completed their training. In August that year, the 99th Fighter Squadron reached full strength at 33 pilots.

Deployed at last in spring 1943, Lt. Col. Davis Jr. and his men operated in the Mediterranean sector, part of the North African prelude to an eventual move into Europe. Over the next two years, Tuskegee Airmen actively participated in the European Theatre, where their many hundreds of additional missions had them flying out of Italy into Germany. Some returned to the service after the war, beginning in 1948 to a desegregating US Air Force, and fought also in Korea and, in some cases, Vietnam. Walter I. Lawson Sr. was one who went on to fight as a military pilot in Korea.

George Edward Hardy saw even greater change over a longer period. After taking postwar time away as a civilian to study engineering, no doubt on the GI Bill, he flew a reported 45 missions in the Korean War and another 70 in Vietnam. His career exemplified the new possibilities brought by World War II—together with the postwar order by President Truman that the armed forces desegregate.

After graduation from high school in Philadelphia in 1942, Hardy had considered modeling his older brother, Burvin, who had joined the Navy as a cook; but his father, wanting better for him, balked. The Tuskegee Airmen supplied a very different path into the military. And yet he always remembered a vivid sense that "the Army's No. 1 job was segregation"; "winning the war was No. 2." Indeed, many White people, especially in the Deep South, had their own Double-V, to defeat the Axis powers abroad and turn back any emerging impulse toward Black equality at home.

Regardless, or even more so, Hardy took pride in how "we did prove that we could do anything that anyone else could do." A program that began with many military leaders skeptical that African Americans would be able to function effectively as military pilots proved, instead, the opposite and smoothed the way for President Truman's decision in 1948 to desegregate the military.

The "Code Talkers" demonstrated a critical contribution to the Second World War by Native Americans from many Nations. Already, in the Great War, Choctaw and Cherokee men had collectively made vital contributions to the US Army in France. In World War II, the Army deployed as code talkers a group of Meskwaki in North Africa and later a group of Comanche men in western Europe during and after the landing at Normandy.

The biggest example of code talkers came with the Marines in the Pacific Theatre, especially "the First Twenty-Nine," a platoon made up of Navajo men from Arizona and New Mexico. Their signal officer later observed: "Were it not for the Navajos, the Marines would never have taken Iwo Jima."

The program swiftly conveyed crucial tactical information under battlefield conditions. Its operations became declassified in 1968, and the Code Talkers Recognition Act of 2008 subsequently honored the war's 500-plus Native code talkers. Years and years of federal efforts to squelch the use of Indigenous languages had evidently—and providentially—failed.

A gigantic war, lasting three or four years and fought on two vast fronts, drew in a wide range of ways upon the members of various social groups in the US, ways that profoundly shaped and reshaped the lives of countless individuals and whole communities.

Rosie the Riveter, Tuskegee Airmen, Code Talkers, these all provided essential input into the war effort, and they each became an essential feature in the historical memory of the war.

2-6
Jimmie Monteith and the D-Day Landing at Normandy

Jimmie Waters Monteith Jr. (1917–1944), following his father and older brother, attended Virginia Polytechnic Institute, although for just two years, 1937–1939. As the school required then, he spent both years in the Corps of Cadets. His experience as a cadet meant that he brought far more preparation than most of his peers could muster when the US moved toward entry into World War II.

Monteith joined the Army in October 1941, two months before Pearl Harbor, and by June 1942 had been commissioned a second lieutenant. The following April, he sailed across the Atlantic, then fought in North Africa (Tunisia) and the Mediterranean (Sicily). He stopped off in England during the final stage of preparation before the long-awaited effort to move across the English Channel and into France.

Letters home from the young soldier reveal his exuberant personality and his wartime observations. In March 1942, from Fort Benning, Georgia, he wrote to his mother and referred to his brother: "When you hear that this place is tough, do not take it with a grain of salt for it is just as hard as you hear it is and maybe harder. In fact you can tell Bob that it rivals the first year at V.P.I."

From Sicily he wrote, with both optimism and irritation, in October 1943, shortly after being promoted to first lieutenant. "I saw the end [of the fighting] in Africa and in Sicily," he observed, before noting: "Frankly I don't think the war will last [until] 1945." But he knew it was far from over, and he vented a bit: "we have been getting news that the people at home think that the war is nearly over and are condu[c]ting themselves rather shamefully[.] I believe I know now why the men who fought the last war never talked about it. It wasn't that the war it self was so horrible [though that too, he no doubt recognized] but because the people at home were so damn dumb." As for the present war, "we have a long ways to go yet and we don't like to hear stories of celebrations that costs us tons of supplies." Then he eased off before closing: "Please excuse the outburst. Guess the old red head got the best of me."

On the last day of May 1944, he wrote from somewhere in England, then signed off as he always did: "Love Jimmie."

Within the week, he was crossing the English Channel. The official version of what soon followed appeared in the citation for his Medal of Honor, awarded "for conspicuous gallantry and intrepidity above and beyond the call of duty on June 6, 1944":

> First Lieutenant Monteith landed with the initial assault waves on the coast of France under heavy enemy fire. Without regard to his own personal safety he continually moved up and down the beach reorganizing men for further assault. He then led the assault over a narrow protective ledge and across the first exposed terrain to the comparative safety of a cliff.
>
> Retracing his steps across the field to the beach he moved over to where two tanks were buttoned up and blind under violent enemy artillery and machinegun fire. Completely exposed to the intense fire, First Lieutenant Monteith led the tanks on foot through a mine field and into firing positions. Under his direction several enemy positions were destroyed. He then rejoined his company and under his

leadership his men captured an advantageous position on the hill.

Supervising the defense of this newly won position against repeated vicious counterattacks, he continued to ignore his own personal safety, repeatedly crossing the two or three hundred yards of open terrain under heavy fire to strengthen links in his defensive chain. When the enemy succeeded in completely surrounding First Lieutenant Monteith and his unit and while leading the fight out of this situation First Lieutenant Monteith was killed by enemy fire.

Other descriptions of the action, coming more directly from fellow soldiers there, more fully and graphically described what Monteith had managed to do that day. The War Department release about his posthumous decoration reflected the significance of his extraordinary performance in advancing the Allies' war effort in Europe:

> Tirelessly, he covered mine and bullet-traversed areas in which no man had the right to hope to live. He died only after he had led the men of his company through the obstacles of barbed wire, mines and fire to a position above shore that meant his unit was established in its objectives. He died leading a charge that strengthened the hard-won position.

For some hours on 6 June 1944, the great gamble at Normandy looked like it might be lost. Jimmie Monteith strode valiantly in, a key figure in averting catastrophe and moving toward Allied victory.

2-7
Control of the Skies and Winning the War

Much of the talk and the policymaking in the lead-up to American entry into World War II assumed that control of the seas and seaports would be central to the course of the war. Yet the Second World War, even more global than the Great War a generation earlier, featured technology far more advanced and far more deadly, none more so than the capacity to wage aerial warfare.

German ground forces took control of much of Europe, climaxing with the fall of France in June 1940. Looking to take over England as well, Germany then rained down bombs over London and much of the rest of Great Britain. In December 1941, Japanese forces brought terror from the skies at Pearl Harbor in the US territory of Hawai'i, an attack on planes, ships, manpower, and territory that finally brought the US into the war against Japan. And when Germany quickly honored its treaty obligations to Japan by declaring war on the US, America was suddenly at war in the European Theatre as well.

Much of the fighting took place either at sea or on land, but control of the skies proved a key feature as well, as when, time and again, Japanese planes attacked US naval vessels in the Pacific. On Guam, for one, the jungle has long since reclaimed airstrips Japan built during the war. In England, Maj. Gen. Cecil R. Moore oversaw the construction of one airfield after another in the two-plus years between Pearl Harbor and D-Day in June 1944.

From England, innumerable American bombers flew from those newly constructed airfields to Germany, where unfathomable numbers of bombs descended on German cities, especially Dresden in February 1945. This was total war. In part these cities were military targets, in part civilian. The destruction of wartime industrial capacity, even aside from the demolition of civilian morale, proved devastating, unprecedented in the history of warfare.

In the war against Japan, meanwhile, against ferocious resistance, US forces made their island-hopping way west across the Pacific Ocean, approaching ever nearer the home islands of Japan, where all Japanese cities could at last be reached by air. In particular, "black snow" enveloped Tokyo in March 1945, as an inferno destroyed the city. Three hundred B-29s caused the fiery deaths of as many as 100,000 people in a single night, a figure never exceeded at any one time before or since.

And then, in summer 1945, came two US planes, one carrying "Little Boy" to Hiroshima (on the biggest island, Honshu) on 6 August, the other taking "Fat Man" to Nagasaki (on Kyushu) on 9 August. Hiroshima seemed a good target, all things considered. As far as American intelligence could tell, no US prisoners of war were located there, and, as an industrial center, the city supplied the Japanese military with the material it needed both on land and at sea in its ever expanding—and then ever shrinking—new empire. President Truman said of the Hiroshima bombing that, if Japan even then failed to surrender, the US would bring "a rain of ruin from the air, the like of which has never been seen on this earth."

Emperor Hirohito announced Japan's surrender in a radio address on 15 August 1945, and Japan signed a formal surrender on 2 September. The bookends of the war between Japan and the US featured dominant displays of air power, from Pearl Harbor at the start to Hiroshima and Nagasaki at the end.

Earlier, as Americans were making their way in 1942 and 1943 east across North Africa, then north across the Mediterranean Sea to Sicily and on to mainland Italy, as well as west across the Pacific, the Russian armies were stopping a German advance deep into Russia and then gradually making their way west toward Germany.

Beginning with the Normandy Landing in October 1944, US forces moved east toward Paris and beyond, making their way toward Germany, as the Russian army closed in from the east. When, between them, they secured Germany's surrender on 8 May 1945, attention could turn to Japan.

Russia had pledged, at the Yalta Conference in February 1945, to join the war against Japan three months after Germany's surrender And it did so, right after the US strike at Hiroshima. Against often heavy resistance, the Soviet Union sent its ground forces sweeping east through Japanese-held Manchuria and on toward the Japanese colony Korea and the northern Japanese island Hokkaido.

As agreed in July 1945, at the Potsdam Conference in Germany (a short distance west of Berlin), Russian forces entered northern Korea, and US forces entered from the south. Recognizing that the postwar demarcation in Europe would be along the boundary between Russian-held territory to the east and American-held areas to the west, Truman's advisors could foresee a similar outcome in Asia.

Russia's joining the fight in Asia came perhaps as less welcome news than the promise of it had been in prospect. The key purpose in dropping the A-bombs has always been generally understood as to avoid the enormous bloodshed, both American and

Japanese, that would inevitably accompany an invasion of the home islands, especially Kyushu and Honshu. Then again, the US had already defeated Japan; Japan had yet to surrender, a key sticking point whether the US would permit the Japanese emperor to continue.

Early August brought an extremely tight timeline, with both of the wartime allies in a hurry, each, it seems, with a view to postwar considerations as much as an urge to finish the current war. The US rushed to drop the first bomb, just before Russia would declare war against Japan, and even as Truman headed back to the US from Germany. Indeed, the USSR promptly declared war to join in the action. The US, only three days after Hiroshima, dropped a second bomb, the last one available.

Thus perhaps the unintended wisdom scrawled at the Hiroshima Peace Memorial Museum, where a visitor can, when exiting, register a response to the experience of having just been immersed in the tale told inside. A young man from New Jersey, visiting the museum from nearby Iwakuni Marine Air Station in late 1979, offered his take on the target's appropriateness, from a perspective centrally framed by the Cold War: "It should of been the Russians." Perhaps it was?

2-8
Good Asians, Bad Asians, and World War II

The Wing Luke Museum of the Asian Pacific American Experience, located in Seattle, Washington, includes a display dating from World War II, designed originally to help non-Asian citizens to distinguish between "good Asians" (people of Chinese descent) and "bad Asians" (people of Japanese descent). In December 1941, two weeks after Japan's devastating attack on US naval vessels at Pearl Harbor in Hawaii, two magazines with mass distribution, *Time* and *Life*, were already advising readers, with images and instructions, how to tell the difference.

So, the Second World War featured a sharp distinction among people of Asian descent living in the US, especially along the Pacific Coast but in fact across the nation. Premonitions of this divergence had come into view in the agonizing aftermath of a horrific invasion of China by the Japanese military in the 1930s, but when the US became directly involved in war in the Pacific, those scenes came much closer to home.

In Asia or the Pacific, the United States was fighting as an ally with China against Japanese forces, which also took over all or much of the Philippines, the Dutch East Indies, the Malayan peninsula, and portions of South Asia. Thus, Japan having attacked both, China became the chief US ally in Asia, Japan the great enemy in the western Pacific.

The consequences were huge for both groups of US residents. Some 120,000 people of Japanese descent living along the Pacific Coast were rounded up and interned at distant locations, whether in Arizona, Arkansas, Montana, or even eastern portions of California, on the other side of the Sierra Nevada Mountains. Well over half of all internees were in fact US citizens, having been born in America.

Regardless of whether they were citizens, they suffered two great liabilities. For one, Whites in the West had long directed hostility toward ethnic Japanese people, and the war supplied an opportunity to remove them and take over their property. For another, wars tend to bring fears of "fifth column" enemies, people within a society who might offer aid and comfort to the enemy.

Meanwhile, some people of Chinese ancestry wore buttons declaring "I am Chinese," whether to ward off threats to them anywhere in America as mistaken targets of possible violence (intended for ethnic Japanese) on the streets and in their homes or, if on the West Coast, to declare themselves exempt from extraction and incarceration. The much smaller numbers of ethnic Koreans sometimes did as well.

Long after 1945, some Americans of Japanese ancestry might say about themselves that they were "born in camp," while their parents were interned. In the 21st century, tourists can visit Manzanar, located in California but east of the mountains, and get a glimpse of what the "relocation centers" looked like. More than that, they can see displays that convey some sense of what life was like, as during month after relentless month, year after year, people were kept incarcerated, making lives best they could out of inhospitable materials.

In the two decades between the end of World War II and passage of the 1965 Immigration Act, step by step changes came, both in federal laws and in wider cultural attitudes, as well as in the growing numbers of immigrants from Korea, the Philippines, and elsewhere.

Already in December 1943, as a gesture toward a wartime ally, Congress made ethnic Chinese residents eligible for naturalization as citizens (the Magnuson Act, also termed the Chinese Exclusion Repeal Act). Continuing to treat all people of Chinese descent as pariahs as a matter of national policy seemed a poor way to treat a wartime ally. FDR had urged Congress to act; now he celebrated the results:

> It is with particular pride and pleasure that I have today signed the bill repealing the Chinese Exclusion Laws. The Chinese people, I am sure, will take pleasure in knowing that this represents a manifestation on the part of the American people of their affection and regard.
>
> An unfortunate barrier between allies has been removed. The war effort in the Far East can now be carried on with a greater vigor and a larger understanding of our common purpose.

Having finally made one group of Asians eligible for naturalization, in 1946, the same year the US recognized the Philippines as an independent nation rather than part of the American Empire, it did the same for Filipinos (the Luce-Cellar Act). Some years after the end of hostilities, as Japan became an ally of the US in the global struggle against communism, ethnic Japanese, too, became eligible for naturalization, in the 1952 Immigration and Nationality Act (the McCarran-Walter Act).

A host of images can capture the emerging possibilities of post–World War II America. Sammy Lee, a Korean American, had been barred from regular use of the local public swimming pool as a child in California in the 1930s. Yet, as a member of the US Olympic team, he won gold in 10-meter platform diving in both 1948 and 1952.

Dalip Singh Saund, who had originally come to the US from India as a graduate student in math, had been barred because of his ethnicity from much of American life, but suddenly he could become a US citizen. He did so in 1949, and voters in his California district elected him in 1956 to Congress. Thrilled at his victory, and what it signified for a new America, he trumpeted: "I am a living proof of America's democracy."

Nearly a half-century after the 1942 internment order, Congress passed the Civil Liberties Act of 1988, sponsored by Congressman Norman Yoshio Mineta of California, who with his family had himself been interned at Heart Mountain Relocation Center in Wyoming, and Senator Spark Matsunaga of Hawai'i, an Army veteran wounded in Italy in 1943. It offered an official apology for the entire internment episode, which it attributed to "race prejudice, war hysteria, and a failure of political leadership," and granted any surviving internee $20,000 in compensation.

2-9
Anna Rosenberg, from New Deal to Cold War

Anna Rosenberg (1899–1983), like Gump in the movie *Forrest Gump*, seemed to show up everywhere in American public life, except in her case she kept filling leadership roles in major political efforts and policy initiatives. Moreover, she started life in Central Europe, a native of Budapest in the old Austro-Hungarian Empire, so she had first to transition to a new society and learn a new language.

Her father, Albert Lederer, joined the massive wave of immigrants out of Europe in the years before the Great War. He arrived in New York City in 1910, then, like so many men who scouted the new country and got himself a bit established before sending for family, had his wife and two daughters follow him in 1912.

As a young woman, even in her twenties, she learned much about labor mediation and election campaigning in Democratic politics. She met Eleanor Roosevelt, then worked on Franklin D. Roosevelt's campaign for the New York State governorship in 1928 and on his 1932 campaign for the presidency.

FDR came into the White House committed to combatting the Great Depression and reforming American society, and he came to rely on Rosenberg as a regional director in New York State, the only woman to hold such a position, first with the National Recovery Administration, then for many years on the Social Security Board.

During the Second World War, she continued with some of her leadership roles and added others. She helped resolve a labor dispute that threatened to undermine the Manhattan Project to build atomic weapons. Her work as the New York State regional director of the War Manpower Commission led President Harry Truman, FDR's successor in 1945, to award her the first Medal of Freedom, with the comment that, without her achievements, the "necessary manpower for war production would not have been attained."

Late in the war, two months after the Normandy Landing—from mid-August through late September—FDR sent her to Europe to talk to US soldiers about what they hoped to see when the fighting had finally ended and they had returned home. The original GI Bill had recently passed when she departed for Europe. After soldiers often told her that they especially hoped for a higher education, she urged enhancing the educational benefits, which amendments to the GI Bill did in 1945.

In late 1950, with the US becoming deeply involved in the Korean War, Truman heeded the advice of Defense Secretary George C. Marshall and nominated Rosenberg to be assistant secretary of defense for manpower and personnel. Serving in that capacity for the remainder of Truman's tenure as president, she strove to build up America's armed forces for the Cold War and, in line with Truman's 1948 Executive Order 9981, to end desegregation in the military.

Roosevelt had offered her a cabinet position in late 1944 to replace Frances Perkins as secretary of labor, but she declined. In the 1950s, though, she served both New York City mayor Robert F. Wagner Jr. and New York State governor W. Averell Harriman in roles similar to those she had filled at the national level under FDR. Across those years and beyond, President Dwight D. Eisenhower sometimes relied on her for advice, as did, later, President Lyndon B. Johnson, whom Rosenberg successfully nudged to appoint women to high positions in his administration.

Regarding her many important roles with the federal government, especially from 1933 through 1953, an obituary in *The New York Times* called her "one of the most influential women in the country's public affairs for a quarter of a century." Gender aside, she proved to be one of the more consequential people in public life in the US, from the Great Depression and New Deal through the Second World War and on into the Cold War.

2-10
Donald Bloss and the GI Bill

F. Donald Bloss (1920–2020) dropped out of the University of Chicago in 1942 to join the Army. At the University of Kentucky, he trained for a time to be an X-ray technician—and also met Louise Land, the young lady he would marry, as soon, that is, as he returned from the Second World War.

A conscientious objector, he did not carry a weapon into battle, but he did his utmost, as a medic in a military hospital in England, to look after the men who did, during the many months after D-Day. His job was to help patch wounded men up, some 4,795 in all according to his count, most of them American, some of them Free French, a great number of them in some way his X-ray patients, so they could, in most cases, head back to the battlefront on the continent.

When finally the war ended, when his war ended, he returned in early 1946 to the States. Waiting for him was not only his beloved Louise, but also the Servicemen's Readjustment Act. Commonly known as the GI Bill, it had become law in June 1944, just after D-Day, and its benefits would be enhanced in 1945 and brought back for later wars.

Reflecting a widespread understanding that it was mobilization for the war that had pulled the US fully out of the Great Depression of the 1930s, members of Congress, and a great many other people in the US as well, had been much concerned that the end of the war, coupled with the return of millions of veterans, would greatly enlarge the ranks of the unemployed, and might jolt the nation back into the Great Depression. Such a jolt would perhaps leave many millions of returning veterans angry and volatile, as had been the case in Germany and Italy in the 1920s, not a good look for a serene postwar nation.

Certainly it seemed prudent to anticipate the likely shape of postwar conditions and try to smooth the double transition, from wartime to postwar, as soldiers were demobilized and the economy made its way to a peacetime footing. Factories would have to be converted away from producing military hardware and into producing consumer goods. How to ease the delays and dislocations?

Moreover, the nation had historically often rewarded veterans of one war or another with various kinds of benefits, and Americans back home tended to view the men and women returning from World War II with a great deal of pride and gratitude.

Some 16 million returning veterans qualified for benefits under the GI Bill of Rights, predominantly White men, but both Black and White, men and women. The vast majority, roughly 80 percent, took advantage of at least one of the benefits the GI Bill offered. A great many made good use of a monthly stipend, made available for the first year after their return as they looked for new employment. More than one-fourth of them used benefits related to buying a house or setting up a business.

Fully half, some 8 million people, took advantage of benefits for training or education, and many of them went to four-year colleges. For a great many people, a higher education suddenly seemed realistic, rather than out of the question.

Enrollment at many colleges promptly doubled and more from prewar levels, as veterans swelled college classrooms and strained housing availability. Black veterans, mostly confined to Black colleges, helped triple the total enrollment in Black colleges between the eve of the war and midcentury. Many among the Black veterans, whether they attended college or not, continued the wartime Double-V for Victory Campaign and became civil rights leaders in the years that followed.

As for Don Bloss, he was one of those who returned to college. With GI Bill support, he finished up his undergraduate work at the University of Chicago, then continued through the graduate studies in geology that prepared him for a career in academia and scientific research. Another benefit helped him and his growing family buy their first house when he began teaching at the University of Tennessee. Bloss embodied the generation of Americans who saw their lives interrupted, went off to World War II, returned, and made a life, in large part, out of what the GI Bill offered.

F. Donald Bloss became one of the nearly countless numbers of people, more than 12 million, whose GI benefits promoted their immediate well-being and, more than that, their longer-term life prospects, not to mention how much all of that did to transform postwar America. The GI Bill went far to help World War II veterans make up much of the nation's rapidly growing middle class of the 1950s and 1960s and beyond.

2-11
Jim Crow's New Deal

One monumental program of the New Deal aimed to restore the construction industry and, with it, carpentry and other building trades, all involving great numbers of workers, as well as the timber, transportation, and nail-making industries. This was the Federal Housing Administration (FHA), established under the National Housing Act of 1934 and designed to work social and economic miracles without costing federal dollars.

The FHA worked from multiple premises: the housing industry lay at the center of the American economy; if people could finance new homes, they would buy them; if mortgages had longer terms, say 30 years, monthly payments would be more manageable; if banks were confident of their investments, they would loan the money to finance such purchases; and therefore builders would confidently go to work knowing that buyers would be able to obtain financing. So the FHA guaranteed mortgages for qualifying homebuyers, provided that those mortgages followed FHA guidelines, and then the entire cycle could kick into operation.

Dating from the origins of the FHA is the 30-year mortgage, together with thousands of suburbs full of detached single-family dwellings. Whereas in the past, mortgages had been short-term only, and builders had typically put up just a few structures at a time, often only one, now large residential subdivisions became readily feasible.

Late in World War II, the Servicemen's Readjustment Act of 1944 (GI Bill) created a counterpart Veterans Administration (VA) program that adopted the FHA concept and criteria. Beginning in the 1930s and surging in the postwar 1940s and beyond, millions of new homes went up in the suburbs, among them the Levittowns of Long Island and Pennsylvania. The dream of a home in the suburbs became a reality for millions of families.

There turned out, however, to be severe limits and drawbacks, in the highly uneven availability of the benefits of the new approach to financing family homes. Experts in the business—bankers, realtors, economists, urban planners—set up the guidelines that governed FHA operations, and they brought their collective wisdom at the time to the task.

The *FHA' Underwriting Manual* identified one of its prohibited "inharmonious land uses" (aside from things like tanneries) as the presence of "inharmonious racial or nationality groups." Therefore, the FHA refused to guarantee mortgages unless properties carried racially restrictive covenants. Those covenants had to prohibit African Americans, and they might bar all non-Caucasians, from buying in areas open to White settlement. As for largely Black areas, the term "redlining" came to refer to mapping acceptable areas and those unacceptable for FHA or VA loan guarantees.

In later years, regarding Black-White ratios in public school enrollments, most people would routinely distinguish between two types of segregation, de jure and de facto, that is, those that were deliberately established by law and those that just happened. The race policies of the FHA and the VA challenge the notion that residential patterns were largely a function of individual preferences and market forces.

As intended, the FHA accomplished many wonderful things. The huge downside was that the FHA's approach to home mortgages can be called Jim Crow's New Deal, one among several facets of Jim Crow's New Deal.

The 1948 Supreme Court case *Shelley v. Kraemer* ruled against the use of courts to enforce restrictive covenants, and the Fair Housing Act (Civil Rights Act) of 1968 aimed to curtail the practice of redlining.

Already in the 1950s, urban reformer Charles Abrams authored the book *Forbidden Neighbors: A Study of Prejudice in Housing* (1955), and academic scholar Clement E. Vose published *Caucasians Only: The Supreme Court, the NAACP, and the Restrictive Covenant Cases* (1959).

2-12
J.D. Shelley and the Right to Buy a Home

J.D. Shelley (1905?–1997) and his family migrated from their native Mississippi to St. Louis, Missouri, on the eve of US entry into World War II. His wife, Ethel, and he both found wartime jobs that permitted them to save enough money to buy, in September 1945, a good home to accommodate their family of six children. Their good fortune lasted only a few weeks, however, before a court summons challenged their legal right to live in their new home.

The neighborhood, they learned, was subject to a racial restrictive covenant, agreed to by 30 of the 39 homeowners living there back in 1911, that barred purchase and ownership by anyone of either the "Negro" race or the "Mongolian" race. Such agreements always targeted African Americans; they often also excluded other groups, in this case people of Japanese and Chinese ancestry.

Fern Kraemer, daughter of an original landowner, whose own house was 10 blocks away, insisted that the Shelleys had to move out, and she wanted the court system to force them to do so.

J.D. declared at the time, "Man, I ain't moving nowhere." Unwilling to give up and go away, only to find similar rejection elsewhere, the Shelleys contested this attempt to evict them, and they actually won at trial. The Missouri Supreme Court, however, overturned the local judge's ruling, and the case made its way to the US Supreme Court.

During that time, Thurgood Marshall and the NAACP assembled a coalition of groups to address the matter. As they struggled to craft a set of arguments that they thought should prevail on what they saw as a truly important issue, they held a series of big conferences.

A host of organizations each brought its own perspectives on what was at stake, how to understand the case, and how best to present it. These included the Congress of Industrial Organizations, the American Civil Liberties Union, the American Jewish Congress, and the Japanese American Citizens' League. Preparation for presenting the Shelleys' case also drew, as Supreme Court cases on constitutional law often do, on the expertise that law professors provided in their publications in law journals.

They all knew it to be an uphill battle. Courts had previously held, as the Missouri Supreme Court did, that restrictive covenants of the sort that the Shelley family had encountered were, as private agreements, exempt from the Fourteenth Amendment's protections against discrimination. The relevant clause prohibited a *state* the authority to "deny to any person within its jurisdiction the equal protection of the laws." It did not, went the traditional argument, bar an *individual* from engaging in discrimination.

The Shelleys' attorneys insisted, to the contrary, that, when Fern Kraemer went into state court to secure enforcement of the covenant, she was calling on "state action" to uphold racial discrimination, something she could not do under the Fourteenth Amendment. President Harry Truman's administration backed the Shelleys, as the solicitor general weighed in as a "friend of the court." In May 1948, by a 6–0 margin, the Supreme Court dismantled Kraemer's supposed right to use the court system to keep the Shelleys from buying in a neighborhood covered (in whole or in part) by a restrictive covenant.

The Court concluded that, as the Shelleys' attorneys had argued, the Fourteenth

Amendment's Equal Protection Clause barred state action of the discriminatory sort that had the Shelleys at risk of being forced to vacate a property that they had demonstrated the financial capacity to buy, from a seller willing to sell. Indicating how widespread restrictive covenants were, the three justices not participating in the case had each recused himself on the grounds that he owned property subject to such covenants.

The Shelleys could, and did, continue to live in the home they had moved into nearly three years earlier. Shelley himself explained the origins and significance of his story: "The way I see it, it was a good thing that we done this case. When all this happened, when I bought the property, I didn't think there was going to be anything about it. But I knowed it was important [to pursue the matter]. We was the first ones to live where they said colored can't live."

By no means did his victory at the Supreme Court bring an end to racial discrimination in housing. The covenants themselves, though courts could no longer enforce them, persisted, decade after decade, in real estate documents. Countless people who wanted to keep from having Black neighbors found alternative tools that could serve. And the fact that the Shelley case, from a segregated state, Missouri, came to the Supreme Court paired with a similar case from Michigan showed that the phenomenon arose in the so-called un-segregated North as well as in southern states.

But the ruling the Shelleys obtained demonstrated that times were changing, that the Constitution could perhaps curtail racial discrimination. The federal government— both the executive branch and the Supreme Court, though not yet Congress—seemed to be changing sides in the struggle over whether it would step back or intervene, uphold or challenge Jim Crow. Congress eventually joined in with the Civil Rights Act of 1968.

When the sit-in movement came in the early 1960s, the "state action" theory proved exactly the right tool to bar private establishments, like department stores with public eating facilities, from calling upon the police to enforce racial segregation through state or city trespass laws. When protesters violated the ban on Black customers eating at drugstore cafeterias and the like, and were then arrested, and convicted of trespass, the Supreme Court drew upon *Shelley v. Kraemer* to overturn those convictions. Racial exclusion could not be the basis for government enforcement of trespass laws.

2-13

Victor Hugo Green, American Automobility, and *The Green Book*

Victor Hugo, the great European novelist, in *Les Misérables* (1862) championed the downtrodden in his native France. An African American young couple, having moved to New York in the late 1880s, in the first great post–Civil War wave of Black Virginians heading north to Washington, DC, or Baltimore, Philadelphia, or New York, no doubt had the novelist in mind when they named their first child Victor Hugo Green (1892–1960).

Across the middle third of the 20th century, Green embodied multiple facets of the American—more particularly African American—past and future, from migration and automobiles to protest and hope. A World War I veteran, Green married a native Virginian, Alma Duke, who had moved to New York from Richmond, and he worked most of his adult life as a letter carrier for the US Postal Service. He kept experiencing—or heard from other people in the New York City area who were experiencing—exclusion from, or harassment at, places of so-called public accommodations, from barbershops and beauty parlors to taverns and nightclubs to restaurants and hotels.

The Negro Travelers' Green Book (1954)

So, emphasizing Metropolitan New York at first, in 1936 he came out with *The Negro Motorist Green-Book* (renamed in 1952 *The Negro Travelers' Green Book*). Quickly expanding its coverage west to the Mississippi River, and then beyond to the rest of the nation, and especially intent on addressing the needs of long-distance travelers, Green and his wife brought out a new edition each year, designed to facilitate safe, convenient, and uneventful travel by advising African Americans where best to take a break. Where might they stop for a meal, or a night's lodging, or to get gas or fix a tire?

From Model T to Model A, from Studebaker or Packard to Buick or Dodge, ever more Black families, like their White counterparts, bought cars in the 1910s or '20s, the 1950s and '60s; and Black athletes, singers, and civil rights lawyers on the road needed places to eat and sleep too. The need especially reflected the world, for example, of Black residents of Chicago heading back south to visit grandparents in Alabama—or going anywhere for a family vacation.

White travelers going any distance might also find a guide useful, and in fact the American Automobile Association (AAA) served them well. They had no occasion for thinking it often advisable, out of safety and necessity, to pack most meals and drive straight through.

With Black motorists in mind, Green mused at the beginning of each *Green Book*: "There will be a day sometime in the near future when this guide will not have to be published. That is when we as a race will have equal opportunities and privileges in the United States." That "near future" took a while, as a new *Green Book* came out every year for three decades (except during World War II), into the 1960s.

The Civil Rights Act of 1964 rendered *The Green Book* an artifact from the receding past, remembered with gratitude and affection.

2-14

Document: The UN Universal Declaration of Human Rights

Throughout the presidency of Franklin D. Roosevelt, First Lady Eleanor Roosevelt (ER) functioned as a social conscience, during both the New Deal and the Second World War. Her presence in the White House came to an end in April 1945 when FDR died, but she lived for many more years, during which time she continued as something of a social conscience for America and the wider world.

FDR's successor, Harry Truman, appointed her as a delegate to the new United Nations. More than that, she found herself unexpectedly filling lead roles in the development of a new international agreement as to a constellation of basic human rights.

In January 1941, in his State of the Union address to Congress and the nation, FDR had spoken of the "four essential human freedoms": freedom of speech and of religion, and freedom from want and from fear. Working with the materials at hand and within the Cold War context of the late 1940s, ER nudged the process along in finding common ground that the many disparate nations in the UN could agree to. In the end, no nation voted against its adoption, though several abstained.

The final document, as ratified by the UN General Assembly in December 1948, contained 30 articles. These included a range of social and economic human rights. Some, including Article 23, reflected ideals pursued in the New Deal. Some—certainly Articles 16 and 21—anticipated substantial change in public policy within much of the US.

The Declaration combined two broad considerations, one quintessentially moral, a matter of right, the other fundamentally pragmatic, a matter of necessity—akin to what FDR had termed "principles of morality and considerations for our own security." If every person were accorded respect and security, then perhaps conflict within a nation state would be less likely to occur, and conflict between one nation and another might also be less likely.

But the 30 articles do not speak to pragmatism so much as to morality, a new era in which not only might each nation frame its own declaration of rights, but a global agreement, an international document, might pave the way for a better future for all:

Article 1 is foundational: "All human beings are born free and equal in dignity and rights."

Article 2 speaks to how these rights are an entitlement to each person "without distinction of any kind, such as race, colour, sex, language, religion, political or other opinion, national or social origin, property, birth or other status."

Article 3: "Everyone has the right to life, liberty and security of person."

Article 5: "No one shall be subjected to torture or to cruel, inhuman or degrading treatment or punishment."

Article 9: "No one shall be subjected to arbitrary arrest, detention or exile."

Article 16: "Men and women of full age, without any limitation due to race, nationality or religion, have the right to marry and to found a family."

Article 21: "Everyone has the right to take part in the government of his country, directly or through freely chosen representatives."

Article 22: "Everyone, as a member of society, has the right to social security and is entitled to realization, through national effort and international co-operation . . . , of the economic, social and cultural rights indispensable for his dignity and the free development of his personality."

Article 23: "Everyone has the right to work, to free choice of employment, to just and favourable conditions of work. . . . Everyone, without any discrimination, has the right to equal pay for equal work. . . . Everyone has the right to form and to join trade unions for the protection of his interest."

Article 25: "Everyone has the right to a standard of living adequate for the health and well-being of himself and of his family."

Article 26: "Everyone has the right to education. Education shall be free, at least in the elementary and fundamental stages. . . . Education shall be directed to the full development of the human personality and to the strengthening of respect for human rights and fundamental freedoms. It shall promote understanding, tolerance and friendship among all nations, racial or religious groups, and shall further the activities of the United Nations for the maintenance of peace."

Article 28: "Everyone is entitled to a social and international order in which the rights and freedoms set forth in this Declaration can be fully realized."

2-15
Harry Truman and Civil Rights

What president of the United States had ever displayed much support for the political or civil rights of African Americans? Why should anyone expect more from Harry Truman? For starters, he came from the officially segregated South, albeit the Border South, the state of Missouri. Yet he proved assertive across a wide spectrum on the civil rights front, helping to set in motion much of what would unfold over the next two decades.

Considerations that fed into his actions included global politics in the early Cold War, a developing sense that it was simply overdue, and also the importance of Black voters living outside the South as a result of the Great Migration, though his stance was sure to lose him many White voters. Back in 1940, when running for reelection to the Senate, Truman had said in a campaign speech: "I believe in the brotherhood of man, not merely the brotherhood of white men." As president he made similar statements, including "When I say Americans, I mean all Americans."

Moreover, the horrific treatment faced by some Black returning veterans, still in uniform, utterly repulsed him. As an example of such mayhem, Isaac Woodard Jr., on his way by bus on 12 February 1946 to his home in South Carolina, having been discharged from the Army earlier that day, endured a brutal beating by police that left him blinded as well as battered. Welcome home; thank you for your service.

Truman's accidental presidency gave him an opportunity to act. In December 1946, Truman's Executive Order 9808 established the President's Committee on Civil Rights, tasked to survey the status of civil rights across the country and make such recommendations as seemed appropriate. In June 1947 he became the first president ever to address an NAACP annual convention. In December 1947, his Committee on Civil Rights released *To Secure These Rights*, a report proposing creation of a Civil Rights Commission and a Civil Rights Division in the Justice Department, as well as a permanent Fair Employment Practices Commission (the one from the 1941 compromise with A. Philip Randolph had ended with the war), an anti-lynching law, and an end to the poll tax as a requirement for voting. In February 1948, Truman gave a speech to a joint session of Congress urging passage of these kinds of proposals.

When Congress did not budge, Truman issued two executive orders. A. Philip Randolph's March on Washington Movement in 1941 had achieved substantial success regarding employment in defense industries, though that benefit was a concession related to a wartime surge in one big category of jobs. Left unaddressed at that time were jobs in the federal bureaucracy and desegregation of the armed forces.

On 26 July 1948, Truman issued executive orders on both fronts. Executive Order 9980 ordered new "regulations governing fair employment practices within the federal establishment." A Fair Employment Board, located within the Civil Service Commission, would make regulations regarding "all departments and agencies of the executive branch." It would enforce compliance and regularly report back to the president.

Executive Order 9981, which made an even bigger splash at the time and remains far more visible in accounts of Truman's time in office, ordered the desegregation of the US military. To direct this huge task, it established "the President's Committee on Equality of Treatment and Opportunity in the Armed Forces."

The task was huge because of the sprawling nature of the military, with its varied branches and authority structures, and because it flew in the face of formidable arguments that generals made all through the Second World War and afterwards. Back in 1941, for example, one general had declared: "Negro pilots cannot be used on our present Air Corps since this would result in having Negro officers serving over white enlisted men." (In short, the general was focusing on a mandate for Black subordination, not any concern over so-called racial inferiority.) Other generals and admirals also voiced strong opposition, both during the war and as late as spring 1948.

Another initiative brought the US Department of Justice into constitutional litigation. In 1948, another Truman committee, the President's Commission on Higher Education, had called for repeal of all state laws requiring segregation of public colleges and universities. Now, the solicitor general, the lawyer who represents the interests of the United States in cases of constitutional law that go before the US Supreme Court, began intervening on the side of Black plaintiffs against their exclusion from graduate and professional programs at historically White institutions. Between 1948 and 1950, the Supreme Court handed down three important decisions regarding separate-but-equal in higher education (in cases from Oklahoma and Texas), plus a decision each that undermined discrimination in housing (*Shelley v. Kraemer*) and in interstate transportation (*Henderson v. United States*).

The Commission on Higher Education, in highlighting a regional fault line on race and higher education, displayed a new federal language on racial identity, public policy, and educational opportunity. As for the three big cases on race and higher education, their significance proved vast, not only in terms of identifying the path the NAACP promptly followed with regard to elementary and secondary education—the road that took the nation to *Brown v. Board of Education*—but also in propelling state after state to embark on modest beginnings in the process of desegregating its institutions of higher education. Then, in turn, *Brown v. Board* propelled still further change.

Meanwhile, those mid-century Supreme Court rulings spurred southern states to invest substantial funds in Black schools at every level in hopes of averting desegregation orders that would rest on the grotesque disparity in funding, facilities, and curricular opportunities for black Southern children and young adults.

President Harry Truman's years in the White House fostered a sea change on Black opportunity in the US armed forces, Black jobs in the civil service, and Black access to higher education. Furious at Truman's assault on Jim Crow, the Democratic Party broke up in 1948 over it. The breakaway faction, the "States' Rights Democratic Party" or

"Dixiecrats," nominated for president and vice-president the governors from the Deepest South, South Carolina and Mississippi, where the commitment to White supremacy and Black subjugation remained especially determined.

The 1948 election season seemed to echo 1860, when the Democrats broke up over slavery and ran two different candidates. The Dixiecrats' appearance in mid-1948 highlighted how far Harry Truman had gone, three years into his presidency. In a tight race, Truman won.

2-16
Document: Roy Wilkins Letter to President Truman, 1953

Toward the end of President Truman's time in office, the head of the NAACP wanted to register his admiration and gratitude for what, to his mind, was a job amazingly well done in the realm of civil rights. Roy Wilkins had excellent reason to see and say that no predecessor had come close to what Truman had attempted nor what he had accomplished. He could only hope—and he expressed confidence—that considerable progress would build on what had recently begun.

Questions: What actions in each area is Wilkins referencing? Based on both the past at that time, and the future, how does Truman stack up against Abraham Lincoln or Lyndon B. Johnson?

January 12, 1953

President Harry S. Truman
The White House
Washington, D. C.

Dear Mr. President:

You must be receiving many letters and your hours in these last days of office must be filled with many duties, but I felt that I could not see you leave Washington without telling you how I feel about one phase of your administration.

I want to thank you and to convey to you my admiration for your efforts in the civil rights field, for your pronouncements and definitions of policy on racial and religious discrimination and segregation.

You have many accomplishments on record during your tenure of the White House (many more by far than is admitted publicly by the Republicans or the majority of the nation's press) but none more valuable to our nation and its ideals than your outspoken championing of equality of opportunity for all Americans without regard to race, color or national origin.

Mr. President, no Chief Executive in our history has spoken so plainly on this matter as yourself, or acted so forthrightly. We have had in the White House great men— great diplomats, great politicians, great scholars, great humanitarians, great administrators. Some of these have recognized inequality as undesirable, as being at variance with the democratic principles of our country; but none has had courage, either personal or political, to speak out or act in the Truman manner.

You spoke, Sir, when you knew that many powerful influences in your own party (and in the party of the opposition) would not heed. You reiterated your beliefs and restated your demands for legislation when political expediency dictated a compromise course. This is sheer personal courage, so foreign to the usual conduct in political office—high or low—as to be unique in the annals of our government. But it was worthy of the Presidency of the United States of America. No little man, no mere politician would have sensed the fitness of such conduct in the nation's leader.

Your great desire was to achieve peace. Your sincere efforts toward this goal have saved us from a Third World War thus far and have laid a foundation on which others, if equally devoted, can bring peace to the world.

In urging that America erase inequality between citizens, as citizens, you were outlining a component of the complex Mosaic for peace in the world: the hope, dignity and freedom that democracies offer mankind in contrast to the offerings of totalitarianism. Your sure realization of the truism that preachment without practice would be powerless as a force for peace is a measure of the quiet greatness you brought to your office.

As you leave the White House you carry with you the gratitude and affectionate regard of millions of your Negro fellow citizens who in less than a decade of your leadership, inspiration and determination, have seen the old order changed right before their eyes.

Their sons are serving their country's armed forces in pride and honor, instead of humiliation and despair.

A whole new world of opportunity in education is opening to their children and young people.

The barriers to employment and promotion on the basis of merit have been breached and will be destroyed.

Some of the obstacles in the way of enjoyment of decent housing have been removed and others are under attack.

Restrictions upon the precious citizenship right of casting a ballot have been reduced and soon this right will be unfettered.

Some of the cruel humiliation and discrimination in travel and accommodation in public places have been eliminated and others are on the way out.

But in addition to these specifics, Mr. President, you have been responsible through the pronouncements from your office, for a new climate of opinion in this broad area of civil rights. By stating a government policy, by relating that policy to the cherished ideals of our nation, you have recalled for the American people that strength of the spirit, that devotion to human welfare and human liberties, that made our country man's best hope for the things all men hold dear.

In their prayers for your health and long life, Negro Americans are joined, I am sure, by hosts of other citizens who have had their spirits renewed and their convictions strengthened by your espousal of the verities of our way of life.

You have said often that the people will act when they have understanding. The people who have had their faith fanned fresh by you will not fail to press toward the goals you have indicated. No change of personnel or party labels will stay them.

May God's blessing and guidance be with you and your new endeavors.

Respectfully yours,
Roy Wilkins
(Administrator, National Association for the
Advancement of Colored People)

2-17
President Truman and the Cold War

The early years after the Second World War took a turn when the two chief nations that defeated Nazi Germany became not allies, but potentially mortal enemies. President Truman shepherded the US through that time, as European economies came near collapse, European empires in Asia crumbled, and the US, as the planet's dominant military and economic power, tried to find its way.

As soon became clear, European powers with vast colonial holdings in Asia would be unable to reclaim the control they had long exercised before Germany warred against them in Europe and Japan moved in on their territories. Resistance within the colonies, combined with great weakness in Europe, led to one newly independent nation after another emerging from its colonial past.

The Dutch, for example, could not retrieve control of the Dutch East Indies, which soon became an independent Indonesia. The British proved incapable of returning to power in South Asia, and India and Pakistan soon emerged as independent nations. And the USA and the USSR would each seek to sway the new nations toward their own sphere of interest.

In spring 1945, as Russian troops moved west and US troops moved east, where they met determined the location of what came to be called the Iron Curtain. As historian Stephen Ambrose once summarized the situation, "The key, of course, was the Red Army." Thus, Eastern European countries, ranging from East Germany and Poland south through Czechoslovakia and Hungary to Romania, Bulgaria, and Albania, fell on the eastern side, the Soviet side, of the Iron Curtain, separated from countries farther west, no matter what side those nations had been on during the war, among them Britain, France, Italy, Greece, Portugal, Belgium, Denmark, and Norway.

The wartime allies divided Germany, with four sectors at first: American, British, French, and Soviet. The three western sectors coalesced as West Germany, with Bonn the new capital city, while the Soviet sector became East Germany. Berlin, formerly the capital of Germany, was also divided, into East Berlin and West Berlin, although physically located inside East Germany.

A series of policy shifts between 1947 and 1949 gave shape to a Western Europe that would last for generations. In early 1947, Truman learned that the British were giving up their attempt to support friendly governments in Greece and Turkey. Both Mediterranean countries featured internal struggles, with outside support for the opponents of the current regime, and the US would be taking Britain's place there. Truman went to Congress in March seeking funds to support the friendly governments in both countries, and Congress agreed to supply necessary funds. Intervention to keep Greece and Turkey within the Western sphere became known as the Truman Doctrine.

Truman soon went back to Congress, this time to propose the European Recovery Plan, conceived by Secretary of State George C. Marshall (therefore called the Marshall Plan). The plan called for massive US funds to fuel an economic recovery in Western Europe, with several major objectives. In humanitarian terms, US aid would ameliorate severe distress in the aftermath of the war's legacy of death and destruction. In terms of politics, desperate citizens were unreliable allies and might well elect governments that the US deemed unfriendly. As for economics, American farmers and other producers could not sell to countries that had no capacity to pay. Reinvigorating the economies of Britain, France, and other countries could help achieve American political and economic interests.

One of the more dramatic episodes in early postwar Europe came after the Soviet Union imposed a blockade on West Berlin, hoping to push the Americans and their allies out of the city by preventing the ground shipment of essential supplies. Instead, the Berlin Airlift of 1948–1949 brought in items like fuel and food by air, so the blockade failed. West Berlin, like West Germany, would remain in the American sphere.

The year 1949 brought the North Atlantic Treaty Organization as well, a mutual defense pact soon countered by the Soviet Union's Warsaw Pact. By then, the broad contours of postwar Europe and indeed global politics and economics had begun to take clear shape. The United States of America faced the Union of Soviet Socialist Republics as the two overwhelming powers, one of them clearly global, the other more regional, although for the Soviet Union "regional" meant great power in both Europe and Asia.

The year 1949 also demonstrated that the US no longer had a monopoly of nuclear power, as the Soviet Union tested its own atomic device. And in Asia, 1949 brought a Communist victory in its civil war against the Chinese Nationalists, who exiled themselves to the island of Taiwan. The new People's Republic of China would, over the years, prove a significant player, in regional politics and eventually in world affairs.

The US soon intervened also in the internal affairs of countries in Southwest Asia and Central America. Seeking to secure a government perceived as friendly to American national and Western interests, the US helped Britain engineer a coup in a fractious Iran in 1953, where, at the behest of British Petroleum (its name today), the Shah of Iran replaced reformer Mohammed Mossadeq; President Truman had opposed US involvement, but his successor, Dwight Eisenhower, approved it. Another coup, this one at the behest of the United Fruit Company, overcame an election in Guatemala in 1954 that had brought reformer Jacobo Arbenz Guzman to power.

In contrast to the Marshall Plan for Europe, these interventions derailed economic reform, wrought social and economic misery and government brutality against the citizenry, and undermined US interests in the long run.

In Southeast Asia, meanwhile, France still hoped to retrieve control of Indochina, but its forces found themselves utterly defeated in 1954 by an insurgent independence movement. The Geneva Accords that year stated Laos and Cambodia to be independent neutral nations. As for the rest of Indochina, Vietnam was soon divided between a Communist-led North Vietnam, supported by China and the USSR, and an anti-Communist South Vietnam. As northern forces threatened to take over the entire country, President Eisenhower, resisting unification under a pro-Communist regime, began in a small way what would grow a decade later into massive US intervention into the affairs of Vietnam.

2-18
Two Koreas, Three Korean Wars

With Korea surrounded by Russia, China, and Japan, headlines during and after June 1950 had a wide horizon and a long backdrop.

Japan, an island nation, had colonized the nearby peninsula for several decades, but in summer 1945 its power on the Asian continent suddenly vanished. In Korea, Soviet troops moved into the northern half, Americans into the southern part.

With the Second World War morphing into Cold War, two competing new Korean governments emerged, one in the North, the other in the South, each claiming authority over the entire country. Korea shared a long border to its north with the new Communist-controlled People's Republic of China, plus a short border to its northeast with the USSR.

The Korean War (or the Korean Conflict, as it is sometimes termed, since Congress never declared war) is generally treated as a single historical unit, but distinguishing among multiple phases helps clarify developments over the next three years. On 25 June 1950, North Korean troops rampaged across the border, sweeping all before them, until only the southeastern port at Busan lay beyond the North's control.

President Truman rushed to the United Nations, where he secured a multinational commitment to turn back what was characterized as an invasion. US troops, having arrived in Japan in 1945, remained stationed there, across the Sea of Japan, and could be quickly deployed to Korea. Soldiers from Turkey, Australia, and many other countries joined the US military to intervene, beginning at Busan.

Opening another front, Gen. Douglas MacArthur engineered a landing on 15 September of US/UN forces at the port town Inchon, on Korea's west coast, not far west of the city Seoul nor far south of what had been the provisional dividing line between Soviet and American spheres.

Between the two strongholds, at Inchon and Busan, Allied forces cut off supplies for North Koreans in the South and retrieved control of the entire South, their stated objective. The US and its allies had thwarted what they perceived as an attempt at expansion of the global Communist sphere. They had achieved "containment."

But they had done so with such relative ease that they decided to continue pushing north, ever closer to the Yalu River, across which lay China. Liberation of the entire peninsula became the objective, to eliminate Communist power and any future threat from the North. Meanwhile, MacArthur began ruminating in public about expanding the war beyond the northern border and bombing the People's Republic of China.

On 19 October, soldiers from China suddenly exploded south across the Yalu River, overwhelmed the US/UN forces in the area, and pushed south. The fighting, scarcely any longer a war among Koreans for control of Korea, became more clearly a proxy war among the world's nations, with the US and its allies on one side, the USSR and China on the other side.

The greatest US/UN casualties took place in this new and much longer phase of military struggle, first, to slow the relentless push southward by Chinese soldiers, then, that failing until much of the peninsula had once again been lost, second, to push northward back toward the 38th Parallel.

Seoul had quickly switched back and forth from South Korean control to North

Korean on 28 June 1950, then South Korean and US/UN by October, then North Korean and Chinese forces in January 1951, and the struggle continued.

When organized fighting came to an end, on 27 July 1953, it did so along just about the same border where it had begun, with the peninsula once again divided around the 38th Parallel. Rollback had failed, for both sides. Containment had succeeded.

In quick succession, the US had spectacularly won the first Korean War, then just as spectacularly lost the second phase. Finally, much more slowly and at far greater cost, the US returned to where it had all started and settled in at stalemate.

Three-quarters of a century later, US troops remain, in large numbers, in South Korea, as they do in Japan. The two Koreas, still divided, have very much gone their separate ways.

2-19
Jackie Robinson and the Color Line in Professional Sports

Perhaps it was unthinkable, but Branch Rickey, president of the Brooklyn Dodgers baseball team, thought of it and then did it. He did not have to guess whether the best Black players could perform as well as their best White counterparts. Professional sports teams need to sell tickets, and Black patrons showed up in force and might be induced to do much more. The whole thing about categorical exclusion seemed to him monumentally unjust. And yet law and custom, attitudes and behavior, virtually the entire culture screamed against the feasibility of challenging the way things were. Or did it?

In August 1945, the same month that World War II came to an end, Rickey approached a young athlete from the West Coast with an offer from an East Coast team. Might he like to play baseball for a Dodgers minor league club? Going that far already broke the "gentlemen's agreement" that no Black player be permitted to join any team in any MLB organization.

Jackie Robinson had, since youth, proved to be a simply outstanding athlete. His mother's decision to move her family from Georgia to California had already made some things possible. Jackie's big brother Mack had come in second to Jesse Owens in the 200-meter event in the 1936 Olympics in Berlin, Germany.

As for Jackie, at the (overwhelmingly White) University of California at Los Angeles, not far from his home, he had twice led the conference in scoring in basketball, had won the NCAA crown in the long jump in track and field, had averaged a first down and then some as a running back during his junior season at UCLA in football, and had done all right, too, in baseball.

Branch Rickey set conditions. Jackie, supremely competitive in sports, had scarcely been known for restraint when he encountered racial slights, as when, having been drafted into the Army during the war, he faced a court martial over his refusal to comply with a driver's command that he move to the back of a military bus in Texas.

Robinson could scarcely escape relentless heckling and worse, whether from opponents, their fans, or even his teammates—not to mention the trials of travel, the challenges of where to eat or spend the night, when on the road for away games. And the experiment had to work, could not blow up. Who knew how it would go as some proportion of Whites would express an urgent need for Black subordination, Black exclusion, a need that stemmed somehow from a fear of what it meant for Blacks to be permitted to operate as equals to Whites and in the same space. Could he rein it in, could he throttle back his emotions, could he do it for three years?

Robinson agreed. In the 1946 season, playing for the Dodgers' top farm team, in Montreal, Canada, he won the league batting championship. He soon headed to the bigs. On opening day, 15 April 1947, there he was, a promising rookie, the starting first baseman, a Major League Baseball player—the first since a lifetime ago, back at an earlier time when things had seemed possible, when Moses Fleetwood Walker played for the Toledo Blue Stockings during the 1884 season.

That summer, Cleveland Indians owner Bill Veeck signed Larry Doby as the second African American in Major League Baseball in the modern era, the first in the American League. All the other MLB teams eventually followed suit, down to July 1959, when infielder Elijah "Pumpsie" Green and pitcher Earl Wilson joined the last holdout, the Boston Red Sox.

Opening the Major Leagues to Black players transformed the game. To be sure, it helped tremendously when, for example, the slugger Hank Greenberg, who had earlier faced comparable fury as a Jewish player, warmly supported Robinson, Greenberg in his final season, Robinson in his first. Soon such superstars as teammate catcher Roy Campanella in 1948 and New York Giants outfielder Willie Mays in 1951 came into the majors.

The Brooklyn Dodgers and Cleveland Indians were not, however, alone in featuring integrated professional teams in the early post–World War II years. Nor was "Number 42" the first Black player to join a non-Black team at the top of professional US sports.

By the time Jackie Robinson took his position on a major league baseball field, four Black men—Marion Motley and Bill Willis with the Cleveland Browns, Woody Strode and Kenny Washington with the Los Angeles Rams—had already completed their first season, 1946, in the National Football League. Notably, before making his mark in baseball, Robinson had starred alongside his college teammates Woody Strode and Kenny Washington on the UCLA football team.

Like MLB, the NFL meandered toward including at least one Black player on every team. By the early 1960s every team but one had, for several years, done so, and President John F. Kennedy's administration found it embarrassing that the nation's capital city continued to sport a Jim Crow team. The Washington Redskins joined the others when owner George Preston Marshall bent to great pressure from Interior Secretary Morris Udall and agreed to end his policy of Black exclusion. The first regular season game of fall 1962 featured three Black players for Washington: Bobby Mitchell, Leroy Jackson, and John Nisby. Mitchell, the star of the game, scored twice on touchdown passes and once on a 92-yard kickoff return.

Within a few years, the National Basketball Association replicated the patterns that the NFL and MLB had pioneered. On 31 October 1950, Earl Lloyd entered the lineup for the Washington Capitols. The next night, Chuck Cooper played for the Boston Celtics. And three days later, on 4 November, Nathaniel "Sweetwater" Clifton made his NBA debut for the New York Knicks.

By the time the youngest, Earl Lloyd, retired in 1960, a growing host of Black players had come into the league, among them superstars Elgin Baylor, Bill Russell, and Wilt Chamberlain. In 1964, the Celtics broke protocol that required at least one starter to be White—a startling contrast with the situation 15 years earlier—by starting an all-Black cast of players, including Bill Russell, Sam Jones, and KC Jones, that won 12 consecutive games.

The NBA announced in early October 2025 that the new season would commemorate the 75th anniversary of the 1950 trio of Nat Clifton, Earl Lloyd, and Chuck Cooper.

On 15 April 1997, on the 50th anniversary of Jackie Robinson's first game with the Dodgers, MLB permanently retired the number, 42, that he wore on that day and throughout his breakthrough career. In 1947, baseball was far and away the "national pastime," and Robinson symbolized what was already beginning to happen in American life.

By demonstrating to fellow Americans, both Black and White, the new possible, he helped transform the nation. Young Black athletes had a model to emulate, a platform for dreaming. Robinson himself, once having made it through his promised three years of restraint, grew into a powerful voice through the remainder of his baseball career and the rest of his life.

2-20
Jim Crow, Jane Crow, and Pauli Murray

Pauli Murray (1910–1985), a triracial child of the South, identified as Black and mostly as a woman, and she kept running into discrimination on both counts. Resisting all such, she tried, eventually with considerable success, to alter American life at every turn.

In her childhood she shuttled between Baltimore, Maryland, and Durham, North Carolina, but then moved to New York City, where she attended Hunter College. She applied in 1938 for graduate study at the University of North Carolina, where her White great-grandfather had studied and his father had been a trustee, but was rejected on racial grounds. She hoped that the NAACP would pursue her case, but it did not.

Twice in quick succession she encountered the South's racial regime in Virginia. In 1940, while taking a bus south to see her family in North Carolina, she was arrested in Petersburg for violating the state law's insistence on segregated bus travel, then contested (though without success) the constitutionality of the law's application to interstate travel. Then she campaigned, again ultimately without success, to prevent the execution of a Black sharecropper, Odell Waller, convicted by an all-White jury on a charge of first-degree murder after a scuffle with his landlord over his share of the crop resulted in the landlord's death.

These experiences pointed her to law school, with what she called "the single-minded intention of destroying Jim Crow." During World War II, while attending Howard University, she led sit-ins to desegregate nearby drugstores and cafeterias.

Hoping to earn a graduate law degree so she could return to Howard as a professor, she applied to Harvard Law School, where her professors, all male, had typically trained, but was turned down for being female. Instead, she earned graduate degrees at the

University of California at Berkeley and at Yale University, with theses titled "The Right to Equal Opportunity in Employment" and "Roots of the Racial Crisis: Prologue to Policy." To provide civil rights lawyers a comprehensive collection of the laws of race in every state, she compiled *States' Laws on Race and Color* (1951).

Murray did far more. In what she called "confrontation by typewriter," she wrote frequent letters to newspaper editors and public officials. As West African colonies became independent nations, she taught for a time at the Ghana Law School and coauthored *The Constitution and Government of Ghana* (1961). A founding member of the National Organization for Women in 1966, she was also ordained in 1977 as one of the first women, and the first Black woman, to be a priest in the Episcopal Church.

She published an account of her family's remarkable history, *Proud Shoes: The Story of an American Family* (1956), and a book of poetry, *Dark Testament and Other Poems* (1970). Her "autobiographical book on Jim Crow and Jane Crow," *Song in a Weary Throat: An American Pilgrimage* (1987), published posthumously, was republished as *Pauli Murray: The Autobiography of a Black Activist, Feminist, Lawyer, Priest, and Poet* (1989).

Late in life she wrote that she had "lived to see my lost causes found," yet she looked in vain for "a truly integrated society," and she entered the ministry in part because, she observed, "we had reached a point where law could not give us the answers."

2-21
Barbara Johns and the Struggle against Separate-and-Unequal Schools

Barbara Rose Johns (1935–1991) grew up in rural Prince Edward County, in Virginia's Southside, a region where counties had historically high proportions, even majorities, of Black residents. Prince Edward had an unusually high rate of Black farm ownership, so Black residents were somewhat less vulnerable there than in most other "blackbelt" counties to White economic retaliation for any expression of dissent against Jim Crow. But dissent there might be.

Black leaders in Prince Edward included Rev. L. Francis Griffin, a combat veteran of World War II, minister at county seat Farmville's First Baptist Church, and leader of the local branch of the NAACP. Barbara Johns had a favorite uncle, Rev. Vernon Johns, an outspoken leader who, having grown up in Prince Edward, preceded Rev. Martin Luther King Jr. at Dexter Avenue Baptist Church in Montgomery, Alabama.

During much of Barbara's young life, her father had been away in the Army during World War II, and her mother worked near Washington, DC, in a government job at the Pentagon, to earn a cash income to help keep the family financially afloat. Barbara, the first-born, served as the household's acting mother. She had a younger sister, Joan, and, at midcentury, two brothers, Ernest and, in first grade in the school year 1950–1951, Roddy.

The county's Black high school, Robert R. Moton High, increasingly overcrowded, lacked all manner of necessities and amenities—from gym to cafeteria to science labs— that the elegant nearby Farmville High School provided White students. Moreover, the temporary buildings put up at Moton High to address the overcrowding—"tarpaper shacks," their inmates termed them—kept most students cold and sometimes wet for much of their school day.

Late in life, Barbara put pen to paper and wrote an account of her childhood and youth—her Prince Edward years—and squirreled it away, intended for her family to find, which they did. She began by recounting her version of a typical childhood in rural America in the 1940s. She next registered her deep long-ago distress at the stark contrast between Moton High, her school, and Farmville High, attended by her White cousins and counterparts.

And she recounted some of the fantasies that had often made their way through her young mind when she contemplated the relentless inequity:

> My imagination would run rampant—and I would dream that some mighty man of great wealth built us a new school building or that our parents got together and surprised us with this grand new building and we had a big celebration—and I even imagined that a great storm came through and blew down the main building and splattered the shacks to splinters—and out of this wreckage rose this magnificent building and all the students were joyous and even the teachers cried.
>
> But then reality would set in and I would be forced to acknowledge that nothing magical was going to produce a new school.

One morning, Barbara, a 15-year-old junior, escorted her three siblings, as she routinely did, down the long driveway to the bus stop, from where they would all be transported along the gravel country road to the distant town of Farmville, where they attended either Moton High or, across the street, the Mary E. Branch Elementary School, far and away the county's best elementary school—the best available, that is, for Black children.

That day, however, she suddenly realized, while her siblings were toting their lunches, that she had left hers back in the kitchen. She rushed up the hill, grabbed the sack, and raced back toward the road, but the bus had pulled away. Might another ride come along? Sure enough, the bus carrying White students, also to Farmville, made its way toward her—and then swiftly passed. We have no report of what the White kids hollered out the bus's windows as it hurtled by. From small events like that one, great consequences can flow.

Deeply troubled, she spent a sleepless night. And an idea took shape, not so much about the day's jangly start but about the entire situation of unequal segregated schools in her part of the world.

Barbara recruited a few classmates, fellow conspirators, to flesh out her idea and plan its implementation. The time to act came late in the school year, in April, shortly after she turned 16. Intent on protecting, as best they could, the faculty from retaliation, they lured the principal away from the school on a pretext, called an assembly, barred the teachers from entering—and announced an intent to go out on strike, 400-plus teenagers in all, until they got a promise of a new school that would be more like the White one.

She reached out for help from the leading civil rights lawyers in Virginia. Oliver W. Hill Sr. and Spottswood W. Robinson III, it turned out, would be passing that way from Richmond anyway within the next few days and again on their return trip. They advised the Black citizens of Prince Edward County that yes, they would take their case to court—but not simply to get an equal school, rather to desegregate the county schools entirely.

Eventually, the case that Barbara Johns initiated made its way to the US Supreme

Court as one of the cluster of cases collectively known as *Brown v. Board of Education*, decided in principle in 1954 and as to implementation in 1955. Meanwhile, hoping desperately to avoid an order to desegregate, county authorities scrambled to supply the new Black high school that, had it been in place a few years earlier, would have meant that Barbara never had to ponder what to do to secure it.

Brown v. Board of Education made clear that even actually securing the "equal" in "separate but equal" would no longer suffice. Then again, Virginia, like several other southern states, responded to *Brown v. Board* by embarking on a program called "Massive Resistance," designed to prevent any White students from ever having Black classmates.

In May 1959, when a federal court order finally came to desegregate the Prince Edward schools, the county board of supervisors did as the Virginia General Assembly had expressly authorized—and shuttered the schools forever. White students began attending a new option, a segregated private academy, supported with public funds. Forever turned out to mean five years. After another Supreme Court ruling, issued in 1964 and specifically related to Prince Edward, local authorities reopened the schools, up and running again and technically desegregated, albeit with very tight funding and only a very few White students.

Meanwhile, after a cross burned at the school, and a death threat against Barbara, her parents sent her off to Alabama for safekeeping with her uncle. Her four siblings— her youngest brother was born about the same time she was exiled—no longer had their big sister around, nor she them. More than that, their house burned to the ground. The family moved to DC, while Joan, living with her grandmother, finished high school in Farmville—in the very nice new school building that Barbara's strike had been all about. As for Barbara, she did her senior year of high school in Alabama, attended Spelman College in Georgia, married and had five children, and lived a quiet life as a school librarian far from Farmville, in Pennsylvania.

The school that Barbara Johns built remains in operation, a centerpiece of Prince Edward County's desegregated public schools.

2-22
Document: Barbara Johns, Memoir of Her Early Years, 1942–1951

Toward the end of her life, Barbara Johns (1935–1991) wrote a memoir of her childhood and youth in rural Prince Edward County, Virginia. Her hand-written manuscript covered the years 1942–1951, between the ages of seven and 16, from when her father went into the Army early in World War II to when she launched her plan for a student strike in protest of her separate-and-unequal high school in the town of Farmville.

My first recollection of Cullen, Virginia was in the year of 1942. I arrived by train from Washington, D.C. to Richmond, VA. In Richmond, we were picked up by my uncle and transported to my grandmother's home in Cullen, VA.

The ride on the train had been exciting—mainly because it was my 1st train ride, but mostly because it was crowded with soldiers. I was fascinated by all of them—in my imagination they were big, tall, not-so tall men who looked so handsome and polished in their uniforms. I was particularly impressed by them because my own Daddy had been called into the army and though I had not seen him in his uniform—I imagined he must look as handsome as these men. In fact, the very reason my Mother, brother, sister and I left Washington to live in Va. was because my Daddy was in the service, and he felt we would fare better in the country.

My days at my Grandmother's house were fun filled and chore filled. In fact, one seldom got a chance to sit down and rest before the familiar cry of Barbree (as she called me came). I then rushed to feed the chickens, pick up chips for the wood stove, run to the spring for a bucket of cool, fresh water, gather the eggs, or do some household chore that was needed. My grandmother owned a 175 acres of land, and farming (raising pigs, cows, tobacco, corn and other crops) was as important to her and my grandfather existence as they became to our own when my Dad returned from the war.

My mother left us in our grandmother's care and returned to Washington to live with her sister and work for the government at the Pentagon. I was enrolled in school at the Mary E. Branch Elementary School in Farmville, VA, where I remained through the 8th grade.

My Dad came home on furlough and we were happy to see him. He brought me a pair of red wooden Dutch shoes which I prized very highly and kept until they were burned in our house on the hill. During his visit, another change took place—we left our Grandmother Croner's house to move to our Grandma Sally's house. It had evidently been decided that the grandmothers would share custody of us while my father remained in the army.

Living at my Grandmother Sally's house was totally different from residing at Ma Croner's house. It was smaller. (This was a puzzlement to me because she had lived in a big two story full basement brick house with my uncle for years.) And she did not farm. I'm not sure what the primary source of her income was, but I do know my grandfather had been a World War I veteran and perhaps received a pension. In addition I think their income was supplemented by their children. Anyway, life became less chore filled, more reading, writing oriented and certainly more enlivened by the spirited exchange of my grandparents. She argued good naturedly, but nevertheless argued about everything from when the War would end, who was likely to win to how much sugar a sane person should put in a cup of coffee.

Sometimes to avoid all the ruckus, I would roam through the woods, wrapping myself in its quiet embrace, listening only to the sounds of the birds, the scattering of the squirrels, rabbits and other small creatures underfoot. Occassionally, a startled deer would lap hurriedly away—or a brace of quail would take flight or some other small creature would scurry about—but mostly it was quiet and peaceful and I sought the woods for solitude and to read in peace.

Finally, my Dad returned from the war and we settled down to family life in a simple white building belonging to my uncle which served as store and as a residence. Attached to it was a living room with fireplace, 3 bedrooms and a kitchen.

Here our chief occupation, Daddy and ours was to run the store, and pump gasoline. Many of our customers ran tickets charging items purchased to a credit account. This type of service often turned us into bookkeepers and bill collectors.

On the surrounding grounds, my Dad raised a garden, my uncle planted a peach tree grove which my dad helped nourish, and I was permitted to have my very own Duck swimming along on a small pond of water in the back of the house. These were happy days. We greeted the customers, fulfilled their needs, ate Big Fours and Johnny cakes, and peanuts when our Dad wasn't looking—and generally lived an uncomplicated life. The fireplace in the living room was flanked by two ceiling to floor book shelves full of books left by my uncle [Rev. Vernon Johns] who had moved to Montgomery, Ala. [pastoring at Dexter Avenue Baptist Church, as Taylor Branch describes in the first volume of his biography of Martin Luther King Jr.]. We spent many nights reading by the warmth of the fireplace. Here I read, "The Postman Always Rings Twice," "H. G. Wells, Wars of the World," and many other good books.

My Grandma Sally had returned to living in the big house at this time and we spent much of our time between her house and ours. In between his trips from Montgomery to VA, my uncle would make sure we spent some of our time devouring the books he kept in the big house—particularly the encyclopedias. We were required to start with Volume A—and work up to Volume Z. Needless to say, I didn't relish this type of imposed and restricted reading—so I managed to circumvent this by inserting a few Archie and Veronica comic books, or some other material between the pages. Of course, one of my brilliant, obedient cousins never took this short cut, and that's why she graduated Phi Beta Kappa and I didn't.

My mother continued working in Washington, while we remained at the store. Soon plans were under way to build our own house on the 127 acres of land my father purchased from his brother.

Finally, the big day arrived. There stood our beautiful white house with a wrap-around porch perched upon a hill. It was a beautiful sight. We were excited and eager to move in—Mom soon arrived and we were assigned to our rooms. My brothers were given a first floor bedroom—across from my parents room—My sister and I were assigned to the second floor attic room as our house was a story and a half. There was also a living, dining room, kitchen and plenty of out door space.

We had a nice new barn. My Daddy bought two horses—a beautiful red one, which we name Sadie Red and a grey one, which we called Gray. Sadie Red was my favorite and we rode up and down the roads across the fields and down to the water brook where she was taken every evening to drink. The horses were gentle with us as children—but not so kind to the adults—Sometime a swift kick would be given by one or the other to my Dad which would anger him enough to get his BB gun + shoot past them.

Alas, [horseback] riding was not all that we did, pitching horse shoes and playing croquet filled many a quiet evening. But the chief source of income still was farming and now that he had his own land—my Dad lost no time in pursuing this career.

We planted tobacco, (a vicious crop), corn, soybeans, watermelons, and a regular garden for family consumption. We planted apple trees, pear trees, Black Walnut trees, shade trees, and sunflowers. Our summertime days were spent "working the tobacco, hoeing the corn, slopping" the pigs, feeding the chickens, gathering the eggs, weeding the vegetable garden, milking the cows, killing chickens for dinner. In the winter—hog killing time was horrible. I always managed to disappear because I could not stand the slaughtering of the hogs. They were shot, their throat slit and then cut up for the meat.

I had to ground sausage, however, and cut pork chops and ribs, etc. all the time staring at the horrible buckets of pig intestines that people greedily eat called chitlings or chitterlings.

From Sept. to May—we went to school daily. I arose early in the morning to fix breakfast and lunch for my sister and brothers and to see that they were properly dressed for school. My mother had returned to her job in Washington to help supplement the income produced by the farm whose primary paying crop was tobacco and the yield from that was realized only once a year after a year of growing it, caring for it and curing it. I never knew what was realized from this crop, but I now know if you were to consider the labor, cost of fertilization, etc. it couldn't have brought that much money. My repulsion to this crop is one reason I don't smoke today.

I was "mother" to my siblings and therefore arrived home each day from school not with frivolous considerations of what I wanted to do—but already I had begun formulating in my mind as I rode the bus home which foods I would prepare for supper that evening.

I had a great deal of responsibility thrust upon my shoulders both outside in the fields and inside the house. In addition, when I needed extra money for another pair of shoes, or club money etc. I went to what was referred to as "the billet woods" where we would cut down a load of timber, take it to town and get paid.

In the meantime my Grandmother Sally + [uncle] Frank moved in with us. My Uncle Robert died and so she and my daddy's cousin Frank were left alone.

Frank slept in the basement and Grandma slept in the room next to ours. My Grandmother was sick—so she could not share the responsibilities of the household with me—but she did provide levity and certain comfort of presence for us.

My Daddy was very strict about homework and each night you had to devote one hour to homework even if you had none. My Grandmother would often suggest that we write about the day's events and then she would grade the papers—and you would receive hilarious comments on the paper—plus we always got an "A."

At school, I enjoyed my French classes, music classes, English classes and History. Math, Science + Gym were not among my favorite classes. Still, I got good grades. I belonged to the debating team, the Student Council and other activities.

I had friends—mostly female. My best friend was killed in a tragic bus crash that killed about 15 members of her family [this was at Elam Crossing, in the northwestern corner of the county, on March 13, 1951, so just weeks before the strike, which she led on April 23, after the plans she describes a few paragraphs below]. I was deeply affected by her death. She was such a beautiful "inside and out" person.

We were fond of our teachers, My favorite and the one who had the greatest impact on my young life—was Miss Davenport—my music teacher who later became Mrs. Jones, wife of the Principal of the school. Besides introducing us to the beauty of classical music, she permitted free expression in her classes, something quite foreign to most of the classes because most teachers taught and you listened and responded when requested. But Miss Davenport felt that everything in life lent itself to a variety of opinions, thoughts, moods, moments—much the same as music—and she encouraged you to respond that way. I got to know her more intimately when she became music teacher for my sister and me when we took piano lessons. I felt I could share my innermost thoughts with her and she wouldn't consider them ridiculous. This is how I happened to mention how unhappy I was with the school [infrastructure] and its inadequacies to her. I told her it wasn't fair that we had such poor facility, equipment, etc. when our white counterparts enjoyed science laboratories, a huge facility—separate gym dept., etc. I warmed to my subject and looked to her for some answer to my frustration—and she paused for a few moments and said, "Why don't you do something about it?" I was surprised at her answer but it didn't occur to me to ask what she meant—I just slowly turned away—as I felt she had dismissed me with that reply.

What one could do with such a situation, I had no idea. But I spent many days in my favorite hangout in the woods on my favorite stump contemplating it all. I sat by the creek while Sadie Red drank and I thought about it. My imagination would run rampant—and I would dream that some mighty man of great wealth built us a new school building or that our parents got together and surprised us with this grand new building and we had a big celebration—and I even imagined that a great storm came through and blew down the main building and splattered the shacks to splinters—and out of this wreckage rose this magnificent building and all the students were joyous and even the teachers cried.

But then reality would set in and I would be forced to acknowledge that nothing magical was going to produce a new school.

And then there were times—I just prayed—"God please grant us a new school." "Please let us have a warm place to stay where we won't have to keep our coats on all day to stay warm." "God, please help us." "We are your children, too."

This type of thinking went on for months—sometimes as I chopped the wood, sometime as I fed the pigs. As I did my work, as I sat quietly, it would crop up in my mind—because I felt we were not treated like any other students. Their classes were not held in the auditorium, they were not cold, they didn't have to leave one building and transfer to another, their buses weren't overcrowded. Their teacher/bus driver didn't have to make the fire before he could start classes.

One morning—I was so busy rushing my brothers and sister down the hill to school, that I forgot my own lunch and had to rush back up the hill to retrieve it. In the meantime, the bus arrived, picked them up and left me standing there by the roadside waiting to thumb a ride with whomever came by.

About an hour later, I was still waiting, when the "white school bus" drives by—half empty— on its way to Farmville High School. It would have to pass by my school to get to that school and I couldn't ride with them.

Right then and there, I decided indeed something had to be done about this inequality—and I still didn't know what. All day my mind and thoughts were whirling and as I lay in my bed that night—I prayed for help—That night, whether in a dream or whether I was awake, but I felt I was awake, a plan began to formulate in my mind. A plan I felt was divinely inspired because I hadn't been able to think of anything until then. That plan was to assemble together the student council members whom I considered the "crème de la crème" of the school—because they were smart and thinkers. I knew them and trusted them and I was a part of them—From this we would formulate plans to go on a strike. We would make signs and I would give a speech stating our dissatisfaction and we would march out the school and people would hear us and see us and understand our difficulty and would sympathize with our plight and would grant us our new school building and our teachers would be proud and the students would learn more, + it would be grand—And we would live happily ever after. Fully confident that all of this would transpire, I arose early the next morning, rushed to get everyone out, could hardly wait to get to school to call this meeting.

I was self-sufficient and independent because my mother was not around to rely upon or consult. My father was too busy plowing + planting and harvesting to have time for any fantasy of mine—and he would have considered it foolish—never agreed with it—but he wouldn't have stopped me. I was permitted free reign in my thinking and actions—as he put it I was too stubborn, too determined to have my way, anyway—so why hassle ourselves.

I didn't consult my Uncle because he wasn't around. And really, I didn't feel a need to consult anyone, anyway. It had been given to me. All I had to do—was do it.

[The memoir concludes, for a final page, with notes toward developing further material, returning to family and community affairs, as occupied the first 11-plus pages of the manuscript—for example: "Went to baseball games formed by neighbors. Sunday afternoons gather at my Grandmothers for homemade ice cream + croquet—court under the big oak tree."]

2-23
Sit-ins, Freedom Rides, and Joan Trumpauer

Joan Harris Nelson grew up in Northern Virginia, just outside the nation's capital, her mother from Georgia and her dad from the Midwest. Perhaps they had no idea early on what path she might take through the 1960s. Then again, she had recoiled from an early encounter with gross racial discrimination at about the age of nine, when visiting family in Georgia.

Born in 1941, she graduated in 1959 from her no-Black high school in Arlington County. By then, the violence at Central High School in Little Rock, Arkansas, in 1957 had jolted her again; and Stratford Junior High School, right there in Arlington County, had become the very first White public school in Virginia to enroll Black students, four in all, on 2 February 1959, nearly five years after *Brown v. Board of Education*.

She had in mind attending a small liberal arts school, Presbyterian-affiliated Muskingum College, in Ohio. But her mother, distressed at the prospect that a Black student might be enrolled at that school, might even become her roommate, put her foot down and pointed Joan toward a safe place, Duke University, in Durham, North Carolina, where, surely, she would never have a Black classmate. Off to Duke she went.

But this was fall 1959, and just a few months later, on the first day of February 1960, not far away in Greensboro, North Carolina, four students from a Black college conducted a sit-in at a Woolworth's lunch counter to protest racial segregation. That touched off a wave of sit-ins that soon swept east to Durham, then into Virginia and through much of the rest of the South.

Her mother had guessed right about Joan's inclination to be critical of the racial regime she had seen growing up. Curious, Joan checked out local people planning a sit-in, attended a mass meeting, then determined that it wasn't enough to express an interest and offer support, that perhaps she too should participate. So, she did, at first by picketing, soon by ordering food at a Whites-only lunch counter and then sharing it with Black students.

Her arrest for trespass on 6 May 1960, together with a male student from Duke plus five students from North Carolina College at Durham, a nearby Black school, proved a turning point, both in her own approach to the world around her and to her relationship with her parents, especially her mother. As she later put it, she had "a feeling of no turning back." The seven appealed their convictions to the North Carolina Supreme Court, which upheld them, and then to the US Supreme Court, which overturned them; the rulings can be found at *State v. Avent*, 253 N.C. 580 (1961), and *Avent v. North Carolina*, 373 U.S. 375 (1963).

She could scarcely go home again, and she decided not to return to Duke for her sophomore year. Rather, she worked in DC for a US senator and spent a lot of time with students from Howard University who formed the Nonviolent Action Group (NAG) and carried out protest activities in the DC area, including both Maryland (for example, Glen Echo Amusement Park) and Northern Virginia (People's Drug Store in Arlington County, Drug Fair at the Lee Highway Shopping Center).

Soon after her arrest in Durham, she also got married. The relationship did not last long (her husband found he could not follow where she needed to be going), but her subsequent protest activities came under her married last name, which gave space to her parents and their families; she meant to reduce the likelihood they would be harassed for her actions. Then she modified two letters in her ex-husband's name to give him space as well, so she became Joan Trumpauer.

Her arrest in Durham came three weeks after dozens of sit-in veterans had gathered in April 1960 at Shaw University, a Black college in Raleigh, North Carolina, and formed the Student Non-violent Coordinating Committee (SNCC). So, she missed that, but she soon joined the group. Then came 1961.

In January 1961, when the University of Georgia, under a federal court order, enrolled its first few Black students, they met with strident resistance, and Joan concluded that integration meant more than having Black students make their way to a hostile or at

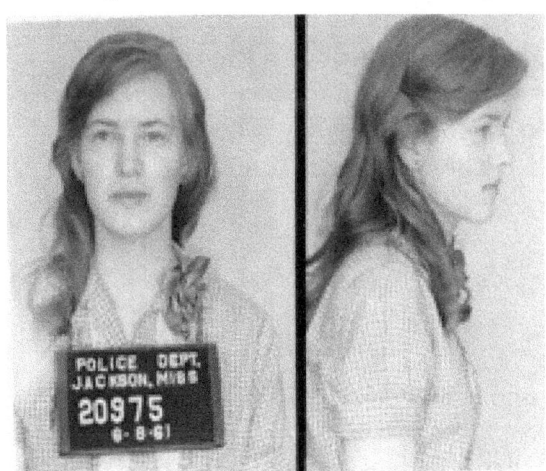

Joan Trumpauer
(1967)

best indifferent White campus. As she later stated, "I thought that if integration meant anything, it should be a two-way street. It shouldn't just be that blacks were allowed into white places, but that whites and blacks did things together." As suggested by fellow members of SNCC, she applied to Tougaloo College, in Jackson, Mississippi. Accepted, she looked forward to the end of summer and a return to school.

But first came the Freedom Rides, organized by the Congress of Racial Equality (CORE). She was not in the initial Freedom Rides, in one Trailways bus and one Greyhound, when integrated groups of riders set off from DC for New Orleans, starting on 4 May 1961. On 14 May, as the Greyhound bus approached Anniston, Alabama, terrorists attempted to burn the bus with the riders inside. Riders on the Trailways bus also met extreme violence that day, in Birmingham, and a call went out for reinforcements.

Joan was ready. She and five of her NAG friends from Howard, among them SNCC national chairman Stokely Carmichael, flew to New Orleans, then took a train east with three other Freedom Riders into Mississippi, to Jackson, the belly of the beast. This time her arrest, on 8 June 1961, was for breach of the peace.

She soon found herself confined at Parchman Penitentiary to serve her two-month sentence, plus longer at $3.00 a day to pay down her $200 fine. But she got out of Parchman in time to begin classes as a transfer sophomore at Tougaloo, where she became a full-fledged member of the campus community and accepted an invitation to join the Black sorority Delta Sigma Theta. She had finally managed to attend a small, liberal arts, church-affiliated college, though not exactly what she or her mother had envisioned during her senior year of high school.

She squired MLK when he came to campus to speak. She worked often at the local offices of CORE and SNCC, also at the NAACP office with Medgar Evers before his assassination on 12 June 1963. She greeted Michael Schwerner on his arrival for the Mississippi Freedom Summer Project on 20 June 1964, the day before he and two fellow volunteers were murdered.

The Jackson Movement engaged in voter registration, boycotts of downtown businesses that discriminated, and acts of civil disobedience, most notably a fraught sit-in at a Woolworth's Department Store lunch counter on 28 May 1963. Three months later, she attended the 28 August 1963 March on Washington for Jobs and Freedom, one among many pilgrims from Mississippi, then returned to Tougaloo for her senior year to finish up her degree in history.

Her mugshot when arrested after the Freedom Ride to Jackson, one of the iconic images of the Civil Rights Struggle, shows a gentle protester, even serene, simply doing what she felt she had been called to do. Another iconic image of her, sitting at the Woolworth's lunch counter in Jackson in the company of her friend Annie Moody and one of her teachers at Tougaloo, shows the nonviolent protesters, with Joan still serene, not just verbally taunted but also physically assaulted and threatened with death.

One other photo captures an utterly devastated Joan Trumpauer, a White face in a sea of Black mourners, at the funeral of four Black girls who, barely two weeks after the euphoria of the March on Washington, died when a bomb detonated at their church in Birmingham, Alabama.

2-24
Document: Ford Johnson and Segregated Courtrooms, 1960–1963

Small acts can lead to big change—a variety of changes. Many types of cases reach the US Supreme Court, though the Court agrees to hear only a very small fraction of those directed toward it. The Court's rulings tend to be structured in a standard format, but most run many pages longer than this one, even, at times, 200 pages.

Focus here on the paragraph regarding "The evidence." Recreate in your mind what took place in traffic court that day, and what might have run through Ford Johnson's mind at the time; then look to the final paragraph to see what the Court decided, and on what basis. The two sides agreed on the core facts; the Court addressed the constitutional question of how to view those facts.

It might help to know that he was an undergraduate at Virginia Union University (VUU, in Richmond) at the time of this court appearance, or that he had been in that same courtroom in 1960 (though it was unsegregated at that time), on a charge of participating in a sit-in at a downtown department store in February that year.

Thirty-three other Virginia Union students also participated in that February

1960 sit-in. Convicted of trespass, they all appealed their convictions and sentencing. Their case went to the Virginia Supreme Court, which as a matter of routine upheld the trial court, and then to the US Supreme Court, which overturned the convictions as an inappropriate—unconstitutional—use of trespass law to enforce racial segregation.

The VUU student whose name topped the list of 34, Raymond B. Randolph Jr., a freshman at the time, also took a second case to the Supreme Court, and, like Ford Johnson, he won that one too: *Thomas v. Mississippi* (1965). Each of them had grown in his resistance to racial discrimination, first enough to participate in direct action at all, then, as a veteran of his initial arrest, taking on a further challenge to Jim Crow. Randolph's second arrest took place in Jackson, Mississippi, after he accepted an invitation to travel there as a Freedom Rider the next year.

Raymond B. Randolph Jr., in front of a newly installed plaque that tells the sit-in story from February 1960

In February 2010, for a 50th anniversary commemoration, many of the surviving members of the Virginia Union 34, or Richmond 34, including Ford Johnson, his sister Elizabeth, and Ray Randolph, returned to the campus for a reunion weekend.

JOHNSON v. VIRGINIA

373 U.S. 61

ON PETITION FOR WRIT OF CERTIORARI TO THE SUPREME COURT OF APPEALS OF VIRGINIA.

No. 715. Decided April 29, 1963.

Petitioner, a Negro, was convicted of contempt of court solely because he refused to comply with a judge's instructions to sit in the section of a courtroom reserved for Negroes. *Held*: A State may not require racial segregation in a courtroom, and the conviction is reversed. Pp. 61–62.

Reversed.

Roland D. Ealey and *Herman T. Benn* for petitioner. *Reno S. Harp III*, Assistant Attorney General of Virginia, for respondent.

PER CURIAM.

The petition for a writ of certiorari is granted, the judgment of the Supreme Court of Appeals of Virginia is reversed, and the case is remanded for proceedings not inconsistent with this opinion.

The petitioner, Ford T. Johnson, Jr., was convicted of contempt of the Traffic Court of the City of Richmond, Virginia, and appealed his conviction to the Hustings Court, where he was tried without a jury and again convicted. The Supreme Court of Appeals of Virginia refused to grant a writ of error on the ground that the judgment appealed from was "plainly right," but the Chief Justice of that court stayed execution of the judgment pending disposition of this petition for certiorari.

The evidence at petitioner's trial in the Hustings Court is summarized in an approved statement of facts. According to this statement, the witnesses for the State testified as follows: The petitioner, a Negro, was seated in the Traffic Court in a section reserved for whites, and when requested to move by the bailiff, refused to do so. The judge then summoned the petitioner to the bench and instructed him to be seated in the right-hand section of the courtroom, the section reserved for Negroes. The petitioner moved back in front of the counsel table and remained standing with his arms folded, stating that he preferred standing and indicating that he would not comply with the judge's order. Upon refusal to obey the judge's further direction to be seated, the petitioner was arrested for contempt. At no time did he behave in a boisterous or abusive manner, and there was no disorder in the courtroom. The State, in its Brief in Opposition filed in this Court, concedes that in the section of the Richmond Traffic Court reserved for spectators, seating space "is assigned on the basis of racial designation, the seats on one side of the aisle being for use of Negro citizens and the seats on the other side being for the use of white citizens."

It is clear from the totality of circumstances, and particularly the fact that the petitioner was peaceably seated in the section reserved for whites before being summoned to the bench, that the arrest and conviction rested entirely on the refusal to comply with the segregated seating requirements imposed in this particular courtroom. Such a conviction cannot stand, for it is no longer open to question that a State may not constitutionally require segregation of public facilities. See, *e. g., Brown v. Board of Education,* 347 U. S. 483; *Mayor and City Council of Baltimore v. Dawson,* 350 U. S. 877; *Turner v. Memphis,* 369 U. S. 350. State-compelled segregation in a court of justice is a manifest violation of the State's duty to deny no one the equal protection of its laws.

Reversed and remanded.

2-25
Gene Gray Sr., Theotis Robinson Jr., and the University of Tennessee

The state of Tennessee entered the 20th century committed to preventing Black students and White students from enrolling together at any state-supported school, and in 1901 a new law extended the ban to private institutions, in particular Maryville College.

The arrangement displayed no change before mid-century. But gradual modifications took place across the 1950s and '60s. Each change reflected initiatives taken by Black Tennesseans to push back against the obstacles and extend the range of the possible. Shifting circumstances sometimes permitted incremental change. Tennessee modeled what was happening, or not, across the South.

In 1936, William Benjamin Redmond II, a graduate of Tennessee's Black land-grant school, Tennessee Agricultural and Industrial State College (renamed Tennessee State University in 1968), wanted to study pharmacy, so he applied to the only such program in the state, the medical branch of the University of Tennessee (UT), located in Memphis. Rejected on racial grounds, he went into state court with the support of the NAACP to make his case.

The NAACP wanted to show that, like other southern states, Tennessee was violating the US Supreme Court's *Plessy v. Ferguson* (1896) standard of "separate but equal." Tennessee was denying to Black citizens a wide range of academic programs for advanced study that it made available to Whites. The state mandated the "separate" but failed to deliver the "equal."

Redmond did not move the judge, but he did mobilize the legislature. A new program offered some scholarship assistance to help Black Tennesseans go out-of-state to a program that would admit them for advanced work in pharmacy—or law, engineering, or architecture, any program available in-state only to Whites. The stipend might cover anything more than what a similar program would have cost in Tennessee. Redmond himself abandoned his quest.

In 1939, in a similar effort, four men applied to the UT graduate school and two others to the law school, both at the main campus, in Knoxville. They, too, saw their case derailed, on the grounds that the state would supposedly soon be creating at the Black school the programs they were seeking at the White school.

In 1950, the US Supreme Court ruled on two cases (especially one from Texas) in a way that made it much more difficult for any state-supported White university to turn down in-state applicants who met all requirements aside from the racial ban—and who were looking for a program not offered at any public in-state Black school. Soon, four Black men, two looking to study law and two to enroll in the graduate school, went to federal district court to challenge their exclusion from UT.

Given the new constitutional dispensation, they won, and in 1952 Gene Mitchell Gray Sr. enrolled as UT's first Black student. The first to complete a degree program at UT was Lillian D. Jenkins, with a master's degree in 1954. R.B.J. Campbelle Jr. graduated in 1959 from the law school, and Harry S. Blanton earned an EdD the same year.

Even then, no Black student had yet enrolled at UT as an undergraduate, and Theotis Robinson Jr. made it his business to end the exclusion. He had recently participated in sit-ins at lunch counters there in Knoxville, and he determined that, though he had planned to start in fall 1960 at the nearby Black college, Knoxville College, he would do what he could to force the matter at UT. For one thing, he wanted to major in political science, not an option at Knoxville College; for another, it was just high time.

In an oral history interview three decades later, Robinson explained how it happened. As part of an effort that went well beyond segregated lunch counters, a group called the Associated Council for Full Citizenship published an ad in July 1960 in the city paper, the *Knoxville New Sentinel*. Among the many local grievances it listed, UT did not admit Black undergraduates, and that one grabbed his attention: "This is something I can deal with."

He recalled writing to the university that very evening, expressing an interest in attending. He did not identify himself by race, but the reply that came back declared the university's policy of Black exclusion. Robinson set up an appointment, and he and his parents met with two people in admissions, who explained that they could not change the policy, but perhaps Robinson and his parents would like to speak with the president, Andrew Holt. They would; they did. He explained that only the board of trustees could change the policy, and if they wished he would bring the matter there. Before leaving, Robinson and his folks made it clear that, if the response proved negative, they would go to court, and they had no doubt that they would win.

That November, in a special meeting, the board brought the old policy to an end. Weeks later, on 3 January 1961, Robinson became a UT undergrad. So did Charles Edgar Blair and Willie Mae Gillespie. None, however, lived on campus, and, as Robinson later observed, he "did not depend" on the campus for his "social life." The first Black student to earn a bachelor's degree there, Brenda Lewis Peel, had transferred into UT in fall 1961 and finished in 1964.

Over the next few years, other racial barriers fell. For example, Dr. Robert H. Kirk became an associate professor of public health in 1967, UT's first African American on the regular faculty. It was all a far cry from when Black Tennesseans at the state university were restricted to custodial work.

But barriers remained. In intercollegiate athletics, as in so many other ways, UT offered a case study in the very gradual shift in what was possible at southern universities.

In 1946, when the UT basketball team went to Pittsburgh, Pennsylvania, to play Duquesne University, the coach pulled the team as soon as he recognized that the home team featured an African American, Chuck Cooper (the Boston Celtics drafted him in 1950, one of the very first Black players in the NBA).

Before the 1950s ended, UT took a first step by agreeing to play an integrated team—if away, at a school in the North. The home campus, however, remained sacred territory, off-limits to Black athletes. In spring 1961, when a visiting track-and-field team included two Black athletes, the renowned UT athletic director Robert Neyland, after failing to get their coach to sit them, refused to permit the meet to go ahead. That fall, he threw a shoe when a new Black student, Avon Rollins, wanted to try out for the basketball team.

One obstacle disappeared when Neyland died the next year, though he was scarcely the only explanation for the slow pace of change, nor was his departure why UT athletics began to change. The Civil Rights Act of 1964 nudged the university in a new direction, as did the competitive pressures that came as other schools began recruiting Black athletes.

In 1966, UT authorities approved recruiting Black athletes with scholarships, and the next year Audry Hardy and James Craig joined the track and field team, where they starred for the 1968 through 1971 seasons.

In a breakthrough in the major sports, Lester McClain joined the freshman football team, also in 1967, and played varsity the next year. Increasingly, Southeastern Conference schools not only played integrated teams at away games, even played integrated teams at home, but, what's more, began fielding teams with one or more Black players themselves. By 1970, his senior year, McClain had six Black teammates. Soon, the UT basketball team also featured Black players.

As for Theotis Robinson, he was already married when he first enrolled at UT, and he never did graduate. But he held a professional position for a great many years with the university, and he continued to champion the place and, in return, received much love from it and the city he had helped change.

2-26
Writings from the 1960s Seeking a(n Even) Better America

Participant observers in the American project have spoken time and again, often eloquently, about what they've seen as the promise of America. Thomas Paine and Thomas Jefferson did so in 1776, Abraham Lincoln in the 1860s.

FDR, as the nation began its pivot from New Deal to World War II, asserted in June 1940: "We need not and we will not, in any way, abandon our continuing efforts to make democracy work within our borders. Yes, we still insist on the need for vast improvements in our own social and economic life."

In the first half of the 1960s, two presidents, JFK and then LBJ, voiced their visions. Many other people weighed in, producing a small shelf of books, as introduced below, that exemplified the deep concerns and great hopes of that time.

Writers write; some write books. They write because they must, or because they hope for a vast readership or big bucks, or because they hope to nudge the world in a direction they yearn for. Upton Sinclair and John Steinbeck represented earlier generations, with their novels *The Jungle* (1906) and *The Grapes of Wrath* (1939), each of which sought both to describe the present and to critique it. The books from the 1960s featured here were all nonfiction.

Rachel Carson, marine biologist, published *Silent Spring* (1962) to bring her scientific expertise to bear on what she saw as a frightening misuse of science. *Silent Spring* sought to alert a wide audience to unnecessary/thoughtless dangers and alter popular attitudes toward, for example, DDT and its disastrous effects on birdlife. Her book quickly became an anthem for a new environmental movement.

I drive, therefore I die—toward a prominent federal role in consumer safety: Ralph Nader, with *Unsafe at Any Speed: The Designed-in Dangers of the American Automobile* (1965), issued a strident call for federal intervention in the realm of product safety. An early response in Congress mandated that automakers install seatbelts in their products.

Tom Hayden and Students for a Democratic Society brought out *The Port Huron Statement* in 1962, an early New Left indictment of mis-directions in American policy, both at home and in foreign affairs.

Two books appeared in 1962 that highlighted what the authors presented as an unconscionable degree of poverty in a prosperous America. Michael Harrington, in *The Other America: Poverty in the United States* (1962), took readers to Harlem and to Appalachia, each more than a metaphor for urban or rural poverty, emphasizing how a great many Americans lived far outside what another writer had recently characterized as "the affluent society." Harrington pointed toward what became the Great Society's War on Poverty.

That same year, Harry Caudill, a lawyer and historian in Eastern Kentucky, tracked the origins and consequences of outside capital under-developing a region that featured vast amounts of coal and timber, wealth extracted for the benefit of people elsewhere and, overall, at great cost to people living in Appalachia. In conjunction with Harrington's book, Caudill's *Night Comes to the Cumberlands* pointed directly toward such legislation as the establishment of an Appalachian Regional Commission to address local ills.

Meanwhile, Betty Friedan's *The Feminine Mystique* (1963) brought a gendered approach to an analysis of American society and culture that emphasized how the new sprawling suburban-based middle class seemed to stultify people born female. Friedan gave voice to the case for what became "second-wave feminism," which promoted female confidence, outside-the-home opportunity, and "consciousness-raising." The decade that followed featured such developments as passage of Title IX and a proposed Equal Rights Amendment.

African American voices sang in various keys, each expressing grave dissatisfaction with where they saw America in the 1960s. James Baldwin, especially in *The Fire Next Time* (1963), spoke from his experience growing up in Harlem. His book constituted a manifesto regarding race in America 100 years after the Emancipation Proclamation.

Martin Luther King Jr., in *Why We Can't Wait* (1964), not only called for a continuing transformation of the nation to make equal space for Black Americans, but also argued that White Americans, too, had a deep interest in seeing substantial change unfold, given an international environment that featured newly independent nations in Africa and Asia, overwhelmingly nonwhite, combined with the continuing global rivalry with the Soviet Union. Therefore the "we" who "can't wait" included all Americans—and change must come now.

Malcolm X, with Alex Haley, authored *The Autobiography of Malcolm X* (1965), a riveting account of the life of the man who started out Malcolm Little and ended up el-Hajj Malik el-Shabazz.

Jonathan Kozol, in *Death at an Early Age: The Destruction of the Hearts and Minds of Negro Children in the Boston Public Schools* (1967), brought a vivid imagination and immersive experience to highlighting what a passionate and compassionate teacher could mean when it came to reaching children and youth who already brought challenges enough to school without getting more grief there than love.

Vine Deloria Jr., with the publication of *Custer Died for Your Sins: An Indian Manifesto* (1969), translated to a broad American public a Native voice with a sustained denunciation of centuries of contorted histories and broken promises.

These various writings all worked from the premise that the American experiment had some distance to go to achieve a felicitous outcome for all—and that citizens and their elected representatives must strive to bring about a wide array of improvements to the great and continuing project of finding an ever more suitable place for all people in the US, and for the US in the world.

2-27
Mr. Rogers, Sesame Street, and the Great Society

Lyndon Baines Johnson brought to the presidency in 1963 three decades of experience in Congress—four years as an enterprising aid to a Texas congressman in the early 1930s, followed by 12 years in the House of Representatives and 12 more in the Senate—and a history of enthusiastically supporting FDR's New Deal. Moreover, he had seen President Harry Truman's push in 1949 for a Fair Deal, a combination of proposals that, going well beyond the New Deal's reform efforts, called for federal aid to schools, a national health policy, and a civil rights program.

Congressional opposition to the Fair Deal stymied its enactment then, as it did also John F. Kennedy's efforts to inaugurate a New Frontier during his abbreviated presidency. As for Dwight D. Eisenhower, he had never supported such policies anyway, though his presidency did feature one towering piece of legislation, the Federal-Aid Highway Act of 1956, which brought about the Interstate Highway System, as well as the National Defense Education Act of 1958. Meanwhile, various books had highlighted areas of American life that called for intervention by the federal government. These included Michael Harrington's *The Other America: Poverty in the United States* (1962).

Then came LBJ. Planning to run for election in 1964, on 22 May that year—six months after becoming president following JFK's assassination—Johnson, in an address at the University of Michigan, called expressly for a "Great Society," a two-pronged program that would, on the one hand, win a "war on poverty" and, on the other, "enrich and elevate our national life." Initiatives that first year resulted in the 1964 Civil Rights Act, an Office of Economic Opportunity, and the 1964 National Defense Education Act.

That fall, LBJ won a landslide victory and brought large Democratic majorities in both houses of Congress. These new Democrats, coming from outside the South, represented a strong impulse in the US for substantial progressive change, leading, for example, to passage of the Voting Rights Act of 1965 as well as a stunning array of other laws, which Johnson had laid out in his State of the Union address on 4 January 1965.

Antipoverty measures enacted in 1965 established the Community Action Program (CAP) and Volunteers in Service to America (VISTA), a domestic counterpart to Kennedy's Peace Corps, as well as the Appalachian Regional Commission (ARC) to attack economic problems in the southern highlands. Regarding health care, Congress created Medicare for the nation's elderly citizens and Medicaid for the poor. And it inaugurated a National Endowment for the Humanities (NEH) and a National Endowment for the Arts (NEA).

Environmental legislation from 1965 included a Water Quality Act and a Motor Vehicle Air Pollution Control Act. Safety concerns led to the Child Safety Act and the Consumer Product Safety Commission. Attention to the needs of big cities brought the Housing and Urban Development Act. The Immigration Act of 1965, radically renovating its predecessor from 1924, led to a dramatic growth in the numbers of new Americans, especially from Asia.

One big prong of the Great Society emphasized federal aid to education. The Elementary and Secondary Education Act provided new resources for the nation's K-12 schools, especially underfunded schools in rural areas and big cities, so in part it reflected the broad goals of the War on Poverty. Similarly, the Head Start and Upward Bound programs originated in 1965 to help younger Americans prepare for educational success, whether in elementary school or in college.

The Higher Education Act of 1965 reflected LBJ's exhortation to Congress that formal education beyond high school was "no longer a luxury but a necessity." In part, the new law created scholarship and work-study programs to assist lower-income young people to attend college. The surge in college enrollment beginning in the mid-1960s largely reflected the post–World War II baby boom, but it also resulted from an increase in prosperity, and financial assistance under the Higher Education Act aimed to broaden access still more, to promote more equal opportunity to attend college.

The spate of reform legislation did not end in 1965, or even with LBJ's presidency. Johnson's final few years in the White House brought the National Traffic and Motor Vehicle Safety Act (1966), for example, and the Public Broadcasting Act of 1967. Richard Nixon's first term in the White House produced the Environmental Protection Agency, or EPA (1970), and the Occupational Safety and Health Administration, or OSHA (1971). Legislation on the environmental front during Nixon's presidency included the Clean Water Act of 1972 and the Endangered Species Act of 1973.

Embodying the Great Society ethos, the TV program "Mr. Rogers' Neighborhood" went on air in 1968, aimed at all households that had children and a television, deploying the new technology and enabled by the 1967 Public Broadcasting Act. Similarly, "Sesame Street," which aimed for preschoolers, began airing on the Public Broadcasting Service in 1969.

In 1972, Congress amended a variety of laws and programs regarding education that had been enacted over the previous decade. The Educational Amendments of 1972, better known as Title IX, modified the Vocational Education Act of 1963, the Higher Education Act of 1965, and the Elementary and Secondary Education Act of 1965. Title IX expressed an emerging commitment to gender equality of opportunity—to protecting female Americans from sex discrimination. In the early going, it focused on higher education, not sports, but over time it became understood as emphasizing athletic opportunity for girls and young women.

Starting with JFK's time, a decade of presidential leadership and congressional action transformed the legal landscape across a broad range of policies, from civil rights to the environment to poverty to consumer safety to medical care to education to immigration to the arts to gender equality.

2-28
Restaurants, Swimming Pools, and the Civil Rights Act of 1964

Into the 1960s, long-distance Black motorists carried *The Green Book* to guide them to places where they might get a meal or spend the night. The sit-ins of the early 1960s mostly took place at low-cost eating establishments. In 1961, the Freedom Riders challenged segregated seating on interstate buses and segregated eating facilities in bus terminals.

These forms of protest had a very long history, dating from the 19th century, both before and after the Civil War, on passenger trains and steamboats, and then in response to the inauguration of segregated streetcars in the first decade of the 20th century. In the 1940s, people from Pauli Murray to Irene Morgan had resisted racial discrimination in interstate travel. The best known of the Black protests against segregated city bus systems took place in 1955–1956 in Montgomery, Alabama, involving Claudette Colvin, Aurelia Browder, Rosa Parks, and others.

The various forms of racial discrimination, public or private, showed up across the US, not only in the officially segregated South. After all, *The Green Book* originated as a guide for the Metro New York area in the 1930s before going national. The Congress on Racial Equality, formed during World War II, used sit-ins to protest segregated restaurants in Chicago. A book titled *Contested Waters*, with the subtitle *A Social History of Swimming Pools in America*, in its treatment of race relations and swimming pools contains no locations farther south than Maryland or Missouri—and supplies many examples of private violence used to enforce Black exclusion from public pools in cities like New York and Chicago.

Sit-ins, mostly associated with Greensboro, North Carolina, in February 1960, had occurred at the city library in Alexandria, Virginia, in 1939, and had cropped up both with Pauli Murray's protests at shops near Howard University in the nation's capital during World War II and among residents in Kansas and Oklahoma in 1958. Joan Trumpauer and Annie Moody were famously assaulted in mid-1963 at a sit-in at Jackson, Mississippi.

The sustained, ubiquitous, nonviolent protests dramatized the everyday exclusion, harassment, disrespect, humiliation, inconvenience, and other faces of Jim Crow's deliberate subordination, marginalization, and exclusion of Black Americans. In 1963, in cases that had been piling up since 1960 and 1961, the Supreme Court overturned the convictions following arrests for trespass at those peaceful protests.

Newspaper coverage of Freedom Rider Jim Zwerg's face, bloody and bruised but smiling, from a hospital bed in Montgomery, Alabama, brought home to White parents in the North how fully committed segregationists could be even against children who looked like theirs. By the 1960s, television was bringing images and stories like that directly into the homes of people across the nation—and around the world.

John F. Kennedy came to realize that, as president of the United States, for reasons moral, domestic, and international, he had to get behind a civil rights bill that would go far beyond anything ever before put in place. What spurred him to action was the extreme violence that authorities in Birmingham, Alabama, visited in June 1963 upon Black citizens, including a great many children. After he died in November 1963, his successor in the White House, Lyndon Johnson, called on Congress to pass the law as a memorial to the martyred JFK, and he pushed the bill through to enactment. He signed it into law on 2 July 1964.

Among the new law's many provisions, Title II outlawed discrimination on the basis of race or religion (Jewish Americans also often ran into discrimination, for example in resort areas in northern New England) in "public accommodations," such as restaurants, motels, and theaters. Title VII barred job discrimination and established the Equal Employment Opportunity Commission to address complaints regarding violations. Title VI, less noted at the time, prohibited racial discrimination in southern public-school districts and in defense contracts—anything involving federal funds—under penalty of being denied those funds.

Courts quickly ruled in favor of the law's constitutionality. *In Heart of Atlanta Motel v. United States* (1964), the Supreme Court said Congress had authority under the Commerce Clause to ban discrimination in motels and hotels. *Katzenbach v. McClung* (also 1964) said that even local restaurants were subject to the law, as some of the food served at such places had crossed state lines.

No more could lunch counters serving the public legally exclude from that public anyone on the basis of racial classification. No longer should it still be advisable for Black motorists to carry an updated edition of *The Green Book*. And in a great many instances, change came virtually overnight. A traveler through Ocala, Florida, any time after 2 July, for example, might be struck by the salt-and-paper arrangement of people who had stopped by for lunch—how readily change could come with the new legal regime.

Authorities in many places found other ways to accommodate White commitment to continue excluding African Americans from public amenities. Town after town in Louisiana, for example, had maintained but one public swimming pool in the years before July 1964. Now came a decision, by Whites, whether to permit Black residents to use a pool that had always been open exclusively to White people. No. Equal access could be supplied in a different way: chain it and drain it; exclude everyone, without discrimination. Thus the 1964 Civil Rights Act propelled many cities and towns out of the business of offering a cool pool as an escape, for Whites, from oppressive summer heat. Private pools, whether in backyards or at private clubs, became the new norm.

But swimming pools might prove the exception; the model from the Ocala lunch counter supplied the more usual response. Higher education reflected that wider response, though more gradually. The Higher Education Act of 1965, for example, which offered very substantial federal assistance, came under the new civil rights law's Title VI. In the second half of the 1960s, the Department of Health, Education, and Welfare used the anti-discrimination requirement to condition federal assistance on institutional compliance, to prod non-Black colleges and universities, private as well as public, to progressively dismantle traditional practices of Black exclusion.

2-29
Voting Rights/Wrongs: Black/White, North/South, Urban/Rural

The Nineteenth Amendment (1920) declared a woman's right to vote in state and federal elections. Over the next half-century, struggles continued over who could vote —and how much that vote might count.

Time and again between the 1920s and the 1940s, down to and beyond the Supreme Court ruling in *Nixon v. Allwright* (1944), Black southerners went to court to secure the right to vote in primary elections. The White Democratic Primary, a 1920s invention, barred Black potential voters from participating in elections to nominate candidates for the general election.

Methods designed to eliminate Black voters included literacy tests and poll taxes. Those methods, however, would also catch many poor and/or illiterate White men. Some states therefore created a loophole: if a man (or his grandfather) could have voted before 1866—before federal law enfranchised Black men—then he could vault over such barriers.

In *Guinn v. United States* (1915), the Supreme Court found this an unacceptably bald attempt to skirt the Fifteenth Amendment.

In practice, literacy and poll tax requirements did indeed eliminate many White as well as Black voters, resulting in quite small (and relatively privileged) electorates in many southern states. These small electorates made it far easier than it would otherwise have been for the same political leaders to get themselves repeatedly elected, not only to state office but also to the US Senate and the US House of Representatives.

In view of the system of seniority in choosing the chairmanships of many congressional committees, White southern conservative Democrats' long tenure gave them outsized power to either support or thwart the legislative priorities that predominated far from the one-party fiefdoms that sent those men to Congress. Beginning by the 1940s, northerners therefore sought to end the poll tax as a voting requirement.

Two events in the 1960s eliminated the poll tax requirement for voting, starting with the Twenty-fourth Amendment, ratified in January 1964, which barred it in *federal* elections. In the case *Harper v. Virginia Board of Elections* (1966), the Supreme Court barred states from demanding a poll tax to vote in state elections, since doing so imposed a wealth or property requirement contrary to the Fourteenth Amendment's Equal Protection Clause.

Other obstacles remained. Time and again, whether in the late 1890s or the early 1960s, White southerners directed violence toward Black southerners—and anyone supporting them—who sought to redeem the promise of voting rights guaranteed under the Fifteenth Amendment. This included murders and, famously, the mayhem inflicted on peaceful marchers in Selma, Alabama, in March 1965. That event spurred passage of the Voting Rights Act in August that year.

The Voting Rights Act authorized federal intervention in districts where voting participation remained unduly low. The new law produced dramatic results in local, state, and federal elections. For the first time since the 1880s or '90s, voters in state after southern state began electing Black legislators.

In Texas, for example, Barbara Jordan lost in the elections of 1962 and 1964, but in 1966 she won the first of three terms in the state senate, and in 1972 she won a seat in Congress. At the other end of the former Confederacy, after an absence since the 1880s, Black representation returned to the Virginia legislature, with William Ferguson Reid elected to the House of Delegates in 1967 and L. Douglas Wilder as a senator in 1969. Other Black legislators elected soon after the Voting Rights Act were Robert G. Clark Jr. in Mississippi and Ernest Nathan Morial in Louisiana, both in 1967.

The right to vote was significant in itself, and it translated directly in statewide elections for president, US senator, or governor. Elections to state legislatures were different, as the scheme of legislative apportionment might greatly enhance or diminish the value of a person's vote.

State after state featured enormous disparities in the population size of legislative districts, so that voters in rural counties with small populations might exercise radically more power than voters in a city like Atlanta or Los Angeles. The ratio between largest and smallest constituencies could be a multiple of 100 or even 1,000.

Resistance to this kind of inequality spurred court challenges in state after state. Before the 1960s, the Supreme Court consistently rejected suits of this kind as involving political questions, inappropriate for judicial oversight. "Equal protection," however, became very much the coin of the constitutional realm in the 1960s, and the Court reconsidered its stance.

In 1964, in the case *Reynolds v. Sims* from Alabama, as well as cases from other states from New York to Virginia to Colorado, the Supreme Court established a "one person, one vote" rule requiring that legislative districts contain roughly equal populations.

After *Reynolds v. Sims,* voters in urban and suburban areas began electing a significantly larger proportion of state legislators, and policy outputs quickly reflected the shift. In Virginia, for example, the 1966 legislature enacted a sales tax that funded significantly greater outlays for public schools and permitted creation of a system of community colleges.

In one last major change in the rules of electoral politics during this period, the Twenty-sixth Amendment lowered the voting age in 1971 to 18.

Over time, rulings by the US Supreme Court eroded the Voting Rights Act. Yet the legacy of the 1960s persisted into the 2020s, as can be seen in the presence of Black legislators in every state across the South, and in the Black congressmen representing districts from Virginia to Texas.

2-30
Dolores Huerta, César Chávez, and the United Farm Workers

New Deal policies and programs of the 1930s brought labor unions to industrial workers in cities like Detroit and Pittsburgh but did nothing for farm laborers. The Civil Rights Struggle brought the Civil Rights Act of 1964 and the Voting Rights Act of 1965 to both the rural and urban South, but it did nothing for migrant farm workers in the West.

Dolores Huerta and César Chávez provided critically important leadership for those western farmworkers, in a struggle that emerged in the early 1960s and brought very considerable success by the end of the decade. Huerta and Chávez were both US citizens with Mexican roots; their biographies, which had begun in New Mexico and Arizona, converged in California in 1962.

As a schoolteacher in Stockton, Dolores Huerta taught farmworkers' children. She observed later of her young charges that "they were so poor, and almost always sick. They came to school in rags, often without breakfast. Most had never seen a doctor or dentist." Huerta concluded that perhaps she could do more good by leaving the classroom and her students and helping to organize their parents in pursuit of higher wages, safer work conditions, better living conditions.

César Chávez grew up one of those workers. He later described the situation: "It was a hell of a life. Working in the fields in the scorching hot summers. Living in a broken-down car, or else in the dark, overcrowded shacks without toilets, electricity, or running water. Farmworkers were in a uniquely bad position. After decades of struggle and bloodshed, unions were established in other industries. But there were no farm unions."

In 1952 Chávez had met Fred Ross—a disciple of community organizer Saul Alinsky, who believed that, while oppressed people could generally see what they needed, they could use help organizing to seek it effectively. The encounter redirected the young Chávez. By the early 1960s, both he and Huerta were doing social work with migrant farmworkers. They joined forces to form a union, but bosses refused to recognize it and used violence to keep workers from joining it..

In 1965, led by Philip Vera Cruz and Larry Itliong, a strike by Filipino grape pickers in Delano began, the start of three years of direct confrontation to bring about the kinds of changes that Huerta and Chávez envisioned. As Chávez voiced it: "I have been driven by one dream, one goal, one vision: to overthrow a farm labor system in this nation which treats farmworkers as if they were not important human beings."

Organizing in the fields was not the only way to bring about change. In March 1966, Chávez garnered national attention to the cause by leading strikers on a long march from Delano to the state capital, Sacramento, in quest of state legislation to address some of the dire needs of his constituency. Meanwhile, Huerta managed to secure an agreement from a winery in Delano. Then the effort went national, with a call for a boycott of California grapes—not a boycott against one discriminatory business but a boycott against all the growers.

Chávez, taking yet another approach, went on a 25-day fast in 1966. Martin Luther King sent a message of solidarity: "Our separate struggles are really one. A struggle for freedom, for dignity, and for humanity." Robert F. Kennedy, as a member of the US Senate, held a hearing on the workers' conditions and their efforts to unionize.

Two years later, Chávez was conducting another hunger strike, and Kennedy was back in California, this time campaigning for the US presidency. As the two met in Delano, RFK declared: "I am here out of respect for one of the heroic figures of our time— César Chávez. I congratulate all of you who are locked with César in the struggle for the farmworker and in the struggle for justice for Spanish-speaking Americans."

The year 1968 brought a constellation of contracts between California growers and the United Farm Workers union. It brought, too, a state law that supported the right of farmworkers to form unions and negotiate collectively over wages, working conditions, and living conditions. The very considerable success that Huerta and Chávez had achieved had taken creative and persistent organizing, gaining highly visible support from icons like King and Kennedy, and effectively taking the campaign to a national audience to participate in and support.

The struggle would go on, but change that had seemed so very improbable had actually come to California agriculture and to the throngs of workers who kept then, and who keep now, going to work to put food on America's dinner tables.

2-31
Mrs. Loving and the Freedom to Marry

He was big-boned and blond, she slender and dark—or "colored" (a catch-all term that mostly assumed Black but also, under Virginia's 1924 Racial Integrity Act, encompassed Native or Asian). In 1958, Mildred Jeter and Richard Loving could have legally married in any of 24 states. Another 24 states, however—all those in the South and many in the North and West—barred a marriage like theirs, and they lived in one of those, in Caroline County, Virginia.

In June that year, she was four-plus months pregnant when they drove 100 miles north to Washington, DC, where the law let couples marry regardless of racial classification. As newlyweds, they turned around and drove back to Caroline County. A month later, the entire local law force, three men, showed up after midnight at her parents' home, where they were living, and hauled them off to jail.

By the time their trial date came along in January 1959, so had Donald Jr., three months old. Of the couple's guilt, having gone out-of-state to marry, then having illicitly attempted to bring their marriage back to Virginia, there could be little doubt. State law mandated a prison term of at least one year and as many as five. So, for a very long time, Mildred and Richard would, it seemed, be forcibly separated, both from each other and from Baby Donald. Judge Leon Bazile perceived another way. Choosing exile rather than incarceration, he ordered them to leave Virginia and not return together for the next 25 years. They moved to DC.

By mid-1963, Mildred's discontent with their plight, and her loneliness for familiar people and surroundings, drove her to try to end their exile. She desperately needed for the family to be able to leave the city and return to Caroline County. But she also needed Richard and herself to stay married *and* out of prison. She found a young lawyer, Bernard Cohen, representing the American Civil Liberties Union, to try to help her. He did what he could, though with limited results.

The next year, 1964, another young lawyer, Philip Hirschkop, who brought experience in civil rights matters, joined Cohen, and they took the case into federal court. There they did not get immediate satisfaction but did gain an ally. The case first had to go through the state court system. Judge Bazile would have to weigh in again on the Lovings' fate, or the federal court would take the case over.

Now that whatever Bazile said would gain wide notice, he was happy to speak up. He got out his legal-size yellow pad and wrote a 12-page manifesto justifying the verdict he had rendered. He closed with an immortal contribution to world culture: "Almighty God created the races white black yellow red and malay and he placed them on separate continents. And but for the interference with his arrangement there would be no cause for such marriages. The fact that he separated the races shows that he did not intend for the races to mix."

Cohen and Hirschkop promptly appealed Bazile's ruling to the Virginia Supreme Court. There, all the justices shared an unshakable commitment to the state law and their authority over its interpretation. They did express one reservation about Bazile's treatment of the Lovings. His authority did not extend to offering them exile rather than imprisonment, although, the Court allowed, they might escape a penalty if they stopped acting like they were married. Regardless, the justices vented on the inappropriateness of any federal court intruding on a state matter. In their view, the law of marriage belonged solely within the purview of each state.

Then again, they doubtless recognized that the next stop for the case would not be for Judge Bazile to reconfigure the sentence, rather it would go now to the US Supreme Court. There, in May 1967, a unanimous Court ruled: "These convictions must be reversed." Under the Fourteenth Amendment, laws like Virginia's could no longer be constitutionally enforced, and the Lovings could live in Virginia, free of further legal threats to their marriage or their freedom. Mildred Jeter really could be Mrs. Richard Loving. And her three children could marry White, Black, or Native—and did, all three.

All Americans, no matter their racial identification, were now free to marry in any state, and free to take their marriage, even if "interracial," across any state line. Black-White couples promptly went ahead and married, in Virginia and other states, too. At first in some states, however, among them Alabama, Black-White couples had to go to federal court to induce a resistant local official to provide a license for them to marry.

In the years to come, Black-White marriages long remained quite few, even in states that had long had no legal restrictions. But the number of "interracial" marriages grew, with Asian-Caucasian couples more numerous than Black-White. Racial freedom in marriage had come to all Americans, thanks to the Lovings' persistence and the US Supreme Court's ruling in the breakthrough way it did.

When Mildred Loving died in 2008, 50 years after her DC marriage and subsequent arrest, many people celebrated what she had accomplished and what she represented: "Your fight has made my marriage possible." "Can't no court system separate them." "Rest well, peaceful warrior."

2-32
Vietnam

In Vietnam, the US found itself caught at the intersection of two powerful currents. One related to how World War II brought an end to European nations' ability to maintain (retrieve) their overseas colonies, with wars of national liberation and struggles over what shape newly independent nations should take. In the other, the aftermath of that war featured an emerging Cold War, a global rivalry of the US with the USSR and the new People's Republic of China.

The Korea War supplied a premonition, with the confluence of a divided nation emerging from colonial status and caught up in the Cold War, thus shaped by forces both internal and external. The year after the Korean War reached stasis in 1953, France suffered a huge military defeat in May 1954 at its stronghold in northern Vietnam, Dien Bien Phu. Akin to Korea's division at the 38th Parallel, Vietnam was provisionally divided at the 17th. As with Korea, the division held for only so long.

President Eisenhower's time in office brought the US into Southeast Asia in a preliminary way. In the 1960s, JFK moved the US in more deeply, and LBJ much more deeply still. Unlike in Korea, the US had no significant military coalition to lead. The US had to look after the economic and political interests of its allies, Japan in Asia and France and Britain in Europe. The Eisenhower administration voiced the notion of a "domino theory," according to which if one domino (Vietnam) fell, others in the region would surely follow, so the US must seek to hold the line.

But the US could not make South Vietnam's government any more popular in the 1960s than it could see its preferred regime in China, the Nationalists rather than the Communists, prevail in the late 1940s. Landlords versus peasants, Catholics versus Buddhists, such intractable social, cultural, and economic fractures in Vietnam were not amenable to US wishes. US involvement in Southeast Asia had no assured happy ending. But the US tried. Perhaps it could achieve at least something along the lines of the Korea model.

An alleged incident along the shores of North Vietnam in August 1964 led to the Gulf of Tonkin Resolution, in which Congress authorized the president "to take all necessary measures to repel any armed attack against the forces of the United States." Aerial bombardment ensued. On 8 March 1965, moreover, several thousand US Marines landed at the port city of Da Nang in South Vietnam.

A US ground war had begun. Predictions had the US prevailing in short order. That did not happen and The "Tet Offensive," which began in January 1968, involved attacks on dozens of cities and US military installations. Neither side at that point was obviously winning, and peace talks, by no means conclusive, began in Paris. From a growing perspective at home in the US, the US was clearly not getting its way. The stakes seemed too limited, the prospects too grim. Americans' support for the war, and for the Johnson administration, sank.

Meanwhile, mass protests against the war took place as early as the May 2nd Movement in 1964, with a huge rally in New York City, and really took off with massive demonstrations as marchers made their way from DC to the Pentagon in spring 1967 and again that fall.

The spreading opposition to the war led to the toppling of a president who had won the 1964 election in a landslide. A sitting president, looking for reelection, faced serious rivals in the primary season, first with Senator Eugene McCarthy of Minnesota (not Joseph!), and then with Senator Robert F. Kennedy of New York (not Jack). Johnson won New Hampshire's Democratic primary, but his small margin of victory stunned him, brought Kennedy into the race, and led to LBJ's surprise announcement, on 31 March 1968, that he would not be seeking another term after all. At that point, US military personnel in Vietnam numbered more than a half million.

The Vietnam War, a central issue in the 1968 presidential election, led to a victory by the Republican Party candidate, Richard M. Nixon. He had let it be known in the run-up to the election that he had a plan, a secret plan, to end the war, something that most voters craved. In practice, his administration soon reduced troop levels some, in a policy that Nixon called "Vietnamization."

But the war dragged on. Polls showed that the proportion of Americans who thought US intervention had been a good idea dropped from two-thirds to one-third. Enrollment in college ROTC programs dropped sharply. In 1971, the *New York Times* published the "Pentagon Papers," a massive collection of documents revealing that much of what Americans had been told about the war had sharply diverged from the truth. The late-1960s mass demonstrations against the war were followed by a crescendo of fury in May 1970, after Nixon widened the war, taking it into Laos and Cambodia, a war that people had thought was winding down.

The 1972 presidential campaign led to a repeat victory by Nixon. He defeated Senator George McGovern of South Dakota despite McGovern's call for withdrawal of US military personnel from Vietnam. But by that point, the American part of the war had effectively ended, and an announcement came in January 1973 of a ceasefire. Things were slogging toward a conclusion. The last US Marines evacuated the US Embassy in Saigon by helicopter on 30 April 1975, marking a sudden inglorious end to it all.

Or not all. In the long aftermath to a decade of massive US intervention in the internal affairs of Vietnam, many hundreds of thousands of refugees made their way to the US or to such other countries as Australia, Canada, and France. Reflecting an argument about young men fighting a war they had no political say in supporting, in

1971 the US dropped the voting age from 21 to 18. The military draft came to an end in 1973. In Vietnam, Agent Orange—a toxic defoliant widely used in the war's aerial campaign so that enemy troop movements could be seen through the trees—left behind an immense destruction of forests and countless human victims. Various impacts of the war reverberated through countless lives and numerous societies in Vietnam, the US, and around the world.

Part Three
1970s-2020s

3-1
Presidents Nixon, Ford, and Carter

Whatever their policy priorities, every president must navigate developments in domestic politics and international affairs. The combination of Vietnam and Watergate towered over the presidents of the 1970s. The Vietnam War ended Lyndon Johnson's thoughts in 1968 of winning a second full term. Watergate led to Richard M. Nixon's tumble in 1974 and Gerald R. Ford's elevation, then contributed in turn to Ford's loss to Jimmy Carter in 1976.

In 1968, after LBJ withdrew from the presidential race, Hubert H. Humphrey, former US senator and sitting vice-president, led the Democratic ticket. Nixon, Dwight Eisenhower's vice-president in the 1950s who had narrowly lost to Jack Kennedy in 1960, was making a big comeback and ran as the Republican. George Wallace, former governor of Alabama, ran as a third-party candidate.

Wallace's campaign and Nixon's victory both reflected a switch among White voters, especially in the South, away from the Democratic Party in response to its championing of civil rights in the 1960s. Nixon won. He proved rather progressive on environmental issues, not so on social matters.

Nixon's presidency started off with a dazzling development a quarter-million miles away, as NASA's Apollo 11 Mission took three Americans to the Moon, a vision first voiced by President Kennedy in 1961.

Three big events related especially to female Americans came within months of each other in 1972–1973 on Nixon's watch, though not reflecting initiatives that he championed: *Roe v. Wade,* Title IX, and congressional approval of the Equal Rights Amendment.

In other domestic policies, Nixon signed the Occupational Safety and Health Act and a Clean Air Act, both in 1970. But he vetoed the universal childcare that the Comprehensive Child Development Act of 1971 would have promoted, and he pushed for a bill to bar the use of busing as a tool to foster integrated public schools.

In the world of diplomacy, the old cold warrior Nixon surprised the world by visiting the People's Republic of China in 1972. The resulting Shanghai Communique stipulated a "one-China" policy very different from the previous one, which had Taiwan representing the entire nation. Then, days after his second term began in 1973, the Paris Peace Accords brought an official end to the Vietnam War.

The 1972 election featured a blowout by Nixon over Senator George McGovern of South Dakota, a leading opponent of the Vietnam War. Yet the incumbent had evidently felt so skittish about his prospects that his reelection campaign funded a burglary of Democratic campaign headquarters, located in the Watergate office building, knowledge of which slowly emerged in Nixon's second term. Also, the Organization of Petroleum Exporting Nations (OPEC) struck in 1973, embargoing the export of oil, and US drivers found themselves waiting in long lines trying to buy scarce gas at prices they had never seen before.

Nixon consistently denied any prior knowledge of the burglary at the Watergate, or any role in trying to cover it up, but the truth gradually emerged. In a case with the telling name *United States v. Nixon*, in July 1974 the Supreme Court directed him to turn over the tapes of White House conversations, and they ended up showing his early and deep participation in the cover up. In the days that followed, the House Judiciary Committee prepared three articles of impeachment, and Nixon ended the process by resigning.

Whatever Nixon accomplished, historical memory of him tends to equate to Watergate, the affair that brought him to the precipice of impeachment and removal. With the elected vice-president having already resigned in disgrace for accepting petty bribes during his term as governor of Maryland, Congressman Gerald Ford had become vice-president and now, therefore, president. His watch brought the image from Saigon in March 1975 of the last helicopter about to lift off from the roof of the US embassy, as a host of Vietnamese people all sought desperately to get safely aboard.

In the 1976 election season, Ford narrowly beat back a challenge for the Republican nomination by former California governor Ronald Reagan. He next faced Jimmy Carter, of Georgia, a centrist Democratic governor from the South. Though running as the incumbent, Ford was an accidental president, stepping into the office after Nixon's ignominious departure. Never having gained election to a higher office than member of Congress, he had no national constituency. Some voters turned against him for issuing a pardon to Nixon. In a debate with Carter, moreover, he made an unforced error, an own goal, when he blurted that he did not believe the Eastern European countries, Poland in particular, to be "dominated" by the USSR. The Democrats, rebounding from their thrashing four years earlier, retook the White House.

Jimmy Carter's presidency brought an improbable but promising breakthrough in Middle East diplomacy in 1978, as Carter brokered a peace agreement between Israel and Egypt in the Camp David Accords. In addition, Carter managed to resolve the long-simmering status of the Panama Canal, with a treaty relinquishing it to Panama after another twenty years, in a process that had begun under Nixon and would not be concluded unless he could get the Senate to ratify it. Moreover, the US followed up on Nixon's 1972 trip and in 1979 gave full diplomatic recognition to the People's Republic of China.

Carter ran into challenges at home and abroad. After a Soviet invasion of Afghanistan, Carter called for a US boycott of the 1980 Summer Olympics, to be held in Moscow. (The US hockey team's memorable run had already taken place in the Winter Olympics.) That year, running for reelection, he had to beat back a strong bid for the Democratic nomination by US Senator Ted Kennedy of Massachusetts, younger brother of Jack and Bobby, before taking on Reagan, who won the Republican nomination this time around.

Carter's loss in November showed how developments in the Middle East might prove central to US domestic politics going forward. In Iran, chickens came home to roost from back at the dawn of the Eisenhower administration, as the people of Iran toppled the Shah from power. The new radical Islamic regime of Ayatolla Khomeini took dozens of Americans hostage at the US embassy in November 1979, and the US proved unable to obtain their freedom.

Also stemming from developments in Iran, an oil shortage in 1979–1980 drove the prices of petroleum products way up. Long gas lines at high prices returned. Oil shortages were chronic, though. Soon after his inauguration in 1977, Carter had gone on television, wearing a sweater and suggesting that, in view of the price of home heating oil, Americans should drop the thermostat to 55 degrees. The oil shortage also brought both high inflation and high unemployment (so-called stagflation). Reagan won decisively.

3-2
Reagan, Bush, and Clinton

The three presidents of the 1980s and '90s held office during a time when, at home, both parties seemed to be leaning to the right. In world affairs, the Soviet Union came unglued, after which a "post–Cold War" world brought new challenges.

In the 1980 race for the presidency, race, gender, and religion all factored into Ronald Reagan's victory, while Jimmy Carter carried heavy baggage related to Iran. Reagan spoke of a return to "morning in America." He rode a wave of "New Right" "evangelical Christians," with promises to seek constitutional amendments to eliminate the new constitutional right (under the 1973 Supreme Court case *Roe v. Wade*) to an abortion, return religion and prayer to the public schools, and end busing as a tool for desegregating those schools.

None of those amendments made their way through Congress. Reagan proposed new laws restricting abortion within the US like the President's Pro-Life Act of 1988. In addition, in 1984 Reagan announced the "Mexico City Policy," whereby the US would supply no funds through nongovernmental organizations to fund abortions outside the US—a policy that, going forward, Democratic presidents would suspend but Republicans would resume. In the Hyde Amendment and Helms Amendment, both dating from the 1970s, Congress had already banned the use of federal funds for abortion services both within the US and in US programs overseas.

Regarding military defense, Reagan performed like a quintessential cold warrior in what turned out to be the final years of the Soviet Union. Reversing the position taken by President Carter, he approved production of the B-1 Bomber. He also promoted what he called the Strategic Defense Initiative (SDI), to supply a shield over the US against possible nuclear attack.

The Reagan years brought a smooth performance by the former actor (he came to be characterized as "the Teflon president," since nothing criminal or unseemly ever seemed to stick). Fearing another Cuba, with its regime oriented toward the USSR, Reagan acted like the US was at war in Central America with Nicaragua's democratic socialist regime, the Sandinistas (who had taken power after overthrowing a dictatorship), trying to bring it down. His administration broke a federal law by secretly selling weapons to Iran, then diverting some $20 million of the proceeds to support the Contras, a right-wing armed group trying to overthrow the Sandinista government. This all led to a running series of congressional hearings on the "Iran-Contra Affair" that brought back memories of the Watergate hearings, but the administration escaped major repercussions.

In June 1987, Reagan went to West Berlin and famously called on Russia to "tear down this wall," referring to the barrier that separated East Berlin from West Berlin as a way of preventing refugees from moving from East to West—something that Berlin residents themselves took care of two years later. Domestically, in 1981 he destroyed a union of federal workers—fired them all—when the air traffic controllers went out on strike. He vetoed a Water Quality Control Act in 1987, but Congress overrode his veto.

In 1988, against a lackluster Democratic candidate, Reagan's vice-president, George Herbert Walker Bush won, bringing to the presidency public service experience of a magnitude that harked back to John Quincy Adams in the 1820s. Bush then presided in an altered world in the aftermath of the Cold War, as the USSR dissolved into Russia and a dozen other constituent nations, including Ukraine.

Big events in other countries included the Chinese Army's massacre, in spring 1989, of hundreds of protesters in a massive rally at Tiananmen Square in Beijing seeking democratization, a horrific end that Bush condemned. After the Berlin Wall came down in November 1989, East Germany and West Germany reunited the following year as one Germany. Much closer to home, US forces invaded Panama in January 1990, to capture its head of state, Manuel Noriega, and bring him to the US on drug trafficking and related charges, for which he was imprisoned.

Bush faced what he understood as a crisis moment in foreign affairs when Iraq invaded its small, oil-rich neighbor Kuwait in August 1990. In something akin to Truman with Korea in 1950, Bush brought together a coalition, led by the US, to safeguard Kuwait's independence: "This will not stand," he declared. And it did not, as Bush managed to persuade Russia and China, as well as the other members of the Security Council, to support or at least permit a huge military action to destroy Iraq's bid to control Kuwait together with its oil reserves.

In domestic affairs, Bush signed the Americans with Disabilities Act and the Clean Air Act, both in 1990. The next year, he changed the future in a very different way when he nominated Clarence Thomas to take Thurgood Marshall's place on the Supreme Court. Despite serious allegations against Thomas for sexual misconduct, the Senate put him on the Court.

But a mellifluous voice from Arkansas came out of the Democratic primaries. Like Jimmy Carter, Bill Clinton was a centrist Democratic governor of a southern state. Bush, like Carter, would be a one-term president. Clinton, like Reagan, served two terms, despite a Republican effort to remove him through impeachment over a sex scandal.

Clinton began his presidency by appointing a Task Force on National Health Care Reform, chaired by his wife, Hillary Rodham Clinton. Congress never accepted its proposals for a universal health care plan, but it did pass the Family and Medical Leave Act in 1993 and approve creation of the Children's Health Insurance Program in 1987.

During this period, women entered several high positions in the federal government for the first time. In 1981, President Reagan had nominated the first female member of the Supreme Court, Sandra Day O'Connor. President Clinton appointed Janet Reno as attorney general and Madeleine Albright as secretary of state, and he named Ruth Bader Ginsburg to the Supreme Court, where she joined Justice O'Connor. Clinton also promoted passage in 1994 of the Violence against Women Act (VAWA).

Unique among modern presidents, Clinton managed to balance the federal budget. In his January 1996 State of the Union address, he announced: "The era of big government is over." Conservative policies from his watch included a "three-strikes" mandatory life sentence for drug crimes (1994); a "war on welfare" (1996), designed "to end welfare as we know it"; a law opposing same-sex marriage (1996); a "Don't Ask, Don't Tell" compromise that permitted gay service members to remain in the military, so long as they stayed in the closet; as well as ratification of the North American Free Trade Act (NAFTA), which Clinton had inherited from Bush.

The Clinton administration featured significant achievements in foreign affairs in two particularly troubled parts of the world. When Yugoslavia broke up into treacherously warring communities, the Clinton administration's intervention—both military and diplomatic—led to the Dayton Peace Accords (1995). The Good Friday Peace Accords, or Belfast Agreement (1998), went a long way toward ending "The Troubles" between Protestants and Catholics in Northern Ireland.

3-3
Bush the Younger and Barack Obama

The first two decades of the 21st century displayed a continuing back-and-forth sequence of Republican and Democratic presidencies, often won by narrow margins. Whatever the numbers, the outcome proved always consequential in domestic policies and often in foreign policies. Much attention on foreign affairs focused on an arc of territory ranging from Ukraine in Eastern Europe, though the Middle East, to Afghanistan in Southwest Asia.

Those years also featured a deepening political and cultural divide, fostered in part by right-wing "talk radio" and in part by the erosion of the kinds of industrial jobs that had fueled the rise of a great middle class in the years following the New Deal and World War II. Unease about a host of other matters, from climate to gender to immigration, also contributed.

The election of 2000 featured Bill Clinton's vice-president, Al Gore, versus George W. Bush, a son of recent president George H. W. Bush. Former auto safety crusader Ralph Nader, running as an independent, siphoned many votes, likely most from the Democratic ticket, in a very close race. Anyway, Gore won the popular vote, but to win in the Electoral College he had to take Florida.

In a technically messy election reflecting the kind of paper ballot employed in that state, the term "hanging chad" became the term du jour, and in the end the Supreme Court abruptly declared an end to the Florida recount at a time when Bush was leading by 537 votes, out of 5.8 million. (A later investigation concluded that, had all the votes been recounted, Bush would apparently still have won, by some 1,665 votes.)

In one of Bush's first acts as president, he declared that the US would not ratify the Kyoto Protocol on climate change. Later that first year, in an event promptly named "9/11" for 11 September, the US came under attack when Middle East terrorists commandeered four passenger planes and turned them into weapons of mass destruction. Two careened through the upper floors of the Twin Towers in downtown New York City. Another crashed into the Pentagon, the Department of Defense headquarters just outside DC. A fourth went down in rural Pennsylvania when other passengers overcame the men who had taken over the plane, perhaps to take out the White House.

In response to this supremely consequential act, Bush declared a "war on terror" (officially the Global War against Terrorism). He first led the way for a military effort in Afghanistan, where Al Qaeda, responsible for the 9/11 attacks, had found sanctuary.

His administration then established a military prison at Guantanamo Bay Naval Station, in Cuba, and engaged in torture there while interrogating men captured during the "war on terror." The great majority of those men were, over the years, released. But legal proceedings in a special military commission against five of them, alleged to have been directly involved in the planning for 9/11, were still going on more than two decades later.

In 2003, the Bush administration asserted (falsely, it later became clear) that Iraq's government had "weapons of mass destruction" of a sort that demanded that it be brought down. Having repeatedly stated, in an October 2000 presidential debate on foreign affairs, that he opposed deploying the US military in efforts at "nation building," and now proving good to his word, Bush displayed a commitment to nation destroying. The Middle East became even more volatile and dangerous.

On the matter of Taiwan's future, Bush took a more aggressive stance than had his recent predecessors. Richard Nixon had agreed to a "one China" policy by which Taiwan, it appeared, would eventually be absorbed into the People's Republic of China. Since then, however, the US had continued to support Taiwan, but Bush went farther and expressly declared that the US would supply military support if necessary to secure the island's continued independence. That huge issue about the future of East Asia would persist very much into the 2020s.

In domestic affairs, Bush resumed efforts by the federal government to restrict abortion, and his administration sought to go farther than the 1996 Defense of Marriage Act against same-sex marriage. With Massachusetts according same-sex couples the right to marry, Bush called for a constitutional amendment to deny any such right. Congress turned back that initiative, but the issue proved crucial to Bush's winning a second term in 2004.

The 2008 presidential election featured a dramatic first in all US history. Barack Obama, who burst on the national scene at the Democratic national convention in 2004 with a mesmerizing speech about "the audacity of hope" of "a skinny kid with a funny name," secured the Democratic nomination four years later. Obama contrasted sharply with any previous US candidate for national office. His mother a White woman from Kansas, his father a Black man from Kenya, Obama was born in Hawai'i (where his parents had met) and raised for a time in Indonesia. He had a law degree from Harvard, years of experience community organizing in Chicago, and a brief time in the US Senate representing Illinois.

With the election returns coming in during his first run, and as his victory became assured, tears of joy streamed down the faces of jubilant elderly Black women in Chicago's Grant Park. But a real estate figure from New York named Donald Trump made a national name for himself by insisting—through both of Obama's two terms—that Obama had been born outside the US and was, Trump contended, therefore not a citizen qualified to serve as president.

Obama's signal accomplishment as president, the Affordable Care Act (the ACA, or Obamacare), which became law in 2010, provided subsidies for health insurance to Americans not otherwise insured. Some kind of national medical system had long since been adopted in Great Britain and many other countries. And the issue had come up repeatedly in the US—during the presidencies of Franklin D. Roosevelt and his New Deal, of Harry Truman and his proposed Fair Deal, of LBJ and the Great Society, and more recently of Bill Clinton as his administration's first main item of business. A constitutional challenge took the law to the US Supreme Court, which upheld it 6–3.

Obama acted on many fronts to address climate change. On other fronts, new legislation included the Hate Crimes Prevention Act in 2009 and the Healthy, Hunger-Free Kids Act in 2010. His nominations put Sonia Sotomayor and Elena Kagan on the Supreme Court. He called for immigration reform. After earlier saying that his position (like that of a great many Americans) was "evolving," in 2012 he announced his support for gay marriage. In 2014, when Russia seized Crimea from Ukraine, Obama called for sanctions against the aggressor.

Much was said, after Obama's first election, about the US having become a "post-racial" society. The evidence did not long sustain the illusion, yet his having fulfilled "the audacity of hope" signaled new possibilities in American life.

3-4
Trump to Biden to Trump

In the 2016 election season, Donald Trump shouldered aside all the more conventional candidates for the Republican nomination and then faced Hillary Rodham Clinton, wife of the former president. In her extraordinary range of experience in public life at the national level, she resembled President Bush the elder. She won the popular election by 2.8 million votes, but she fell short in the Electoral College. Trump became president.

In office, Trump pushed with great success for a massive tax reduction bill. He failed, however, in his effort to bring an end to Obamacare, and he never supplied a long-promised substitute for it. With the vital assistance of Senate majority leader Mitch McConnell, he managed to secure not just one or two but three new appointments to the Supreme Court, a feat that would reap great rewards for him going forward.

Trump's four years left an enduring collage of images: at the Mexican border, the separation of young children from their parents; in Singapore, meeting alone with North Korean leader Kim Jong-un; in Helsinki, Finland, publicly taking Putin's word, as opposed to US intelligence, about allegations of Russian interference in the 2016 election; his phone call to Ukraine's President Volodymyr Zelensky holding US aid hostage to an inappropriate demand; a phone call to Georgia's secretary of state imploring him to "find" just enough additional popular votes to win that state's Electoral College votes in the 2020 election.

In the early months of 2020, a pandemic, Covid-19, struck the US and the world, causing more than one million deaths in the US and huge social costs and economic distortions, as schools closed and businesses had to suspend operations. In that year's election season, Joe Biden, formerly a long-term US senator and then Obama's vice-president, emerged in the Democratic primaries as the seasoned centrist who might best bring Trump's time in the White House to an end.

The popular vote demonstrated Biden's very clear victory. The incumbent refused to concede. Rallying to his call, many thousands of avid supporters descended on DC with the avowed intent, by any means necessary, to prevent Congress from officially counting the votes of the Electoral College on 6 January and thus completing the process of naming the next president.

In the end, the transfer of power to Biden took place, though only after much mayhem, both around the Capitol building and inside it. A subsequent series of high-profile congressional hearings would outline the breathtaking range of innovative ways in which the former president had desperately tried to hold onto the White House.

For these efforts, the House brought impeachment charges (for a second time) against Trump, although (as before) not enough senators supported the charges to reach the requisite two-thirds supermajority to convict.

Much as Trump had promptly sought to reverse a series of Obama initiatives, Biden reversed Trump's. Early executive orders, for example, had the US rejoining the World Health Organization and the Paris Climate Accord.

Biden's presidency featured great challenges in both domestic policy and foreign affairs. On the domestic front, the Democratic president, working with the narrowest of margins in both houses of Congress, managed to enact bills during the first two years that had the look of another New Deal. One key impulse behind these initiatives had to do with pulling the nation out of a deep economic funk resulting from Covid-19, but they also addressed priorities like clean energy and internet access. The new laws included the American Rescue Plan, the Infrastructure Investment and Jobs Act, the CHIPS and Science Act, and the Inflation Reduction Act.

Biden also signed the Emmett Till Antilynching Act, the Safer Communities Act (addressing gun violence), and a bill making Juneteenth a national holiday. In contrast to the Defense of Marriage Act back in 1996, the Respect for Marriage Act, passed in late 2022, gave federal statutory protection to both same-sex and interracial marriage, a legislative response to suggestions earlier that year that both might be in jeopardy as matters of constitutional right.

In foreign affairs, the first half of the 2020s brought a series of huge challenges to the US and to various parts of the globe. For one, the People's Republic of China continued its meteoric rise not only as a regional economic and military power but to world power status. In 2024, the US began refurbishing World War II runways on Tinian Island in the western Pacific (where the planes carrying atomic bombs to Hiroshima and Nagasaki in 1945 had lifted off) as part of its effort to thwart Chinese expansion in the region.

For another, Russia's invasion of Ukraine in February 2022 put at great risk Ukraine's continuing sovereignty, as well as the security of other neighboring nations, and the Biden administration slowly ramped up US assistance to the beleaguered nation.

The 45th and 46th US presidents, Trump and Biden, were both elderly, even in their first term, but in 2024 each sought another term. Biden had positioned himself in 2020 as a one-term bridge to another generation. Days after the 2022 midterm elections, however, Trump declared himself a candidate to take back the presidency. In view of the manifold charges against him, it might be the only way to guarantee staying out of prison for his behavior during his previous time in office.

Five months later, Biden made an historically poor judgment and responded by declaring that he, too, would run again, as if once again he was the strongest candidate to defeat the former president. Biden had already failed to recognize that fairly open immigration across the southern border, an overreaction to Trump's harsh actions, was turning some of his former supporters against him.

Once again, moreover, an event in the Middle East, a series of events starting in October 2023, contorted US domestic politics. A gruesome attack from Gaza across the border into Israel in October 2023, killing some 1,200 civilians and abducting another 251, elicited a monumental and continuing military campaign against all of Gaza. Under Biden, the US continued to support Israel, but a great many Americans, Muslim or not, could not abide the death and destruction that, month after month, they were seeing relentlessly unfold.

In 2024, Trump persuaded the Supreme Court in the case styled *Trump v. United States* that presidents should have nearly unlimited power, that they should be immune from criminal prosecution for any "official" action. And then Trump won the second term that had eluded him before.

This time, nearly an octogenarian himself, Trump took office with an ominous blueprint for America's future, masterminded by others for whom he acted as the enthusiastic instrument: Project 2025, a call to undo much of the Great Society, the New Deal, the Progressive Era, the 1883 Civil Service Act, even the Fourteenth Amendment from 1868. Immigration—legal, not just illegal—would flip to willy-nilly mass deportation. NATO, too, would be at risk, as well as the global image of the US as a reliable friend and ally and a beacon of stability, democracy, peace, and opportunity.

3-5
Roe v. Wade

Pregnancy can be exhilarating, daunting, yearned for, unwelcome—whatever else it is, it is dangerous and comes with no guarantees. It puts a prospective birth and a potential mother in a relationship that can be uneventful and go as planned, or that might pit a potential life against a mature one. What role the law plays with respect to women and pregnancy—whatever roles the law has historically played—has varied very much over time and place.

Twin matters of *preventing* a pregnancy or *terminating* a pregnancy have long appeared in the news as well as in countless private lives. The late 1950s not only preceded "the pill," which came on the market in 1960 but remained legally restricted in many places, it also also featured twin scourges of pregnancy: rubella (German measles) and thalidomide, a drug given to women as a sedative or to ease morning sickness. Either could have devastating consequences.

Topping the news in summer 1962, a pregnant resident of Arizona, Sherri Finkbine, came to realize that the thalidomide she had unwittingly taken might result in a severely malformed child. In desperation, she flew to Sweden, where she managed to get an abortion—which confirmed that yes, it would have been a "thalidomide baby."

In *Griswold v. Connecticut* (1965), the Supreme Court ruled against a state law that banned the distribution of birth-prevention items or information to married couples. And in *Baird v. Eisenstadt* (1972), the Court extended that liberty to single individuals. The Court had built on rulings from as early as the 1920s that recognized Americans' individual claims on liberty, privacy, autonomy. What about the right of a woman to terminate a pregnancy?

Several cases regarding abortion arrived at the Supreme Court from Texas and Georgia in the early 1970s. At the time these cases were making their way toward resolution, *Washington Post* reporters Bob Woodward (he of the Watergate investigation as it played out soon afterward) and Scott Armstrong were working on a book, *The Brethren: Inside the Supreme Court*. In-depth interviews with Court personnel permitted them to track with extraordinary detail not only how the Court goes about its business—the personalities, the back-and-forth process, the roles played by the clerks of the various justices—but also how nine men trained in law made their way toward the ruling known as *Roe v. Wade*, which set new ground rules for pregnant women and for their medical professionals.

The issues—moral, religious, legal, constitutional, medical, political, jurisdictional—were volatile and complex, and the justices, each and together, made an extremely difficult journey toward their decision, handed down at last in January 1973, days after the inauguration of Richard Nixon for a second term as president. Nixon, who opposed the easing of restrictions on abortion, had appointed two new justices he hoped would secure the ruling that he wanted from the Court.

Assigned to draft an opinion for the Court majority, Justice Harry Blackmun worked for months on it. Having been for many years legal counsel for the Mayo Clinic in his home state, Minnesota, Blackmun had long acquaintance with skilled figures in the medical profession, and he had often advised about how the law related to medical decisions. As he worked on the abortion cases, he at first emphasized the perspectives of physicians and of legislators, not so much of women.

But he came to see that, to navigate the issues at hand, he had to address the interests of a state, the viability of a fetus, and the health—and autonomy—of a woman. He discovered that laws restricting abortion were historically quite recent, and that they seemed to have emerged from a concern for the well-being of pregnant women, given the enormous dangers associated with abortion in the 19th century. He learned that, in the modern day, women who had abortions early in their pregnancy had lower rates of death from their pregnancy than those who carried the fetus to term.

Regarding a constitutional right to privacy, and to abortion, Blackmun and his colleagues could look, for example, to the Fourteenth Amendment and its language that "no State shall . . . deprive any person of . . . liberty . . . without due process of law." The Ninth Amendment of the Bill of Rights stated that, just because the Constitution specified some rights, it did not "deny or disparage others retained by the people." Certainly, words like pregnancy and abortion nowhere appeared in the Constitution, but perhaps individual rights to autonomy could imply a right to have children—something already established— or to end a pregnancy.

While the abortion cases were at the Court, a federal district judge in a similar case ruled that any moral position on abortion "must remain a personal judgment," not a judgment that anyone has a right to "impose upon others by force of law."

Justices could agree that a state law could demonstrate both an interest in protecting a pregnant woman's health and an interest in protecting the potential life of a fetus. But those considerations were quite different. In a 7–2 decision, the Court divided the nine months of a pregnancy into trimesters, an understanding common to doctors. In the first three months, the state had no constitutional interest in protecting a fetus, since it was not yet "viable," and women and their doctors must be left to make their own determinations about continuing a pregnancy. A woman now had that constitutional right.

In the second three months, the state had a legitimate interest in intervening, but it extended only to protecting the pregnant woman's health. In the third trimester, with the fetus presumably viable, the state could step in to protect the potential life of the fetus.

Justice Blackmun and his fellow members of the Court had no doubts that the decision, when announced, would kick up a storm no matter which way the ruling went. The Court had recognized a woman's right to act as she saw fit through much of any pregnancy, but many people instinctively recoiled against permitting such female autonomy. From the Catholic Church as an institution came outraged denunciations.

At the time, however, public opinion had been shifting in the direction that the Court majority had taken. A growing number of states had already legislated considerable autonomy for women regarding pregnancy. *Roe v. Wade* accorded any woman in any state the legal autonomy, well into a pregnancy, to make her own decision and act on it.

But controversy by no means came to an end, and many states sought in various ways to limit the reach of *Roe*. Moreover, Congress soon legislated a ban on the use of federal funds for an abortion. The constitutional right to terminate a pregnancy remained in place.

3-6
"Female Individuals" and the US Military

In 1948, Senator Margaret Chase Smith of Maine successfully championed the Women's Armed Services Integration Act. Building on the limited integration of women in the US military during World War II, the new law pointed toward greater opportunities for women to participate in US military affairs and contribute to national defense.

Yet not a lot changed, a fact underscored by women's continued exclusion, into the 1970s, from all the service academies, plus the Corps of Cadets at Texas A&M University and at Virginia Tech, as well as The Citadel and Virginia Military Institute.

Movement toward further change came into view in March 1972, when Congress proposed the Equal Rights Amendment, with the expectation that ratification would shortly follow. That did not happen, but that same month Senator Jacob Javits of New York nominated a young woman to the Naval Academy, which promptly rejected her, upon which Congress passed a resolution that gender should no longer be a basis for selecting students at the service academies. The three Department of Defense (DOD) service academies (West Point, Annapolis, and Air Force) reluctantly prepared for a possible order to inaugurate a coeducational student environment.

In late 1972, DOD approached Virginia Tech about possibly starting an ROTC program for women, evidently with a pilot program in mind. Tech agreed; and fall semester 1973 featured two dozen female cadets, including junior Deborah Noss, sophomore Cheryl Butler, and freshman Emily Pillsbury. Adjustments were not routinely smooth, but the experiment worked.

The University of North Georgia enrolled several "cadettes" in fall 1973, at the same time as Virginia Tech, and Texas A&M enrolled female cadets starting in 1974. Meanwhile, cases filed in federal court in September 1973 challenged female exclusion at Air Force and Annapolis.

Pressed by Patricia Schroeder, first-term congresswoman from Colorado, the Merchant Marine Academy, under the Department of Commerce, admitted its first female cadets in 1974. Next, leadership at the Coast Guard Academy, under the Department of the Treasury, decided in August 1975 to embark on a similar change.

As for the Department of Defense, in October 1975, when President Gerald Ford signed the Appropriations Act for DOD for the coming year, it became national policy that the three DOD service academies open their ranks to "female individuals" starting with fall classes in 1976.

Cheryl Butler's commissioning at Virginia Tech as a second lieutenant in the Air Force came several months before the first "female individuals" enrolled in the Air Force Academy. But change was clearly coming at most schools with military programs. In 1980, the inaugural cohorts of female students completed their studies at all three DOD schools, among them Janet C. Wolfenberger at the Air Force Academy.

Two military colleges, The Citadel and Virginia Military Institute, deflected any change in gender policy into the 1990s, but a ruling by the US Supreme Court in 1996 brought an end to female exclusion at both of those schools, that year or the next. Much had changed since 1973, even more since 1948.

3-7
Judith Heumann and Americans with Disabilities

Judith Ellen Heumann (1947–2023), "Mother of the Disability Rights Movement," exemplified the roughly 20,000 US children who came down with polio each year—with approximately 2,000 of them dying and many more paralyzed—before a vaccine against the disease, developed by Dr. Jonas Salk, became available in 1955. Having contracted polio as an infant in 1949, she lived much of her life in a wheelchair.

Heumann grew up with neighbor children who adapted their play to include her, but formal education proved another matter. Her parents had to fight for her to gain admission to New York City's public schools, first for elementary school and again for high school. Each summer for many years, she attended a summer camp for children with handicaps, an experience that taught her that she was not alone in her frustration that so many opportunities were inequitably denied. In college in the late 1960s, she and other students, both with and without disabilities, campaigned for the right for students with handicaps to live in the dorms and to have ramps that made classrooms accessible. When denied a license to teach elementary school because of her reliance on a wheelchair, she sued, won, and became a pioneer on that front.

So, when she took on a quest to gain rights for all people with handicaps, she was accustomed to running into obstacles and then overcoming them. The nationwide publicity surrounding her suing to be permitted to teach led her to co-found Disabled in Action (DIA) to lobby and protest until securing civil rights legislation for people with disabilities.

The Rehabilitation Act of 1973, a major first step, aimed to end discrimination against "handicapped people" in federal programs. Heumann then worked to secure the 1975 Education for All Handicapped Children Act (EHA), renamed in 1990 the Individuals with Disabilities Education Act (IDEA), designed to provide all children an appropriate education in the nation's public schools, as well as the more comprehensive Americans with Disabilities Act (ADA) of 1990.

Section 504 of the 1973 Rehabilitation Act barred discrimination against individuals with a disability in any program receiving federal funds, akin to the 1964 Civil Rights Act's declaration on race. But the US Department of Health, Education, and Welfare under both Presidents Ford and Carter stonewalled implementation and enforcement. To dramatize the issue, Heumann and other Disability Rights Movement leaders planned direct action at HEW offices in ten cities. She had charge of the "Committee to Save 504" in San Francisco.

To draw people to a rally outside the HEW building, they came up with the slogan "People with disabilities: The federal government is trying to steal our civil rights!" A couple of hundred people assembled, many featuring white canes, sign language, or wheelchairs. Speakers included Heumann, who spoke of the right of people with disabilities to be fully "included in the American Dream." Then many headed inside and up to the fourth floor to meet with an HEW official who, when they asked about the status of Section 504, drew a blank.

When HEW staff left for the night, Heumann's group of protesters did not. It was time to invite everyone to stay, to plan next steps, to organize into committees to look after food, medicine, reaching out to allied organizations, and communicating with the press. The rally might be turning into a sit-down strike.

A newspaper headline the next day reported that "An Occupation Army of Cripples Has Taken Over the San Francisco Federal Building." Protesters could come and go that first full day. The group called a press conference inside the building and schooled reporters on the issues and appropriate language, like "people with disabilities," not "cripples."

Afterwards, each of the protesters, now more than one hundred, was asked, "Can you stay one more night?" All agreed to stay. In other cities, official resistance, like denying access to food and medicine to sit-in activists, was bringing sit-ins to an early end and, by the next morning, the San Francisco building, too, was closed to incoming traffic.

There, however, "one more night" became another, and another. Even without phones, the group could communicate, by sign language, out the windows with supporters below. Governor Jerry Brown publicly announced his support. So did César Chávez of the United Farm Workers. Passover came, and Heumann remembered, as she looked around her, "the deliverance of the Israelites from slavery."

Six men from the Black Panthers brought food. One explained, "We told the security guards we would stop at nothing to bring the media's attention on HEW if they didn't let us in and you guys got starved out." The Panthers continued to bring food as long as the sit-in lasted.

Congressman George Miller showed up and urged the group: "Stay in this building and don't leave until you've won." Then he arranged for a congressional hearing to be held there. Julian Bond, then a Georgia state senator, stopped by. San Francisco mayor George Moscone brought supplies and a cadre of medical professionals. Other supporters, from local pharmacists to an international labor union, put additional air beneath their wings. On it went, through 24 days.

And then, suddenly, the protest had worked. On 28 April 1977, HEW secretary Joseph Califano signed the long-awaited Section 504 regulations to put ADA to work. Universities, like other institutions, would have to work toward equal accessibility.

Back in San Francisco, the hundred-plus protesters inside the federal building were disbelieving, relieved, jubilant. They weren't even sure they wanted to leave. Said one to a reporter, "We all fell in love with each other." Said another, "Instead of seeing myself as a weak person, I found my strength reinforced by others like me." Together they had created the belonging and community that they hoped the wider society could model. Heumann wrote many years later: "They decided to spend one last night together in the building, to celebrate."

Heumann extended her mission in multiple directions. In 1983 she co-founded the World Institute on Disability. She served in related capacities in President Bill Clinton's Department of Education, the World Bank, the District of Columbia, and President Barack Obama's State Department. In 2017, the new administration abolished her position at State, deleted references to the ADA from the White House website, and took down the Department of Education's policy guidelines that had explained student rights under the IDEA.

Heumann appeared in the documentary films *The Power of 504* (2008), *Lives Worth Living* (2011)—on disability rights from World War II veterans to the 1990 ADA—and *Crip Camp: A Disability Revolution* (2020) and authored *Being Heumann: An Unrepentant Memoir of a Disability Rights Activist* (2020), adapted the following year for younger readers as *Rolling Warrior*.

3-8
Wong Kim Ark and Birthright Citizenship

In November 1911, Clara Elizabeth Chan Lee and Emma Tom Leung went together to exercise, with excitement and determination, their right to register to vote, newly granted to all citizens of California, even if female.

In 1942, Fred Korematsu, born in California, Gordon Hirabayashi, born in Oregon, and Minoru Yasui, born in Washington State, each went to court with determination to assert his right, as a US-born citizen, not to be treated as an enemy alien and forced, as a person of Japanese ethnicity, to leave his Pacific Coast community and be confined in an internment camp far from the coast.

These episodes all related to the outcome of the case *Wong Kim Ark*, decided by the US Supreme Court back in 1898, about a man born in San Francisco who had gone to China and tried to return, but was turned back because, as a person of Chinese ancestry, he surely could not be a citizen, and, under the Chinese Exclusion Act, he had no right to enter the US as an immigrant.

The new discipline of anthropology in the late-19th century divided humanity into five races, among them "Mongolian," a category that included people from Japan, China, and Korea. Under US law, no Mongolian could become a naturalized citizen, that is, transfer his or her allegiance from Japan or China to the US, because American law dictated that only people of European or (beginning after the Civil War) African ancestry qualified to do any such thing. But each of these individuals had been born in the US. Were they citizens, or not? And if citizens, how did they get to be that way?

The ruling in Wong Kim Ark's case has huge significance, both historical and contemporary. It resonates into the 21st century, as the Supreme Court's decision in 1898 about birthright citizenship has come under sharp attack. Calling it a faulty interpretation of the Fourteenth Amendment's statement that all people born in the US, and subject to its jurisdiction, are citizens, the Trump administration went to court in 2025 in quest of a reversal of *Wong Kim Ark*, a rejection of birthright citizenship.

In a curious way, Wong Kim Ark continues to be an alien; that is, his name not understood in terms he would have recognized. A recent book about him and his case is catalogued by the Library of Congress as though the family name were Ark. YouTube features a collection of short videos on his story, typically rendered by experts on immigration including from China, all of which seem uniformly to render his name as a single unit, as if it were all one word, Wongkimark.

But Mr. Wong was the son of a man by the name of Wong Si Ping, and in characteristic Chinese fashion, the family name precedes the personal name. Mr. Wong, we will call him here to give him back his actual name, was born in San Francisco. His parents were unusual, in that far and away most immigrants from China at that time were men, so women of Chinese ancestry were always scarce (and California law prohibited Chinese men from marrying White women). Yet Mr. Wong Senior found Wee Lee. Their son Kim Ark was born in October 1870, followed by a younger son, and the family lived over their shop in Chinatown.

His parents, however, found life in America unduly onerous, even highly dangerous for ethnic Chinese, and returned to China. If Wong the younger were to see his parents, he would have to go to where they were, and so he did as a young man, more than once. When he returned from China in August 1895, however, customs officials barred his entry. They would not let him return to his California home. Wong, refusing to accept their decision, found himself interned at length on a ship in San Francisco Bay, awaiting resolution of his case. When his dilemma attracted press attention, he secured legal counsel as well as his freedom pending the outcome.

Was the US his country, or was it not? The question arose at a time when many Americans feared that people of Chinese ancestry were so different as to remain unassimilable and so numerous as to constitute a threat. What would the courts say?

His case made its way to the US Supreme Court, where in March 1898 a Court majority (the decision was 6–2) sided with Wong, ruling that, having been born in the United States, he was indeed a citizen. The Court minority did not see Wong as "subject to the jurisdiction thereof." The majority was having none of that. Back in the 1860s, framers of the Fourteenth Amendment included the phrase "subject to the jurisdiction thereof" to exclude the children of diplomatic personnel, or the children of Native Americans living on reservations.

Mr. Wong's parents had not been born in the US, and only people of European or African ancestry could become naturalized citizens. So, they could never be citizens. But the Court ruled all that to be irrelevant.

Wong Kim Ark had been born in the United States. Under the Fourteenth Amendment, therefore he was a US citizen.

3-9
Asian Americans, 1965–2025

"Asian American" is a catch-all term that scarcely existed in 1965, when Congress enacted a radically altered immigration law that opened the nation to greatly increased immigration from Asia. During much of the first half of the 20th century, the small numbers of ethnic Koreans could scarcely think of themselves as sharing an identity with ethnic Japanese, when Japan dominated Korea as a colony. Much the same held for ethnic Chinese during the 1930s and '40s when Japanese forces were brutalizing much of China.

Despite such differences, US policy scarcely distinguished one group from another. None was eligible to become a naturalized citizen before China became a US ally against Japan during World War II. Immigration restriction targeted China by 1882, and similar policies barred ethnic Japanese and other groups from Asia as their numbers later surged. The Immigration Act of 1924 put an end to legal immigration from anywhere in Asia. The sole exception, and it lasted for only a decade, was the Philippines, as part of the American Empire; and several states enacted laws in the 1920s or '30s that barred Filipino men from marrying White women.

The 1965 Immigration Act undid the 1924 law. Some other largely Caucasian and English-speaking nations similarly moved to open their doors to immigrants from Asia. Canada had initiated a Chinese Immigration Act in 1885, followed by a harsher one in 1923, also called the Chinese Exclusion Act, but relaxed its restrictions after World War II and in 1962 did away with national origins as a criterion for admission. Australia greeted the 20th century with a "White Australia policy," an approach to immigration gradually relaxed after World War II and largely abandoned in 1966, though proponents of the traditional policy persisted.

The term "Asian American" gained traction in 1968, when coalitions of students at the University of California at Berkeley and at San Francisco State University developed the Asian American Political Alliance to include all Americans of Asian descent, their varied aims to make their political voices more effective, promote social change and economic opportunity, resist the Vietnam War, and push for ethnic studies classes.

Catalysts of immigration to the US from Asia in subsequent years have included— aside from the end of the legal ban—the many refugees after the Vietnam War, the attractions of higher education in the US, and the persistent push factor to escape extreme poverty in people's countries of birth.

The 21st century contrasts profoundly with such earlier times as the 1880s or 1920s. As one indication of mainstream acceptance of Asian cultures, Americans of all ethnicities and in most areas can and often do choose to go out to dinner at restaurants specializing in Chinese, Japanese, Thai, Korean, or Indian cuisine. In electoral politics, in the early years of the 21st century, candidates of various Asian ethnicities have won elections for state governor or a seat in Congress, not only in Hawai'i and California but also in South Carolina, Louisiana, and elsewhere. Yet poverty continues to beset many immigrants from Asia, and hostility against ethnic Asians can surface at any time.

3-10
Latinos across America, 1965–2025

Various terms in use in the 21st century—Latino, Hispanic, Latinx—posit a readily defined social group in the US. The concept, whatever the term, is of fairly recent origin.

In the 1960s, New York City's main "nonwhite" group, aside from "Negroes," were "Puerto Ricans." The people in California that Dolores Huerta and César Chávez sought to organize into the United Farmworkers Union were mostly "Mexican." Refugees from Fidel Castro's new regime in the Caribbean were "Cubans." Meanwhile, immigrants from the wider Caribbean, many of them from earlier in the 20th century, and often from Jamaica or some other English-speaking island, were "West Indians."

The different groups scarcely shared an umbrella, whether historical or rhetorical, that could cover all of them, or even the mostly Spanish-speaking groups. But "Hispanic" came along, and "Latino" (and then "Latinx"), either of which might cover groups in the US with 20th-century origins from "Latin America" (together with people of Mexican origin, recent or long ago). One term emphasized a shared language, Spanish (thus generally excluding Portuguese-speaking Brazil, much the largest South American country). The other term emphasized geographical origins, most places in the Western Hemisphere south of the US.

A broader grouping like either of these might reflect a self-identification as belonging to a wider group than from a particular country. Or it might reflect a habit of the wider culture to homogenize disparate groups, classify them as more or less the same, like "Europeans" or "Asians."

Especially in the years after the Immigration Act of 1965, newcomers to the US from Central and South America, as well as the Caribbean, grew greatly in numbers. They came, for varying combinations of reasons and clustered at different times and different places, from the Dominican Republic, from Venezuela, from Honduras, and so on.

The terms did not capture the differences among people coming from a common area or speaking a more or less common language. Where should descendants from the many people brought in as laborers from Asia back in the 19th century, whether now speaking English (as in Jamaica) or Spanish (anywhere in Latin America), be grouped? Moreover, how should people coming from the Philippines, mainly speaking Spanish, be placed in the social and rhetorical universe? The term "Latino" might, and often did, racially homogenize all "Hispanics," in the act erasing their Indigenous or African lineage.

One striking phenomenon related to these matters came in the 2024 presidential election with commentators often resorting to the term "the Latino vote." If that behavior by reporters and analysts did not reveal a perception of the homogenization of a broad range of historically disparate groups, it is hard to know what might.

The general non-Latino perception of Latino people has sometimes oscillated between Brown and White. In the Southwest, the US had seized much of Mexico back in the 1840s; the border had suddenly migrated hundreds of miles to the south, and great numbers of "Mexicans" found that they and their descendants were in the US. They might from then on be legally categorized as White and yet, in their day-to-day lives, they tended to be tremendously discriminated against in their school situations, job opportunities, residential patterns, and vulnerability to official or private Anglo violence.

Experiences in one part of the country did not necessarily equate to those in another part. The South, especially during the long reign of Jim Crow, where the Black-White binary worked with the greatest ferocity, had to slot Latinos into one or the other of those two racial categories. In the states between Florida at one end and Texas at the other, the numbers of Latinos remained for quite some time quite small. There, "Black" appearing Latinos became effectively Black, while "White" appearing Latinos might obtain provisional status as White, because non-Black.

By the 1980s, though, as the numbers of Latinos in the region doubled and then doubled again and again, all Latinos became increasingly perceived as belonging to a distinct group. On the receiving end of mounting animosity, disrespect, and discrimination, they themselves increasingly grouped themselves under a larger rhetorical umbrella. The phenomenon brought those areas of the South in greater alignment with previous developments farther west.

A large majority of all people classified as Latino are citizens who, however, experience various forms of discrimination, especially in recent times a fear, for themselves or members of their families and communities, of being seized, incarcerated, and deported to some random country. Even citizens might be seized. Or they might be left behind when, as the spouse or child of an "illegal" resident, they are subject to being suddenly and forcefully separated. Whether citizen or not, members of such communities are often, then, very much on edge.

3-11
Anne Scott, Gerda Lerner, and the Discovery of Women's History

In the 1970s, a young scholar attending the annual conference of the Southern Historical Association sat down for lunch with a relatively senior couple, Thomas B. Alexander, noted historian of 19th-century US politics, and his wife, Elise. Tom introduced Elise as the smarter member of the family, who collaborated with him on his many projects, but, he explained, he could get an academic job; she could not. (Phi Beta Kappa, she taught high school English.)

There had previously been notable female historians, among them Angie Debo (1890–1988), who grew up in Oklahoma and wrote much of its history. In 1934, Debo published her University of Oklahoma PhD dissertation as *The Rise and Fall of the Choctaw Republic*, an innovative and empathetic approach to the Native past based on oral histories as well traditional archival materials. She later published other important books on Native American history. The only post-secondary teaching post she ever had, however, was at a teachers' college, prior to her dissertation.

The name Mary Ritter Beard (1876–1958) appeared together with that of her husband, Charles A. Beard, a professor at Columbia University, as co-authors in 1930 of a magisterial and innovative reconceptualization of US history, *The Rise of American Civilization*. Her husband insisted that not only had she been a full collaborator, but also that she had done much to emancipate him from the discipline's traditional emphasis on military and political history. And yet Columbia University had no women on its history faculty and no place for her. Pushing ahead without a university affiliation, she published under her own name *Woman as Force in History* (1946), a consequential anthem that clearly demonstrated a woman doing women's history.

By the 1970s, women were becoming a force in the study of history, and many among them transformed the entire field by introducing a missing element, the experiences of what Congress in 1975 termed "female individuals." Anne Firor Scott, Gerda Lerner, and Darlene Clark Hine exemplified the change, even led the way.

Anne Firor Scott (1921–2019), a Georgia native, early on came across Mary Beard's book, also Simone de Beauvoir's *The Second Sex*, both of which planted seeds in her mind that went on to sprout. She earned her PhD at Radcliffe College, where she wrote about southern progressives, who had been thought not to exist, but "kept stumbling over women," who were also not supposed to be there.

After her husband, political scientist Andrew Scott, secured a teaching position at the University of North Carolina, the history department at nearby Duke University invited her to teach for them starting fall 1961, on a temporary basis, until the department could find a suitable long-term person. Decades later, still at Duke, she would note with pleasure that they apparently never were able to find that more suitable person.

Looking back years later, Scott mused that she had rather accidentally embarked "upon a study for which there was almost no historiographical tradition and no network of established scholars." She also came to see "the effect of education upon women's lives and the effect of a growing body of educated women on American society."

Scott's book *The Southern Lady: From Pedestal to Politics*, 1830–1930, came out in 1970. Her later works included *Making the Invisible Woman Visible* (1984), *Natural Allies: Women's Associations in American History* (1991), and an edited collection, *Pauli Murray and Caroline Ware: Forty Years of Letters in Black and White* (2006).

Gerda Lerner (1920–2013), a Jewish exile from Nazi Austria, brought a German accent, more than that a female perspective to US history—a perspective inspired in part, she pointed out, by the work of Mary Beard. Lerner's first book as an historian developed a dual biography of two White sisters from the pre–Civil War South who, repelled by the system that surrounded them and privileged them, became race traitors, renegades, moved north and became active abolitionists. Lerner titled it *The Grimké Sisters from South Carolina: Rebels against Slavery* (1967). A revised edition altered the subtitle in a revealing way: *Pioneers for Women's Rights and Abolition*.

Teaching at Sarah Lawrence College from 1968 to 1980, Lerner inaugurated a pioneer master's program in the new academic field of women's history, before moving to the University of Wisconsin, where she organized the first PhD program in women's history. She also helped establish "Women's History Week," forerunner of Women's History Month. Her other books included *The Majority Finds Its Past* (1979), *The Creation of Patriarchy* (1986) and *The Creation of Feminist Consciousness: From the Middle Ages to 1870* (1993).

Gerda Lerner and Anne Firor Scott proved instrumental in opening the academy to women as historians and to the study of women. Meanwhile, the field of African American history had begun to flourish and go mainstream, incorporated as an integral dimension of US history. Building on the pioneering work of George Washington Williams in the late 19th century, then Carter G. Woodson in the 1910s through the 1940s, John Hope Franklin (1915–2009) did much, from the 1940s on, to recreate the field. One key question became: what about people who were both female and Black?

In stepped a younger cohort of scholars who themselves were both female and Black, as exemplified by Darlene Clark Hine, whose books include *Black Women in White: Racial Conflict and Cooperation in the Nursing Profession*, 1890–1950 (1989) and *Hine Sight: Black Women and the Re-construction of American History* (1994). In later years she might tell how, skeptical at first but eventually brought around, she took on the task of writing the history of a Black women's group in Indiana. Placing her hand on her hip, she affectionately mimicked the women who pulled her into writing their history and redirecting her professional trajectory.

Long before the 2020s, the field of women's history had taken a prominent place in the academy. Thavolia Glymph's book *The Women's Fight: The Civil War's Battles for Home, Freedom, and Nation* (2020) exemplifies how bringing women's history to the center of an inquiry, in from the margin, or from beyond the margin, can transform traditional understanding of the past.

Nor, of course, was the new field of women's history limited to the United States. Gerda Lerner herself branched out across time and space from the 19th-century US. The movement she did so much to establish and lead also resonated through time and space.

3-12
John Adams and Contested Elections

US presidential elections, by definition, have always been contested, with the exception of George Washington, who twice swept the Electoral College. Elections that stand out are those where the outcome and aftermath were contested.

It is often said that President Washington left a great legacy by declining to run for a third term in 1796, thus setting a precedent long followed (and today stipulated in the Constitution's Twenty-second Amendment). It was no small thing, a strong symbol of the intended impermanence of any national leader, though a matter of happenstance, as Washington had done his duty and had no interest in dying in office.

A greater precedent came in 1800, when the Federalist Party candidate, President John Adams, Washington's vice-president and successor, sought a second term, at a time of bitter political division. Adams had narrowly won in 1796, despite the huge thumb-on-the-scale that the Three-Fifths Clause gave his Republican opponent, Thomas Jefferson. In 1800, by contrast, Adams learned he had lost in a rematch with Jefferson, when the workings of the Three-Fifths Clause put a Virginian back in the presidency.

What did Adams do? He quietly prepared to pack up and move back home to Massachusetts. His uneventful departure—the peaceful transfer of power from one president to the next, also from one political party to the opposition—was, as one writer has put it, "a gift of tremendous magnitude." Adams had run for a second term, but he could not gather it in, and he stepped aside for his victorious opponent. In 1828, his son, John Quincy Adams, replicated his father's performance when he lost a bid for reelection.

US history has featured an occasional contested election of the sort where the outcome could not be determined through the Electoral College. The four-way 1824 election, in which no candidate received a majority of Electoral College votes (as required under the Constitution), went to the House of Representatives, which chose John Quincy Adams. The 1876 election featured three states where both the Republicans and the Democrats claimed to have won; in the end, a special commission gave all the contested electoral votes to the Republican candidate, Rutherford B. Hayes.

In later years, defeated for reelection in 1888, Grover Cleveland vacated the White House and headed home to New York; in 1892 he ran again, and won. In the 20th century, President Herbert Hoover, when Franklin Roosevelt trounced him in 1932, just left for his home in California.

Gerald Ford, disappointed in failing to secure a term all his own in the 1976 race, went home to Michigan. In turn, Jimmy Carter followed his failed bid in 1980 for a second term by returning to Georgia. As for George Herbert Walker Bush, defeated in a three-way race in 1992 while seeking a second term, he unobtrusively left DC and headed back to Texas.

Through the next several presidencies, Bill Clinton served two terms, as did George W. Bush and Barack Obama. Democrats did, however, find themselves conceding the White House in 2000, when the voters, and the electors, divided in such a way that it was the Supreme Court that handed George W. Bush the presidency, after cutting short a recount in Florida, and thus a Republican took the White House, rather than the Democrats holding on. Then came 2020, when, for the first time, the loser, more particularly the incumbent, refused to acknowledge he had lost.

John Adams's legacy from 1800 had a magnificent run.

3-13
James Buchanan and the Apotheosis of Pure Capitalism

In 1859, a man named James Buchanan, president of the United States at the time, vetoed the first stab at what three years later became the Morrill Land-Grant College Act. He did so on the basis, in part, that education was better left to the states; the national government should play no role. One hundred and ten years later, another person named James Buchanan, an economics professor, brought a similar orientation to matters of public policy when he came to Virginia Tech, where he spent the entire decade of the 1970s.

At Virginia Tech he set up shop at The Grove, vacated when President T. Marshall Hahn Jr. moved to a new house away from campus. Buchanan brought an aura of high-powered researcher, though in fact much of his research career focused on navigating ways to insinuate his views into the worlds of big business and policy makers. He had earlier taught at the University of Virginia and would leave Virginia Tech for George Mason University (GMU), an up-and-not-yet-coming institution at that time whose leadership anticipated that Buchanan could enhance the school's prestige; and, there again, he benefited from free rein and ample private resources. During his time at Virginia Tech, and again at GMU, he had an institutional home that supported the development of his ideas and influence.

In the 1880s and into the 1920s, the United States had experienced something approaching unregulated industrial capitalism, much as, in the Slave South in the 1840s and 1850s, it had featured something akin to unregulated agricultural capitalism. But then came the New Deal and its reorientation of the heft and goals of government.

Buchanan represented and led a powerful backlash that sought to strip federal regulation of the economy and promotion of social well-being, including the New Deal's labor policies and Social Security. Another impulse behind the effort emerged from *Brown v. Board of Education*, in that instance directly focused on race, also on education, and an aspect of federal power making a difference in American life. As consumer protection and environmental sustainability became significant concerns, statutes and regulations addressing these concerns, too, came under fire.

Government, in Buchanan's view, must protect property rights, particularly the immediate interests of large corporations, but definitely not the well-being of groups, large or small, of voters and other mere people.

Two principal writings of recent years have, in combination, highlighted the origins and implications of the work that Buchanan and his cohort brought—and continue to bring—into being. Adam Winkler unearthed the mendacious origins of the conceit that corporations are citizens under the Fourteenth Amendment (so much for "originalism"), and he went on to trace corporations' "civil rights movement" down to the present.

Nancy MacLean focused on Buchanan himself; the central role he played in proselytizing his viewpoint regarding politics and policies; and like-minded mega-donors buying up institutions ranging from economics departments to law schools—including GMU's school of law, renamed in 2016, with funds from Charles Koch, in honor of Supreme Court justice Antonin Scalia after his death that year.

MacLean's work points toward a (behind-the-scenes) deliberately constructed world the central objective of which is to make corporations—not humans—the only real citizens, where constitutional law is renovated to the point that it trammels even the possibility of progressive change, electoral or legislative. In that world, public education—K-12 and universities alike (therefore government responsibilities at the state level, not just the federal)—is best marginalized, defunded, privatized, neutered or repurposed.

3-14
James Obergefell's Freedom to Marry

In 2013, James Obergefell married his longtime love, John Arthur, in Maryland. Gravely ill at the time, Arthur soon died, and Obergefell found that, since their home state, Ohio, did not recognize same-sex marriage, he could not appear on Arthur's death certificate as the surviving spouse. Obergefell went to court to contest the constitutionality of Ohio's refusal.

His resort to court action had a long history, with various twists and turns. One early indicator of the obstacles that couples like Obergefell and Arthur encountered dated from 1971. Did a same-sex couple have the "freedom to marry"? The question came up in several states in the aftermath of *Loving v. Virginia* (1967), in which the Supreme Court ruled that, no matter that the state of Virginia made it a felony for a "White" man like Richard Loving to marry a "colored" woman like Mildred Jeter, they had a constitutional "freedom to marry" that overrode the state law.

In a case titled *Baker v. Nelson* (1971), the Minnesota Supreme Court became the first of several state appellate courts to reject the argument that the US Supreme Court's interpretation of the Fourteenth Amendment four years earlier in *Loving v. Virginia* should be applied not only to interracial marriage but also to same-sex marriage, so that a gay couple could obtain a license to marry. Richard John Baker appealed the state ruling to the US Supreme Court, which, in 1972, turned him down cold.

By the mid-1990s, by contrast, state judges in both Hawai'i and Alaska appeared close to interpreting language in their state constitutions in a fashion that would permit gay couples to marry there. In response, however, two consequential actions took place.

First, in 1996, Congress passed, and President Bill Clinton signed, the Defense of Marriage Act (DOMA). It had two wings. For one, it expressly permitted any state to deny recognition of a same-sex marriage that a couple had entered into elsewhere. And two, it denied all same-sex couples, even if married, any federal benefits that a heterosexual married couple would routinely enjoy.

And second, in 1998, voters in both Hawai'i and Alaska approved a "Marriage Amendment" to their constitution that barred any legislative effort to permit same-sex marriage and also, more immediately, changed the constitution's language that a state judge might have interpreted in a way that would end the traditional impediment.

But the next year, in *Baker v. State of Vermont*, the Vermont Supreme Court, quoting *Loving v. Virginia* about the "freedom to marry," directed the state legislature to extend to same-sex couples "the common benefits and protections that flow from marriage under Vermont law." To comply, the Vermont legislature adopted what it called "civil unions," equivalent under state law to marriage but not carrying the name.

Before a state could approve any sort of same-sex marriage, it would have to first remove any legal basis for criminal prosecutions for same-sex sex. Back in 1986, in *Hardwick v. Bowers*, the Supreme Court upheld a Georgia sodomy statute when it was being applied to same-sex sex. In 2003, by contrast, in *Lawrence v. Texas*, the Court overturned that ruling and, instead, threw out all sodomy laws in any state, including one in Texas that specifically targeted same-sex couples.

That same year, 2003, the highest state court in Massachusetts, in a case called *Goodrich v. Department of Public Health*, went beyond Vermont's civil unions. Based partly on *Loving v. Virginia* and partly on the Massachusetts state constitution, the court determined that even civil unions were not enough and called for full marriage rights under Massachusetts law for same-sex couples.

As with Vermont, Massachusetts could only go as far as state authority reached. Whether called civil unions or marriage, same-sex couples' rights would be delimited by DOMA. Other states could refuse to recognize the validity of same-sex couples' new legal relationship, and all marriage benefits under federal law would remain off limits.

But change kept occurring. In 2012, in a radically different approach to the issue than had characterized developments back in the 1990s, voters in Maryland, Washington State, and elsewhere approved legislative action to inaugurate same-sex marriage.

In 2013, the US Supreme Court, in a ruling on same-sex marriage, took a very different approach than back in 1972. *United States v. Windsor*, from New York, challenged the constitutionality of DOMA's denial of federal benefits, in that instance related to a tax on inheritance. Although by only 5–4, the Court ruled in support gay rights.

The implications of the ruling against DOMA quickly rippled out. Social Security benefits became available to same-sex married couples living in states that recognized their marriage; and same-sex married couples could file joint federal tax returns, no matter where they lived.

That same year, moreover, the Hawai'i legislature enacted same-sex marriage, and New Mexico's state supreme court ruled that restricting marriage to heterosexual couples violated the state constitution. By late 2013—a decade after *Lawrence v. Texas* and *Goodrich v. Department of Public Health*—more than a dozen states plus DC recognized same-sex marriage, whether through court decisions or legislative action. The number was small but growing. And then Mr. Obergefell sued for the right to have his Maryland marriage recognized in Ohio.

James Obergefell's name identifies the case at the Supreme Court, but a convergence of cases and issues encompassed how much had been occurring, or not, in US law and culture as the nation moved fitfully from a consensus against same-sex marriage in the early 1990s to a patchwork that, by the 2010s, had seen such marriages become legally possible in more and more states. The various cases addressed a range of issues: adoption, birth certificates, death certificates, the ability to import a marriage valid elsewhere, and the underlying question of being able to enter into a legal marriage anywhere.

James Obergefell, for one, had taken advantage of his freedom to travel to go elsewhere—there had to be an elsewhere—to get married, but then faced the challenge of having his home state recognize that marriage. Similarly, many of the other couples were seeking to gain recognition of marriages they had entered into in Massachusetts, Connecticut, New York, Iowa, or California.

The plaintiffs in *Obergefell* had all won at trial in US district court. Across the country, in most circuits the court of appeals had upheld the lower court ruling in cases like theirs. In the Sixth Circuit, however, by a 2-to-1 vote, the majority judges held to what they saw as the controlling case, *Baker v. Minnesota*, from 1972. Couples bringing the cluster of cases grouped under *Obergefell*, all from states in that circuit, lived in Ohio, Michigan, Tennessee, or Kentucky.

With the circuits divided, the Supreme Court set out to resolve the issue for every state. As in the *Windsor* case, the Court proved closely divided. Writing in June 2015 for a 5–4 majority, Justice Anthony Kennedy ruled that no state could constitutionally refuse to recognize an out-of-state same-sex marriage. More than that, no state could any longer deny a same-sex couple the right to obtain a license to marry. Questions about birth certificates, death certificates, and adoption were, of course, no longer at issue.

James Obergefell had his court victory. His name could go on his deceased husband's death certificate as surviving spouse. Beginning in 2015, moreover, every state had to grant same-sex couples a license to marry in that state, unlike when Obergefell had to leave Ohio and go to Maryland to marry.

Within two decades of DOMA's passage in 1996, the US Supreme Court had (narrowly) overturned both parts of it, one part in 2013 in *United States v. Windsor*, the other in 2015 in *Obergefell v. Hodges*. In less than two decades, same-sex marriage had gone from no states to every state.

3-15
Earth Day, Doomsday, One Planet

Environmental concerns, though by no means new, became an ever more pressing policy issue, in the US and elsewhere, from the 1960s. And increasingly they emphasized climate change, what it is, how to account for it, what to do about it.

Inside of one decade, Congress passed a Clean Air Act (1963) and a Clean Water Act (1972) and established the Environmental Protection Agency (1970). During the same time, Rachel Carson brought out a book, *Silent Spring* (1962), to call attention to the dangers of the chemical DDT, a synthetic insecticide that protected humans from mosquitos that transmitted malaria but that carried severe downsides as well, such that the US banned its use in 1972.

The first Earth Day, on 22 April 1970, invited citizen action; it both reflected and heightened awareness of a constellation of environmental challenges. Many streams fed into Earth Day. Peace activist John McConnell had secured support for an idea along those lines from the United Nations secretary general, U Thant. US Senator Gaylord Nelson of Wisconsin thought teach-ins of the sort that had focused on campus opposition to the Vietnam War might animate college students to take on environmental concerns, so the date should come after spring break. Denis Hayes shouldered the task of organizing an effort that soon went national and reached beyond college campuses to bring in community rallies. A leading advertising writer, Julian Koenig, came up with the name Earth Day. Walt Kelly, from his daily comic strip *Pogo*, contributed the phrase "we have met the enemy and he is us." Walter Reuther, president of the United Auto Workers, stepped in with both stature and funds to support a big communications effort that first year.

Meanwhile, mounting concern about climate change made its way into scientific journals and policy discussions. In 1965, shortly after Lyndon Johnson gained a landslide election, the President's Science Advisory Committee asked Roger Revelle, a leading climate scientist, to educate them on what he saw as the potential impact of global warming caused by rising levels of carbon dioxide in the atmosphere. He focused on the dimension that he could be most sure of at that early time, sea level rise from melting icecaps.

In a 1983 publication, Revelle wrote: "The oceans would flood all existing port facilities and other low-lying coastal structures, extensive sections of the heavily farmed and densely populated river deltas of the world, major portions of the state[s] of Florida and Louisiana, and large areas of many of the world's major cities."

The National Climate Act of 1978, one example of congressional action, called for a national research program on climate science. An Intergovernmental Panel on Climate Change followed in 1988.

Throughout the years, however, a handful of dissenting scientists, in particular William Nierenberg, Fred Seitz, and Fred Siegel, worked assiduously to undermine public belief in the science of climate change. News reporters tended, in the interests of "balanced" reporting, to give them equal or even greater weight than the emerging overwhelming consensus among actual climate scientists.

The three worked so hard to neutralize action on climate change precisely because so much evidence suggested that real action was very much needed and just might take place.

Addressing a future in which climate change would drive refugees from regions that "lose their capacity to support people," scientist Alvin Weinberg wanted to know: Did anyone "believe that the United States or Western Europe or Canada would accept the high influx of refugees from poor countries that have suffered a drastic shift in rainfall pattern?"

The Senate Committee on Energy and Natural Resources held a hearing in summer 1988 on "Greenhouse Effect and Global Climate Change," at which Senator J. Bennett Johnston of Louisiana, in his opening statement, explained the topic's urgency:

Today, as we experience 101° temperatures in Washington, DC, and the soil moisture across the midwest is ruining the soybean crops, the corn crops, the cotton crops, when we're having emergency meetings of the Members of the Congress in order to figure out how to deal with this emergency, then the words of Dr. [Syukuro] Manabe and other witnesses who told us about the greenhouse effect are becoming not just concern, but alarm.

The next quarter-century, like the preceding one, featured back-and-forth actions, generally halting and limited but also holding some promise. The UN Earth Summit of 1992 in Rio de Janeiro concluded with a pledge, signed within the next two years by nearly 200 nations, including the US, to work toward preventing "dangerous anthropogenic [human-induced] interference in the climate system."

Yet, as the Kyoto Protocol, an international pledge to reduce reliance on fossil fuels and thus reduce carbon dioxide emissions and therefore global climate change, took shape in 1997, a congressional resolution to block the US from embracing it passed by a whopping 97–0 vote. Naomi Oreskes, coauthor of the book *Merchants of Doubt: How a Handful of Scientists Obscured the Truth on Issues from Tobacco Smoke to Global Warming* (2010), on which the 2014 movie *Merchants of Doubt* was based, observed about the vote: "Scientifically, global warming was an established fact. Politically, global warming was dead."

But perhaps not yet. In the 2000 presidential race, Al Gore, who had become a convert to the threat of climate change when taking an undergraduate course at Harvard in the 1960s with Revelle, won the popular vote and came within a hanging chad of the presidency. In view of all he had done on the subject in the previous decade and more, Gore would no doubt have made the issue a top priority of his administration. And some years later, with Barack Obama in the White House, the US helped secure the 2015 Paris Agreement, in which almost all nations came together to pledge reductions in fossil fuel emissions.

The 21st century brought ever hotter ocean surfaces and thus the threat of ever more powerful hurricanes. It brought ever higher agricultural commodity prices, as climate change threatened productivity in coffee from Brazil, cacao from Ivory Coast, olive oil from Spain.

It also brought books like *A World Without Ice* (2009), *World Without Fish* (2011), *The Attacking Ocean* (2013), *Baked Alaska* (2025), and *Here Comes the Sun* (2025), as well as such films as *An Inconvenient Truth* (2006), *Chasing Ice* (2012), and *Chasing Coral* (2017).

In 2020, the 50th anniversary of the inaugural Earth Day came just weeks after a global shutdown over Covid. Perhaps, after the plague receded, positive action on the environment in general, and on climate change in particular, would pick up? Instead, the 55th anniversary brought an avalanche of retrenchments in the US, including withdrawal from the 2015 Paris Agreement.

The science had not changed. Nor had there been any lessening of what Joe Biden said in the run-up to the 2020 presidential election and after, that climate change posed an "existential threat" for humans (and other life on Earth). Roger Revelle was not around to see what had become of his scientific research or his warnings about what it told him.

3-16
George Floyd and Public Commemoration Revisited

The 21st century brought a growing sense among a great many Americans that change was long overdue in how public places commemorated US history. A series of jolts spurred the process along: the shooting murders of nine worshipers by a White supremacist at Emanuel African Methodist Episcopal Church in Charleston, South Carolina, in June 2015; the "Unite the Right" violence in Charlottesville, Virginia, in August 2017; and the public murder of a Black man, George Floyd, by a uniformed White police officer in Minneapolis, Minnesota, in May 2020.

George Floyd's death, especially on top of the earlier episodes—and vividly displayed on footage from the phone of a teenager at the scene—transformed the political and cultural landscape. It made change far more likely in many places across America. But change had already begun.

In August 2015, in New Haven, Connecticut, Yale University president Peter Salovey welcomed incoming freshmen. Referencing the recent events in South Carolina, he linked them to one of Yale's residential colleges, where many students lived and dined, named for John C. Calhoun. A long-time US senator from South Carolina before the Civil War, Calhoun had been a political giant in support of state rights, nullification, secession, and, at the center of it all, slavery. The Emanuel African Methodist Episcopal Church, site of the bloodshed in Charleston, is on the city's Calhoun Street, also named in his honor.

Dissatisfaction with the Calhoun name had long simmered. The Yale administration set up a webpage and invited members of the Yale community to weigh in on whether, this time, a change of name might be appropriate. Whatever the input, the president announced in April 2016 that Calhoun College was keeping its name.

Resistance came from many quarters, with hundreds of students staging a renaming ceremony for "the college formerly known as Calhoun." Reconsidering, Salovey appointed a special committee to develop "a set of well-articulated principles according to which a historical name might be removed or changed." Committee members drew on their own scholarly expertise, as well as the perspectives stemming from their roles on campus and their ethnic identities, as they evaluated the evidence and the arguments. They sought to develop guidelines for use not only at Yale but at any institution.

The intersection of evidence and principles led to a reversal of the original decision. A headline in the *Washington Post* explained: "Yale renames Calhoun College because of historical ties to white supremacy and slavery." The new name, announced in February 2017, would be Grace Hopper College, honoring a White woman who had earned graduate degrees at Yale in the 1930s in mathematics, had gone on to superlative careers as teacher, mathematician, and computer scientist, and had also reached the rank of rear admiral in the US Navy. In both the denaming and the renaming, Yale scrupulously followed the principles that its committee had painstakingly developed. At the same time, Yale established a new college, named for Pauli Murray, a towering African American female figure from the 20th century.

Mitch Landrieu, recent mayor of New Orleans, published a book, *In the Shadow of Statues: A White Southerner Confronts History* (2019), to recount his experience in leading and then implementing a decision to remove three statues valorizing big men of the Confederacy, including Robert E. Lee and Jefferson Davis, from public places in the city. An appendix to the book supplies his speech on 19 May 2017 explaining the removal of those monuments from their prominent public places.

"It is self-evident," he declared that day, "that these men did not fight for the United States of America, they fought against it." He called the Confederacy a "four-year, brief historical aberration" in the city's 300-year history, one that had "sought to tear apart our nation and subjugate our fellow Americans to slavery." Such a past, he insisted, must be remembered, but must not be revered. A friend, he said, had urged him to consider the perspective of "an African American mother or father trying to explain to their fifth-grade daughter who Robert E. Lee is and why he stands atop of our beautiful city."

"Relocating" those monuments allowed the city to "reclaim" the spaces they had long occupied. Their purpose had been to "purposefully celebrate a fictional, sanitized Confederacy, . . . ignoring the enslavement, and the terror." Aiming to "rewrite history to hide the truth," they were "a part of that terrorism as much as a burning cross on someone's lawn; they were erected purposefully to send a strong message to all who walked in their shadows about who was still in charge in this city." No more.

Some 3,000 miles west of Yale, a controversy suddenly burst onto the scene regarding the name Boalt at the law school of the University of California at Berkeley. There, the questions did not date back to slavery and the Confederate South, but rather to the late-19th century West and the origins of a federal law banning the immigration of most people from China.

On 18 May 2017, the new law school dean, Erwin Chemerinsky, read an article in the *San Francisco Chronicle* revealing that John Boalt, namesake of the main classroom building, was a prime mover, even *the* prime mover, in pushing an anti-Chinese immigration agenda, in California and across the nation, in the late 1870s and early '80s. Boalt Hall carried that name not in celebration of his attitudes or behavior in the 1870s or '80s but because his widow, years later, made a substantial contribution to the school on condition that her husband be recognized.

Regardless, the revelation jarred, all the more so because many of the students taking classes in Boalt Hall were themselves ethnic Chinese. The report from Yale, made public six months earlier, offered guidance in organizing a process for developing potential responses. What to do with the name of the law school's alumni association and several professorships, as well as the classroom building, plus the informal name of the school itself? Charles Reichmann, faculty member and author of the original article in the *San Francisco Chronicle*, published a more detailed account the next year, in the *Asian American Law Journal*, of John Boalt's activities and significance as a propagandist for Chinese exclusion. A town hall in February 2018 gave people a public forum for voicing their views.

As at Yale, the question occasioned sharp differences over whether to make a change, underwent a thoughtfully constructed process, and resulted in small steps before the larger one. In November 2018, 18 months after the original news piece first stirred the pot, the dean recommended removing Boalt's name. When a campus worker chiseled "Boalt" off the Berkeley building long identified by that name, the "unnaming" was well under way, but neither the dean nor the committee members saw the work as finished.

The special Committee on the Use of the Boalt Name had expressly called for a "visible public record," and the first of three new exhibits, "A Time for Change," which opened for fall 2021, introduced viewers to the background of "Boalt Hall," the reasons for the change, and considerations going forward. Said a spokesman, it was important to show "how we got from one place to another," to have a public display "for people to walk by and learn from."

The chair of the special committee explained: "New students, as well as alumni returning to the building for reunions, will come to understand the complex history of what's in a name." A committee member called for "term limits" on all such names, so that honors of that sort not necessarily be "perpetual" but periodically be given fresh consideration. Another person involved in the process observed: "Simply taking a name from a building is only an important first step, and the university needs to follow through with more substantive actions." At Berkeley, these had already included more scholarship aid to recruit Native and Black students to the law school, what one person called "an amazing array of lunchtime workshops on various aspects of race and the law," and recruitment of new African American and Asian American professors.

George Floyd's death spurred change across the nation. In Northern Virginia, for example, a public park took a new name. In December 2020, following up on a proposal from the previous summer, Arlington County renamed what had been Henry Clay Park, honoring one of the leading politicians of the first half of the 19th century, for Zitkala-Sa (Red Bird, or Gertrude Simmons Bonnin), a great Native leader, activist, and writer of the first half of the 20th century, who had lived nearby for some years.

In Richmond, Virginia, once the Capital of the Confederacy, a row of statues celebrating the Confederacy, including Robert E. Lee and Jefferson Davis, long towered over Monument Avenue. In July 2020, however, after the killing of George Floyd, Richmond city mayor Levar Stoney directed that those monuments be removed, something soon done.

But Richmond failed to work up a suitable alternative use of the space. Meanwhile, some people wanted the monuments put back up. Many wanted something to show what had been there but was no more, and how residents had demonstrated with success to make it gone. Many of those people expressed deep dissatisfaction given what failed to happen next. "Have some historical markers up. Explain what happened and why it happened. Show . . . pictures of the people that came out here and used their voice and made this change," urged one area resident, Caroline Bowers, in 2024. Though pleased with the removal, she still found herself "disappointed with the outcome."

In sum, as this sample demonstrates, reconsideration of traditional names took place across the country and related not only to Black and White but also to Native and to Asian.

Not all the changes in the years around 2020 proved permanent. At President Trump's direction in 2025, one military base after another in the South, having been recently renamed from a Confederate general, had its former name restored. Much the same happened with an occasional public school. In Richmond, some people expressed concern that, though parks and streets were local, therefore not obviously subject to federal authority, George Floyd's moment might be reversed. Much was different. But some changes had reverted or at least appeared to be unstable, uncertain.

3-17
The Undoing of *Roe v. Wade*

From the moment in 1973 that the Supreme Court handed down its ruling in Roe v. Wade, that women had a constitutional right to choose abortion during at least the first trimester of a pregnancy, perhaps two trimesters, opposition challenged the new legal and constitutional environment. The most obvious place to hedge the ruling had been in effect invited, to take legislative charge of the third trimester, and next the second one. Even the first trimester might be hemmed in, for example requiring parental consent for an under-age daughter to obtain an abortion.

Running for president in 1980, Ronald Reagan called for a constitutional amendment to overrule the Court's interpretation in *Roe* and permit states to make policy, as had been the situation before *Roe*. The leading later case to reach the Supreme Court, *Planned Parenthood v. Casey* (1992), modified *Roe v. Wade's* viability standard, which had put viability of a fetus outside the womb at perhaps twenty-six weeks, but left in place the substance of the ruling in *Roe*. Lower courts routinely rejected State laws perceived as unduly restricting the exercise of that right. Anti-abortion groups kept looking for a case that might reach the Supreme Court for reconsideration and the possible overturn of *Roe v. Wade*.

Then came a 2018 Mississippi law, the Gestational Age Act, which banned all abortions beyond fifteen weeks of pregnancy except in situations of a severe threat to the woman's health, or a severe fetal abnormality such that ever getting to viability seemed impossible. The Mississippi statute directly challenged *Roe v. Wade*. The Jackson Women's Health Organization, the only clinic offering abortion services in Mississippi, promptly sued state health officer Thomas E. Dobbs.

The state of Mississippi claimed that the viability test should be thrown out, that the state had an interest in the matter beginning at the very "onset of pregnancy." The state lost in federal district court, lost resoundingly again in the Fifth Circuit Court of Appeals, then appealed to the US Supreme Court, which agreed in May 2021 to hear the case, focused on one question: "Whether all pre-viability prohibitions on elective abortions are unconstitutional."

Seeking to keep the substance of *Roe* whatever the outcome in the *Dobbs* case, the US House of Representatives passed the Women's Health Protection Act. Even if the constitutional right to an abortion vanished, a federal law might offer women protection, but the Senate, along party lines, narrowly defeated the bill. Everything hung on what the Supreme Court majority decided.

Meanwhile, President Donald Trump had appointed three new justices to the Court. In nomination hearings, they generally refused to answer questions related to abortion. One of them, though, Brett Kavanaugh, privately assured skeptics that he considered *Roe v. Wade* "settled law," not to be second-guessed. In the end, all three new justices, including Kavanaugh, did as Trump and his supporters had expected and, together with three other justices, formed a majority that overturned *Roe v. Wade*.

Justice Samuel Alito, writing the majority decision in *Dobbs v. Jackson Women's Health Organization*, declared in June 2022 that "*Roe* was egregiously wrong from the start."

And he transformed the language. A "pregnant woman" was now already a "mother," and a "potential life" was an "unborn human." The "mother" had no right under the US Constitution to an abortion, and laws related to her health and pregnancy must be left to "the people's elected representatives." He left uncertain whether he meant to put authority over such matters back in the hands of state legislative majorities—what anti-abortion groups had insisted upon ever since Roe—or bring Congress into the mix, making law for the entire nation. At the very end, he specified "state" legislators, though that hardly settled the question.

Other justices in the majority wrote separate opinions. Brett Kavanaugh noted that a woman would still have a constitutional right to travel outside her home state to obtain an abortion elsewhere—an assertion very soon emphatically rejected in some states, where legislatures passed laws making it illegal for a woman to do so.

Justice Clarence Thomas made it clear he thought other privacy cases should also be reconsidered: the contraception cases from the 1960s (*Griswold v. Connecticut*, for example) and the cases that had recognized the right to same-sex sex (*Lawrence v. Texas*) and same-sex marriage (*Obergefell v. Hodges*). Thomas left out *Loving v. Virginia*, the decision that had thrown out bans on interracial marriage (Thomas, a Black man, was married to a White woman).

After *Dobbs*, more strident opponents of *Roe* abandoned the argument that the laws regarding pregnancy should be left in the hands of each separate state. They instead called for Congress to nationalize a ban on access to abortion, so no state would be able to recognize female reproductive rights, a radically different proposition.

One means of securing such an outcome might be for the federal government to rigorously enforce a law that had been on the books (though occasionally amended) since the 19th century, the Comstock Law, which banned the distribution through the mail of items ranging from pornography to means of preventing a pregnancy or aborting a fetus.

Soon after *Dobbs*, voters in several states, including Republican states like Missouri, voted in referendums to try to secure legal access to abortion, including by amending their state's constitution. Some state legislatures, by contrast, effectively ended legal access to an abortion by enacting draconian penalties on any doctor providing one, including fine, imprisonment, and loss of license to practice medicine.

Both the prevention of pregnancy and the termination of pregnancy were under assault. In the harsh new environment, when doctors hesitated to jeopardize their liberty and their livelihoods by performing emergency procedures, women died, among them Nevaeh Crain, Porsha Ngumezi, and Josseli Barnica, all in Texas. A ten-year-old girl in Ohio, raped and pregnant, had to go out-of-state to get an abortion.

Students today, when asked for how long "your constitutional right to obtain an abortion" is good—zero weeks, six weeks, three months, six months—few choose "zero," even though that answer is the only factually correct one. According to the Supreme Court, as far as the US Constitution is concerned, they no longer have any rights on that question. Even any current rights in their state are at risk.

3-18
Alignment with American Interests and American Values

On 20 January 2025, former president Donald Trump, returning to the White House after four years away, took the oath of office to uphold the Constitution of the United States of America. Later that day, he issued Executive Order 14169, "Reevaluating and Realigning United States Foreign Aid," which opened by declaring: "The United States foreign aid industry and bureaucracy are not aligned with American interests and in many cases antithetical to American values."

The United States Agency for International Development (USAID) felt the impact immediately and thoroughly. Pending a 90-day review, the US would disburse no further foreign aid funds. Contractors in foreign countries, having in good faith followed through on their end of the bargain and then billed the US for the previous month's time and outlays, found themselves defrauded of their compensation. The people's representatives in Congress had appropriated money with the usual expectation that those funds would reach their intended beneficiaries and serve their intended purposes.

The next day, after taking the oath of office as the new secretary of state, Marco Rubio affirmed the nation's new posture on foreign aid. The current structure, "not in alignment with . . . American values," had been summarily suspended, would be reexamined, and might go away, which it soon effectively did.

Each new administration gets to set policy priorities. Rubio highlighted a theme, which he said had been central to the president's campaign, of ensuring "that our foreign policy is centered on one thing, and that is the advancement of our national interests, . . . anything that makes us stronger or safer or more prosperous"—a worthy goal indeed, and a yardstick by which to calibrate performance. News stories in the months to follow pointed up some of the consequences that came in the aftermath of the US change of regime. Predictably, stories out of Asia and Africa indicated costs or benefits, offered glimpses of the future being created.

International relations scholar Joseph S. Nye Jr. gave the term "soft power" considerable currency. He assesses its meaning and significance for the US in a changing and always volatile world in such books as *Bound to Lead: The Changing Nature of American Power* (1990), *Soft Power: The Means to Success in World Politics* (2004), and *Soft Power and Great-Power Competition: Shifting Sands in the Balance of Power between the United States and China* (2023).

In brief, from an American perspective (or any nation's), soft power is the use of cultural or economic programs, rather than military force, to nudge other peoples and nations toward a favorable view of the US, rather than a coercive approach that depends on naked power—and it has historically tended since World War II to reflect an altruistic, humanitarian bent toward alleviating misery where feasible. Back in the late 1940s, in the aftermath of the Second World War and with a view to the emerging Cold War, the Marshall Plan in Europe, together with a counterpart program for Japan, embodied these dual considerations, one definitely calculating, the other simply generous.

On a macro level, that includes efforts to promote agricultural productivity to increase food supplies. Or more generally, foreign aid not only fosters good will but also might promote the economic strengthening of one nation after another toward the status of equal trading partner. In a more immediate, more micro way, it offers emergency medical or nutritional assistance to discrete individuals who, in the absence of such aid, in an acute environment, simply die difficult and unnecessary deaths.

Back in 1961, another new president, John F. Kennedy, inaugurated two programs to address the US role in the world: the Peace Corps and USAID, one new, the other to reorganize existing efforts to project soft power in the Cold War with the Soviet Union. The program, which took up a minuscule share of the US budget, had ever since received bipartisan support, including from Marco Rubio as a member of the Senate.

In the decades since 1961, China has emerged as a major political rival to the US. The Trump administration has focused on China's military and economic power, not the political. Within weeks of his executive order, *Politico* published a piece titled "As USAID Retreats, China Pounces," in which China expert Michael Sobolik—author of *Countering China's Great Game: A Strategy for American Dominance* (2024) and once an assistant to Senator Ted Cruz—observed: "Beijing is hoping we do exactly that." In short, some early assessments had it that, rather than enhancing US security, deep-sixing USAID jeopardized it.

At a congressional hearing held on 21 May 2025 by the House Foreign Affairs Committee, Secretary of State Rubio, now also acting administrator of USAID, faced a barrage of questions regarding the administration's abrupt cutoff of US contributions to health programs around the world. Rubio hit back with a combative line about the consequences of killing USAID programs that "no one has died." Rather than reconsider, he soon doubled down: "No children are dying on my watch."

Bereaved individual fathers and mothers of very recently deceased sons and daughters, as well as experienced people involved in running groups like Doctors without Borders, disputed the claim that "no one has died." They all knew better. One estimate has put the average figure of lives saved in each of the previous twenty years, as a direct result of various aspects of USAID, at 4.6 million. So, millions of people, most of them in Africa and Asia, seemed destined to die each year if denied the medical and nutrition program of USAID.

Investigative reporters tried to track down what was becoming of supplies— emergency food, medical materials, contraceptive items—that US taxpayers had bought and paid for, with funds that Congress had appropriated expecting that they would be fully and prudently spent, items that had been promised to agencies and individuals around the globe, and that were critical for promoting the health and well-being of many millions of people.

They found evidence of many millions of dollars' worth of such supplies being wasted rather than sent on for distribution. The story broke in July that $9.7 million worth of contraceptive supplies held in a warehouse in Belgium were slated for destruction, at the cost of millions more dollars, at a special facility in France. These items had been intended for women typically in situations of desperate poverty, continuous warfare, sexual violence, refugee status, or some combination.

Uncertain whether the destruction had actually occurred, reporters continued their efforts into November and found a great deal more material, stored elsewhere and set to be destroyed. Regarding birth control, one false response from the administration had it that US policy did not permit the distribution of materials designed to terminate pregnancies, when the items in question were designed to prevent pregnancy in the first place.

Congressman Gregory W. Meeks, ranking member of the House Foreign Affairs Committee, wrote to Rubio in August urging a response to a news report that 500,000 tons of food supplies had not been distributed but instead were to be destroyed. He expressed deep concern about the apparent negligence, compounded by the prospect that the president's policy would operate to make America much diminished: "The Administration has displayed a troubling pattern of squandering lifesaving foreign assistance resources and commodities rather than using them to reach people in need around the globe to extend American influence and goodwill. This is a textbook example of government waste and an affront to the generosity of the American people."

Reporting from Rohingya refugee camps along the Thai border with Myanmar (Burma), AP journalist Kristen Gelineau told tale after tale contradicting Rubio's declaration to Congress in May that "no one has died." Two weeks prior to his defiant assertion, Mohammed Taher's two-year-old son Hashim had died begging for food: "I lost my son because of the funding cuts," insisted the toddler's dad; "without rations, we have nothing—no food, no medicine, no chance to live." Or as another man, Mahmud Karmar, put it, "We will all die if it continues like this. . . . We can't do this forever." And yet another: if food won't come, "then please drop a bomb on us—because we can't continue this way."

Coda
John Steinbeck and Woody Guthrie

John Steinbeck (1902–1968) and Woody Guthrie (1912–1967) both emerged in the years around 1940 as major figures in popular culture, and they've never gone away. They continue to resonate because what they had to say, and how they said it, continue to matter.

Steinbeck won a Pulitzer Prize for his best-selling *The Grapes of Wrath* (1939), and he won the Nobel Prize in Literature in 1962 "for his realistic and imaginative writings, combining as they do sympathetic humour and keen social perception."

Grapes of Wrath recounts the saga of a fictional but representative Tom Joad returning home in Oklahoma only to find his family getting under way to head west on Route 66 to California. Living in Dust Bowl Oklahoma cannot sustain a family, not when the crops don't come in, the bank forecloses on the farm, and the roaring dust makes it about impossible to see or breathe. Besides, news had it that California provided green land, good jobs, a great place to begin again. Not much of that turned out to be true, and Steinbeck sets out to guide his readers to see the despair crowding out all hope, or almost all hope. A 1940 film based on the novel and starring Henry Fonda as Tom Joad won multiple Oscars, including for Best Director, and is included on many "best of all time" lists.

John Steinbeck's World War II saw him writing not only as a novelist but also as propagandist, recruitment writer, and war correspondent. *The Moon Is Down* (1942) imaginatively constructed experiences rooted in Nazi occupation and local resistance in what appeared to be Norway.

Bombs Away: The Story of a Bomber Team (also 1942), assisted by the Office of War Information and based on travels to eight states becoming acquainted with the planes and their crew members in training for the Army Air Forces, rendered a composite of each—pilot, navigator, gunner, bombardier, radio man, crew chief—all working smoothly together as a team.

The year 1943 took him as a war correspondent for the *New York Herald Tribune* to London, England, with its continuing blitz, then to North Africa, and on to Sicily and Italy, first observing the war-making from near the front lines, then embedded. His wartime dispatches later came out as a book, *Once There Was a War* (1958).

Quite aside from *The Grapes of Wrath*, Steinbeck wrote such early novels as *Tortilla Flat* and *Of Mice and Men*, with themes of good and evil and capturing aspects of the labor and lives of people scraping by in Steinbeck's native California. Later he brought out the novels *Cannery Row* and the monumental *East of Eden*, as well as a travelogue from a many-month tour of the US in 1960, accompanied by his dog, *Travels with Charley in Search of America* (1962).

Woody Guthrie's narrative writing included a novel and a riveting autobiography, *Bound for Glory* (1943), addressing his early years, and he produced considerable artwork.

But his main medium of expression, singing and songwriting, made him into a towering figure in the world of folk music, with songs like his "Dust Bowl Ballads" and, perhaps his best known, "This Land Is Your Land." His music stemmed from his experiences in his native Oklahoma as well as his time in Texas, California, New York City and elsewhere. Washington State's official state folk song is Guthrie's "Roll On Columbia, Roll On," written for a film on the Grand Coulee Dam. His "Oklahoma Hills" ("where I was born") is Oklahoma's.

Guthrie crossed paths with Steinbeck while living and working in California in the late 1930s. The John Steinbeck Committee to Aid Farm Workers invited Guthrie to play in 1940 for a benefit to help migrant workers. His song "The Ballad of Tom Joad," inspired by Steinbeck's novel and by the 1940 movie, provides a wondrous poetic distillation of the book and the film.

Guthrie first faced World War II armed with a guitar carrying the slogan "this machine kills fascists." Later, he spent a year with the Merchant Marine, crossing the Atlantic on convoys of merchant vessels or troop carriers, whether to Tunisia, England, or France. Of course he brought along his guitar, this time named "Hoping Machine." His wartime songs included "Sally, Don't You Grieve" and "Sinking of the Reuben James."

Shortly after his death in late 1967 of Huntington's disease, "A Tribute to Woody Guthrie" at Carnegie Hall in New York City in early 1968, presented again later at the Hollywood Bowl in California, included performances by a host of friends and admirers, all deeply influenced by Guthrie and his music, among them Pete Seeger, Judy Collins, Bob Dylan, Odetta, and his son Arlo Guthrie.

For a radio show in 1944, he explained why he wrote and sang what he did: "I am out to sing songs that will prove to you that this is your world and that if it's hit you pretty hard and knocked you for a dozen loops, no matter what color, what size you are, how you are built, I am out to sing the songs that make you take pride in yourself and in your work."

Timeline, 1857–2024

To assist readers in locating in time various incidents referenced in the modules and documents, presented here is a broad outline of selected events or periods.

1857	Supreme Court ruling in *Dred Scott v. Sandford*
1860–1861	Election and inauguration of Abraham Lincoln
	Secession of 11 of the 15 slave holding states:
	Deep South, then Upper South, but not Border South
1861–1865	War of the Rebellion
1862	Morrill Land-Grant College Act
1863	Emancipation Proclamation
1865–1900	Post–Civil War Era
1865	13th Amendment
1866	Civil Rights Act of 1866; 14th Amendment proposed
1867	Congressional Reconstruction in 10 states
1870	15th Amendment
	Last of the former Confederate states restored
	Public school systems inaugurated in southern states
1872	Yellowstone National Park
1882	Chinese Exclusion Act
1890	Second Morrill Act
1898	Spanish-American War
	Wong Kim Ark
1900	Black electoral power in the former Confederate states has vanished
1900–1920	Progressive Era
1906	Pure Food and Drug Act
	Antiquities Act
1913	Federal Reserve Act
1914	Smith-Lever Act (Agriculture Extension Act)
1917–1918	US in First World War
1917–1922	Russian Revolution
1920	Women's right to vote in every state
1924	Immigration Act of 1924
1929–1941	Great Depression
1933–1938	New Deal
1933	Tennessee Valley Authority Act
1934	Federal Housing Administration
1935	Social Security
	National Labor Relations Act
1941	March on Washington Movement
1941–1945	US in Second World War
1944	GI Bill
1945	United Nations established

1945–1991	Cold War
1947	Truman Doctrine
	Jackie Robinson plays baseball with the Brooklyn Dodgers
	To Secure These Rights
1948	Desegregation of the US military
	Dixiecrats
	Shelley v. Kraemer
1948–1951	Marshall Plan
1949	North Atlantic Treaty Organization
	People's Republic of China
1950	*Sweatt v. Painter and McLaurin v. Oklahoma*
1950–1953	Korean War
1954/1955	*Brown v. Board of Education*
1955–1956	Montgomery Bus Boycott
1956	National Interstate and Defense Highways Act
1960	Sit-Ins
1961	Freedom Rides
	Peace Corps
1962	Cuban Missile Crisis
1963	Clean Air Act
1960s/1970s	Great Society
1964	Civil Rights Act of 1964
1965	Voting Rights Act
	Medicare Act
	Higher Education Act of 1965
	Immigration Act of 1965
1960s/1970s	War in Vietnam
1966	National Traffic and Motor Vehicle Safety Act
1967	*Loving v. Virginia*
	Public Broadcasting Act of 1967
1970	Environmental Protection Agency
1971	Occupational Safety and Health Administration
1972	*Roe v. Wade*
	Clean Water Act
	Title IX
1974	President Nixon resigns over Watergate
1990	Americans with Disabilities Act
2001	"September 11"
2010	Affordable Care Act (Obamacare)
	Citizens United v. Federal Election Commission
2015	*Obergefell v. Hodges*
2022	*Dobbs v. Jackson Women's Health Organization*
2024	*Trump v. United States*

Presidential Elections, 1860–2025

Year	Top Candidates	Popular Vote	Electoral Vote
1860	**Lincoln (R)**	1,867,198 (39.8%)	180 (59.4%)
	Douglas (D)	1,379,434 (29.4%)	12 (4.0%)
	Breckinridge (SD)	854,258 (18.2%)	72 (23.8%)
	Bell (CU)	591,658 (12.6%)	39 (12.9%)
1864	**Lincoln (R)**	2,220,846 (55.1%)	212 (90.6%)
	McClellan (D)	1,809,445 (44.9%)	21 (9.0%)

Andrew Johnson (15 April 1865–)

Year	Top Candidates	Popular Vote	Electoral Vote
1868	**Grant (R)**	3,013,650 (52.7%)	214 (72.8%)
	Seymour (D)	2,708,744 (47.3%)	80 (27.2%)
1872	**Grant (R)**	3,598,468 (55.6%)	286 (81.9%)
	Greeley (D)	2,835,315 (43.8%)	(died before EC met)
1876	**Hayes (R)**	4,033,497 (48.0%)	185 (50.1%)
	Tilden (D)	<u>4,288,191 (51.0%)</u>	184 (49.9%)
1880	**Garfield (R)**	4,453,611 (48.3%)	214 (58.0%)
	Hancock (D)	4,445,256 (48.2%)	155 (42.0%)

Chester A. Arthur (20 September 1881–)

Year	Top Candidates	Popular Vote	Electoral Vote
1884	**Cleveland (D)**	4,915,586 (48.9%)	219 (54.6%)
	Blaine (R)	4,852,916 (48.2%)	182 (45.4%)
1888	**Harrison (R)**	5,449,825 (47.8%)	233 (58.1%)
	Cleveland (D)	<u>5,539,118 (48.6%)</u>	168 (41.9%)
1892	**Cleveland (D)**	5,554,617 (46.0%)	277 (62.4%)
	Harrison (R)	5,186,793 (43.0%)	145 (32.7%)
	Weaver (Pop)	1,029,357 (8.5%)	22 (5.0%)
1896	**McKinley (R)**	7,105,076 (51.1%)	271 (60.6%)
	Bryan (D)	6,370,897 (45.8%)	176 (39.4%)
1900	**McKinley (R)**	7,219,193 (51.7%)	292 (65.3%)
	Bryan (D)	6,357,698 (45.5%)	155 (34.7%)

Theodore Roosevelt (14 Sept. 1901–)

1904	**T Roosevelt (R)**	7,625,599 (56.4%)	336 (70.6%)
	Parker (D)	5,083,501 (37.6%)	140 (29.4%)

1908	**W H Taft (R)**	7,676,598 (51.6%)	321 (66.5%)
	Bryan (D)	6,406,874 (43.0%)	162 (33.5%)

1912	**Wilson (D)**	6,294,327 (41.8%)	435 (81.9%)
	T Roosevelt (Prog)	4,120,207 (27.4%)	88 (16.6%)
	W H Taft (R)	3,486,343 (23.2%)	8 (1.5%)
	Debs (Soc)	900,370 (6.0%)	0

1916	**Wilson (D)**	9,126,063 (49.2%)	277 (52.2%)
	Hughes (R)	8,547,030 (46.1%)	254 (47.8%)

1920	**Harding (R)**	16,151.916 (60.3%)	404 (76.1%)
	Cox (D)	9,134,074 (34.1%)	127 (23.9%)
	Debs (Soc)	914,191 (3.4%)	0

Calvin Coolidge (2 August 1923–)

1924	**Coolidge (R)**	15,724,310 (54.0%)	382 (71.9%)
	Davis (D)	8,386,532 (28.8%)	136 (25.6%)
	LaFollette (Prog)	4,827,184 (16.6%)	13 (2.4%)

1928	**Hoover (R)**	21,432,823 (58.2%)	444 (83.6%)
	Smith (D)	15,004,336 (40.8%)	87 (16.4%)

1932	**FD Roosevelt (D)**	22,818,740 (57.4%)	472 (88.9%)
	Hoover (R)	15,760,425 (39.6%)	59 (11.1%)

1936	**FD Roosevelt (D)**	27,750,866 (60.8%)	523 (98.5%)
	Landon (R)	16,679,683 (36.5%)	8 (1.5%)

1940	**FD Roosevelt (D)**	27,243,218 (54.7%)	449 (84.6%)
	Willkie (R)	22,334,940 (44.8%)	82 (15.4%)

1944	**FD Roosevelt (D)**	25,612,610 (53.4%)	432 (81.4%)
	Dewey (R)	22,014,160 (45.9%)	99 (18.6%)

Harry S. Truman (12 April 1945–)

1948	**Truman (D)**	24,105,810 (49.5%)	303 (57.1%)
	Dewey (R)	21,970,064 (45.1%)	189 (35.6%)
	Thurmond (St Rts)	1,169,114 (2.4%)	39 (7.3%)
1952	**Eisenhower (R)**	33,777,945 (54.9%)	442 (83.2%)
	Stevenson (D)	27,314,992 (44.4%)	89 (16.8%)
1956	**Eisenhower (R)**	35.590,472 (57.4%)	457 (86.1%)
	Stevenson (D)	26,022,752 (42.0%)	73 (13.7%)
1960	**Kennedy (D)**	34,226,731 (49.7%)	303 (56.4%)
	Nixon	34,108,157 (49.5%)	219 (40.8%)
	Byrd (Dem)	0	15 (2.8%)

Lyndon B. Johnson (22 November 1963–)

1964	**Johnson (D)**	43,129,566 (61.1%)	485 (90.3%)
	Goldwater (R)	27,178,188 (38.5%)	52 (9.7%)
1968	**Nixon (R)**	31,785,480 (43.4%)	301 (55.9%)
	Humphrey (D)	31,275,166 (42.7%)	191 (35.5%)
	Wallace (Am Ind)	9,906,473 (3.5%)	45 (8.4%)
1972	**Nixon (R)**	47,169,911 (60.7%)	520 (96.7%)
	McGovern (D)	29,170,383 (37.5%)	17 (3.2%)

Gerald R. Ford (9 August 1974–)

1976	**Carter (D)**	40,830,763 (50.1%)	297 (55.2%)
	Ford (R)	39,147,793 (48.0%)	240 (44.6%)
1980	**Reagan (R)**	43,904,153 (50.7%)	489 (90.9%)
	Carter (D)	35,483,883 (41.0%)	49 (9.1%)
	Anderson (Ind)	5,720,060 (6.6%)	0
1984	**Reagan (R)**	54,455,075 (58.8%)	525 (97.6%)
	Mondale (D)	37,577,185 (40.6%)	13 (2.4%)
1988	**GHW Bush (R)**	48,886,097 (53.4%)	426 (79.2%)
	Dukakis (D)	41,809,074 (45.6%)	111 (20.6%)
1992	**Clinton (D)**	44,909,326 (43.0%)	370 (68.8%)
	GHW Bush (R)	39,103,882 (37.4%)	168 (31.2%)
	Perot (Ind)	19,741,657 (18.9%)	0

1996	**Clinton (D)**	47,402,357 (49.2%)	379 (70.4%)
	Dole (R)	39,198,755 (40.7%)	159 (29.6%)
	Perot (Reform)	8,085,402 (8.4%)	0
2000	**GW Bush (R)**	50,455,156 (47.9%)	271 (50.4%)
	Gore (D)	<u>50,992,335 (48.4%)</u>	266 (49.4%)
	Nader (Green)	2,882,738 (2.7%)	0
2004	**GW Bush (R)**	62,040,610 (50.7%)	286 (53.2%)
	Kerry (D)	59,028,444 (48.3%)	251 (46.7%)
2008	**Obama (D)**	69,456,897 (52.9%)	365 (67.8%)
	McCain (R)	59,934,814 (45.7%)	173 (32.2%)
2012	**Obama (D)**	65,899,660 (51.1%)	332 (61.7%)
	Romney (R)	60,932,152 (47.2%)	206 (38.3%)
2016	**Trump (R)**	62,955,340 (46.2%)	306 (56.9%)
	HR Clinton (D)	<u>65,788,564 (48.2%)</u>	232 (43.1%)
	Johnson (Libertarian)	4,487,570 (3.3%)	0
2020	**Biden (D)**	81,268,773 (51.3%)	306 (56.9%)
	Trump (R)	74,216,728 (46.9%)	232 (43.1%)
2024	**Trump (R)**	77,303,568 (49.8%)	312 (58.0%)
	Harris (D)	75,019,230 (48.3%)	226 (42.0%)

Note: Presidents' names are bolded. Popular vote victories are underscored here (four times) when failing to result in winning the presidency.

Source: The American Presidency Project (presidency.ucsb.edu); corrected for 1884 and 1896; added Debs for 1920.

For Further Reading

Beyond books identified within individual modules, here are 100 readings on topics or themes from between the 1860s and the 2020s: books that stretch across much or all of that period; books related primarily to the first sixty years or so; books exploring the years 1930s–1960s; and books more on topics beginning in the 1970s.

General

Berry, Daina Ramey, and Kali Nicole Gross. *A Black Women's History of the United States*. Boston: Beacon Press, 2020.

Blackhawk, Ned. *The Rediscovery of America: Native Peoples and the Unmaking of U.S. History*. New Haven: Yale University Press, 2023.

Clarren, Rebecca. *The Cost of Free Land: Jews, Lakota, and an American Inheritance*. New York: Viking, 2023.

Coleman, Arica L. *That the Blood Stay Pure: African Americans, Native Americans, and the Predicament of Race and Identity in Virginia*. Bloomington: Indiana University Press, 2013.

Dunbar-Ortiz, Roxanne, and Dina Gilio Whitaker. *"All the Real Indians Died Off" and 20 Other Myths about Native Americans*. Boston: Beacon Press, 2016.

Eig, Jonathan. *The Birth of the Pill: How Four Crusaders Reinvented Sex and Launched a Revolution*. New York: W. W. Norton, 2014.

Foley, Edward B. *Ballot Battles: The History of Disputed Elections in the United States*. 2016; updated edition, New York: Oxford University Press, 2024.

Frost, Amanda. *You Are Not American: Citizenship Stripping from Dred Scott to the Dreamers*. Boston: Beacon Press, 2021.

Gregory, James N. *The Southern Diaspora: How the Great Migrations of Black and White Southerners Transformed America*. Chapel Hill: University of North Carolina Press, 2005.

Grundy, Pamela, and Susan Shackelford. *Shattering the Glass: The Remarkable History of Women's Basketball*. 2005; revised edition, Chapel Hill: University of North Carolina Press, 2025.

Heilbrunn, Jacob. *America Last: The Right's Century-Long Romance with Foreign Dictators*. New York: Liveright, 2024.

Immerwahr, Daniel. *How to Hide an Empire: A History of the Greater United States*. New York: Farrar, Straus and Giroux, 2019.

Irons, Peter. *The Courage of Their Convictions: Sixteen Americans Who Fought Their Way to the Supreme Court.* New York: Free Press, 1988.

Kahrl, Andrew W. *The Black Tax: 150 Years of Theft, Exploitation, and Dispossession in America.* Chicago: University of Chicago Press, 2024.

Keyssar, Alexander. *The Right to Vote: The Contested History of Democracy in the United States.* New York: Basic Books, 2000.

LaFeber, Walter. *The Panama Canal: The Crisis in Historical Perspective.* New York: Oxford University Press, 1978.

Lee, Erika. *The Making of Asian America: A History.* New York: Simon and Schuster, 2015.

Loewen, James W., and Edward H. Sebesta, eds. *The Confederate and Neo-Confederate Reader: The "Great Truth" about the "Lost Cause."* Jackson: University Press of Mississippi, 2010.

Livesay, Harold C. *American Made: Men Who Shaped the American Economy.* 1979; 3rd edition, Boston: Little, Brown, 2011.

Nye, Joseph S., Jr. *Do Morals Matter? Presidents and Foreign Policy from FDR to Trump.* New York: Oxford University Press, 2021.

Suarez, Ray. *Latino Americans: The 500-Year Legacy That Shaped a Nation.* New York: Penguin, 2013.

Takaki, Ronald. *Strangers from a Different Shore: A History of Asian Americans.* Boston: Little, Brown, 1989.

Urofsky, Melvin I. *The Affirmative Action Puzzle: A Living History from Reconstruction to Today.* New York: Pantheon Books, 2020.

Wallenstein, Peter. *Blue Laws and Black Codes: Conflict, Courts, and Change in Twentieth Century Virginia.* Charlotteville: University Press of Virginia, 2004.

Wallenstein, Peter. *Cradle of America: A History of Virginia.* 2007; 2d edition, Lawrence: University Press of Kansas, 2014.

Wallenstein, Peter. *Virginia Tech, Land-Grant University: History of a School, a State, a Nation.* Blacksburg: Virginia Tech Publishing, 2026.

Westad, Odd Arne. *The Cold War: A World History.* New York: Basic Books, 2019.

Woodard, Colin. *American Nations: A History of the Eleven Rival Regional Cultures of North America.* New York: Viking, 2011.

Part I, 1860s–1920s

Blackmon, Douglas A. *Slavery by Another Name: The Re-enslavement of Black Americans from the Civil War to World War II*. New York: Doubleday, 2008.

Brinkley, Douglas. *The Wilderness Warrior: Theodore Roosevelt and the Crusade for America*. New York: HarperCollins, 2009.

Eller, Ronald D. *Miners, Millhands, and Mountaineers: Industrialization of the Appalachian South, 1880–1930*. Knoxville: University of Tennessee Press, 1982.

Freehling, Willliam W. *The South vs. the South: How Anti-Confederate Southerners Shaped the Course of the Civil War*. New York: Oxford University Press, 2001.

Gorn, Elliott J. *Mother Jones: The Most Dangerous Woman in America*. New York: Hill and Wang, 2001.

Guelzo, Allen C. *Robert E. Lee: A Life*. New York: Knopf, 2021.

Hager, Ruth Ann (Abels). *Dred & Harriet Scott: Their Family Story*. St. Louis: St. Louis Public Library, 2010.

Haney Lopez, Ian F. *White by Law: The Legal Construction of Race*. New York: New York University Press, 1996.

Kolko, Gabriel. *Railroads and Regulation, 1877–1916*. Princeton: Princeton University Press 1965.

Leonard, Elizabeth D. *Men of Color to Arms! Black Soldiers, Indian Wars, and the Quest for Equality*. New York: W. W. Norton, 2010.

Levine, Bruce. *Confederate Emancipation: Southern Plans to Free and Arm Slaves during the Civil War*. New York: Oxford University Press, 2006.

Lewis, David Levering. *W. E. B. Du Bois: Biography of a Race, 1868–1919*. New York: Henry Holt, 1993.

Livesay, Harold C. *Andrew Carnegie and the Rise of Big Business*. Boston: Little, Brown, 1975.

Livesay, Harold C. *Samuel Gompers and Organized Labor in America*. Boston: Little, Brown, 1978.

Luxenberg, Steve. *Separate: The Story of Plessy v. Ferguson, and America's Journey from Slavery to Segregation*. New York: W. W. Norton, 2019.

McCullough, David. *The Great Bridge: The Epic Story of the Building of the Brooklyn Bridge*. New York: Simon and Schuster, 1972.

Nackenoff, Carol, and Julie Novkov. *American by Birth: Wong Kim Ark and the Battle for Citizenship*. Abridged edition; Lawrence: University Press of Kansas, 2022.

Powers, Thomas. *The Killing of Crazy Horse*. New York: Alfred A. Knopf, 2010.

Salvatore, Nick. *Eugene V. Debs, Citizen and Socialist*. Urbana: University of Illinois Press, 1982.

Taylor, Philip. *The Distant Magnet: European Emigration to America*. New York: Harper and Row, 1971.

Varon, Elizabeth R. *Appomattox: Victory, Defeat, and Freedom at the End of the Civil War*. New York: Oxford University Press, 2014.

Wallenstein, Peter. *From Slave South to New South: Public Policy in Nineteenth-Century Georgia*. Chapel Hill: University of North Carolina Press, 1987.

Part II, 1930s–1960s

Allport, Alan. *Advance Britannia: The Epic Story of the Second World War, 1942–1945*. New York: Alfred A. Knopf, 2026.

Altschuler, Glenn C., and Stuart M. Blumin. *The GI Bill: A New Deal for Veterans*. New York: Oxford University Press, 2009.

Arsenault, Raymond. *Freedom Riders: 1961 and the Struggle for Racial Justice*. 2006; abridged edition, New York: Oxford University Press, 2011.

Banks, Ann, ed. *First Person America*. New York: Alfred A. Knopf, 1980.

Boyle, Kevin. *The Shattering: America in the 1960s*. New York: W. W. Norton, 2021.

Carlos, John, with David Zirin. *The John Carlos Story: The Sports Moment That Changed the World*. Chicago: Haymarket Books, 2011.

Downey, Kirstin. *The Woman Behind the New Deal: The Life and Legacy of Frances Perkins—Social Security, Unemployment Insurance, and the Minimum Wage*. New York: Doubleday 2009.

Eig, Jonathan. *Ali: A Life*. Boston: Houghton Mifflin Harcourt, 2017.

Eig, Jonathan. *King: A Life*. New York: Farrar, Straus and Giroux, 2023.

Eig, Jonathan. *Opening Day: The Story of Jackie Robinson's First Season*. New York: Simon and Schuster, 2007.

Fisher, Ada Lois Sipuel, with Danney Goble. *A Matter of Black and White: The Autobiography of Ada Lois Sipuel Fisher*. Norman: University of Oklahoma Press, 1996.

Fussell, Paul. *The Boys' Crusade: The American Infantry in Northwestern Europe, 1944–1945*. New York: Modern Library, 2003.

Gaillard, Frye. *A Hard Rain: America in the 1960s, Our Decade of Hope, Possibility, and Innocence Lost.* Athens: NewSouth Books, 2018.

Gluck, Sherna Berger. *Rosie the Riveter Revisited: Women, the War, and Social Change.* Boston: Twayne, 1987.

Gorham, Christopher C. *The Confidante: The Untold Story of the Woman [Anna Rosenberg] Who Helped Win World War II and Shape Modern America.* New York: Citadel Press, 2023.

Hoose, Phillip. *Claudette Colvin: Twice Toward Justice.* New York: Melanie Kroupa Books, 2009.

James, Rawn, Jr. *The Double-V: How Wars, Protest, and Harry Truman Desegregated America's Military.* New York: Bloomsbury Press, 2013.

Kanefield, Teri. *The Girl from the Tarpaper Shack: Barbara Rose Johns and the Advent of the Civil Rights Movement.* New York: Abrams, 2014.

Lemann, Nicholas. *The Promised Land: The Great Migration and How It Changed America.* New York: Alfred A. Knopf, 1991.

Lewis, Andrew B. *The Shadows of Youth: The Remarkable Journey of the Civil Rights Generation.* New York: Hill and Wang, 2009.

McGuire, Danielle L. *At the Dark End of the Street: Black Women, Rape, and Resistance—A New History of the Civil Rights Movement from Rosa Parks to the Rise of Black Power.* New York: Alfred A. Knopf, 2010.

Meier, August, and Elliott Rudwick. *Black Detroit and the Rise of the UAW.* New York: Oxford University Press, 1979.

Murphy, Audie. *To Hell and Back.* New York: H. Holt, 1949.

O'Brien, M. J. *We Shall Not Be Moved: The Jackson Woolworth's Sit-In and the Movement It Inspired.* Jackson: University Press of Mississippi, 2013.

O'Brien, Tim. *The Things They Carried.* Boston: Mariner Books, 1990.

Otsuka, Julie. *The Buddha in the Attic.* New York: Alfred A. Knopf, 2011.

Piascik, Andy. *Gridiron Gauntlet: The Story of the Men Who Integrated Pro Football in Their Own Words.* Lanham, MD: Taylor Trade Publishing, 2009.

Roediger, David R. *Working toward Whiteness: How America's Immigrants Became White—the Strange Journey from Ellis Island to the Suburbs.* New York: Basic Books, 2005.

Sanders, Crystal R. *A Forgotten Migration: Black Southerners, Segregation Scholarships, and the Debt Owed to Public HBCUs.* Chapel Hill: University of North Carolina Press, 2023.

Saxby, Troy R. *Pauli Murray: A Personal and Political Life.* Chapel Hill: University of North Carolina Press, 2020.

Scott, James M. *Black Snow: Curtis LeMay, the Firebombing of Tokyo, and the Road to the Atomic Bomb.* New York: W. W. Norton, 2022.

Shetterley, Margot Lee. *Hidden Figures: The American Dream and the Untold Story of the Black Women Mathematicians Who Helped Win the Space Race.* New York: William Morrow, 2016.

Sokol, Jason. *There Goes My Everything: White Southerners in the Age of Civil Rights, 1945–1975.* New York: Alfred A. Knopf, 2006.

Swift, Earl. *The Big Roads: The Untold Story of the Engineers, Visionaries, and Trailblazers Who Created the American Superhighways.* Boston: Houston Mifflin Harcourt, 2011.

Terkel, Studs. *"The Good War": An Oral History of World War Two.* New York: Pantheon Books, 1984.

Titus, Jill Ogline. *Brown's Battleground: Students, Segregationists, and the Struggle for Justice in Prince Edward County, Virginia.* Chapel Hill: University of North Carolina Press, 2011.

VanDeMark, Brian. *Kent State: An American Tragedy.* New York: W. W. Norton, 2024.

Wallenstein, Peter. *Race, Sex, and the Freedom to Marry: Loving v. Virginia.* Lawrence: University Press of Kansas, 2014.

Winkler, Allan M. *"To Everything There Is a Season": Pete Seeger and the Power of Song.* New York: Oxford University Press, 2009.

Young, Marilyn B. *The Vietnam Wars, 1945–1990.* New York: HarperCollins, 1990.

Part III, 1970s–2020s

Coontz, Stephanie. *The Way We Never Were: American Families and the Nostalgia Trap.* New York: Basic Books, 1992.

Demmer, Amanda C. *After Saigon's Fall: Refugees and US-Vietnamese Relations, 1975–2000.* Cambridge: Cambridge University Press, 2021.

Dierenfield, Bruce J. *The Battle over School Prayer: How Engel v. Vitale Changed America.* Lawrence: University Press of Kansas, 2007.

Duane, James. *You Have the Right to Remain Innocent: What Police Officers Tell Their Children about the Fifth Amendment.* New York: Little A, 2016.

Elmore, Bart. *Country Capitalism: How Corporations from the American South Remade Our Economy and the Planet.* Chapel Hill: University of North Carolina Press, 2023.

Gerry, Gail Burrell. *Here to Stay: The Story of the Class of Women Who Coeducated the University of Virginia.* Charlottesville: University of Virginia Press, 2025.

Gomez, Laura E. *Inventing Latinos: A New Story of American Racism*. New York: New Press, 2020.

Issenberg, Sasha. *The Engagement: America's Quarter-Century Long Struggle over Same-Sex Marriage*. New York: Pantheon Books, 2021o.

King, Billie Jean, with Johnette Howard and Maryanne Vollers. *All In: An Autobiography*. New York: Alfred A. Knopf, 2021.

Kruse, Kevin M., and Julian E. Zelizer. *Fault Lines: A History of the United States since 1974*. 2019; 2d ed., New York: W. W. Norton, 2025.

Landrieu, Mitch. *In the Shadow of Statues: A White Southerner Confronts History*. New York: Viking, 2018.

Oreskes, Naomi, and Eric M. Conway. *Merchants of Doubt: How a Handful of Scientists Obscured the Truth on Issues from Tobacco Smoke to Global Warming*. New York: Bloomsburg Press, 2010.

St. John, Allen. *Clapton's Guitar: Watching Wayne Henderson Build the Perfect Instrument*. New York: Free Press, 2005.

Sanger, David E. *The New Cold Wars: China's Rise, Russia's Invasion, and America's Struggle to Defend the West*. New York: Crown, 2024.

Santoli, Al, ed. *New Americans, An Oral History: Immigrants and Refugees in the U.S. Today*. New York: Ballantine Books, 1988.

Seidule, Ty. *Robert E. Lee and Me: A [White] Southerner's Reckoning with the Myth of the Lost Cause*. New York: St. Martin's Press, 2020.

Summitt, Pat, with Sally Jenkins. *Sum it Up: 1,098 Victories, a Couple of Irrelevant Losses, and a Life in Perspective*. New York: Crown, 2013.

Trado, Linda. *Hand to Mouth: Living in Bootstrap America*. New York: G. P. Putnam's, 2014.

US Department of Justice, Civil Rights Division. *The Ferguson Report: Department of Justice Investigation of the Ferguson [Missouri] Police Department*. New York: New Press, 2015.

Woodward, Bob, and Scott Armstrong. *The Brethren: Inside the Supreme Court*. New York: Simon and Schuster, 1979.

Illustrations

Mississippi State Sovereignty Commission, "Mississippi State Sovereignty Commission Photograph," 11 May 1967, SCRID# 3-11-0-25-1-1-1-cph, Series 2515: Mississippi State Sovereignty Commission Records, 1994-2006, Mississippi Department of Archives and History, 20 April 2006, <http://mdah.state.ms.us/arlib/contents/er/sovcom/sovcomphoto/photo.php?display=item&oid=318628> (6 January 2023).

Vannerson, Julian. (1859). Justin S. Morrill, representative from Vermont, thirty-fifth Congress, half-length portrait. Library of Congress. https://www.loc.gov/pictures/item/2010648581/.

Acknowledgments

I don't suppose it happens often that a publisher gets an email, the first week of October, the gist of which goes: "I have an idea for a book I'd like to write, for a class that begins in January. Might you be interested?" Even less often, I'm guessing, does such an inquiry elicit a reply displaying both receptivity and equanimity.

So, without Lori Graham, at Pocahontas Press, there is no book. I had worked with the press two owners and nearly three decades ago, on a comparable quest, so I had confidence this could be done, as long, of course, as I could produce what I had in mind.

To follow through and complete the race, I drew upon the talents, grace, and expertise of several people to make it more likely that "newbook" would not only do what I had in mind but do it well. My collaborators included longtime fellow college teachers and also a special few recent or current undergrads.

Rose Puschnik, former best student and continuing exemplary poet and scientist, expressed her keen approval of an early module, confirming that hey this works.

Grace Lawson, perennial best student, thought she'd like to use materials like this in the high school classes she plans to be teaching in another couple of years.

Penny Livesay, wordsmith extraordinaire, made a series of highly astute observations about passages that she saw needed reconsideration and revamping.

Ai Le, she of the most amazing observational powers and command of the language, vetted a majority of the modules. She also sketched the Statue of Liberty, which faces the other direction from how her parents arrived on these shores.

J. William Harris, whom I've known since grad school days back in another life, took on almost all the modules. A highly accomplished scholar of the American past, he bolstered content, corrected missteps, streamlined language, and, like the others, confirmed that this seemed a race well worth running.

My fall 2025 graduate teaching assistant Elliot Sheehan and I somehow converged on the notion that he take the lead on the saga of Shepard Mallory's quest for freedom.

Inspirations throughout relate to sparks flying from books by other scholars, things my long-ago teachers said or exposed me to, a raft of people I've known and admired, travels hither and especially yon, and statements I heard myself saying in class as a young teacher (because they were known to be true and important) that suddenly sounded preposterous, so there must be a better way to understand the topic.

As for Sookhan, I don't know that she read any modules. But she kept the home fires burning while I was immersed in this project.

Index

www.ingramcontent.com/pod-product-compliance
Lightning Source LLC
Chambersburg PA
CBHW081658120626
46550CB00010B/2939